# CORPORATE SOCIAL RESPONSIBILITY

***Edited by***

**Dr. Lourdes Poobala Rayen**

*Faculty Research*
*Dept. of Commerce*
*St. Xavier's College, Palayamkottai*
*Manonmaniam Sundaranar University*
*Tirunelveli, (Tamil Nadu)*
*(India)*

**&**

**Prof. J. Jeya Ani**

*Assistant Professor*
*Department of B.com Corporate Secretaryship*
*St. Xavier's College*
*Palayamkottai (Tamil Nadu)*
*(India)*

**DISCOVERY PUBLISHING HOUSE PVT. LTD.**
**NEW DELHI-110 002**

*Published by:*
**Tilak Wasan**
**DISCOVERY PUBLISHING HOUSE PVT. LTD.**
4383/4B, Ansari Road, Darya Ganj
New Delhi-110 002 (India)
*Phone* : +91-11-23279245, 43596064-65
*Fax* : +91-11-23253475
*E-mail* : discoverypublishinghouse@gmail.com
sales@discoverypublishinggroup.com
parul.wasan@gmail.com
*web* : www.discoverypublishinggroup.com

*First Edition:* **2013**

**ISBN: 978-93-5056-244-4**

**Corporate Social Responsibility**



*Printed at:*
**Aditi Fine Art Press**
**Delhi**

# Foreword

Corporate Social Responsibility (CSR) is an important function to accelerate the process of overall development and nation-building. It is a joint and shared responsibility of civil society, activist groups, Government and corporate sector to create appropriate means and avenues for the marginalised and bring them to the mainstream. The success of CSR lies in practising it as a core part of a company's development strategy. It is also important for the corporate sector to identify, promote and implement successful policies and practices that achieve results. The companies need to ask themselves how best they can bring about social justice, and protection of the environment in co-operation with other sectors of the economy. To create a win-win situation, it is essential for all of us to work together to alleviate poverty and improve miserable living conditions that exist in rural India.

I congratulate Dr. Lourdes Poobala Rayen, the Dean of Arts and the Coordinator of Corporate Secretaryship for bringing out an edited volume of the papers presented in the state level seminar organised by the Department of Corporate Secretaryship on the title "Corporate Social Responsibility". I am sure this book will help the students to understand the concept and the different dimensions of Corporate Social Responsibility.

**Rev. Dr. ALPHONSE MANICKAM,S.J**
*Principal*
*St.Xavier's College (Autonomous)*
*Palayamkottai- 627 002, Tamil Nadu*

# Foreword

Corporate Social Responsibility (CSR) is an important function to accelerate the process of overall development and nation building. It is a joint and shared responsibility of civil society, activist groups, Government and corporate sector to create appropriate means and avenues for the marginalised and bring them to the mainstream. The success of CSR has brought to light its a core part of a company's development strategy. It is also important for the corporate sector to identify, promote and implement successful policies and practices that achieve results. The chapters here try to discover and show how best they can bring about social harmony and protection of the environment in cooperation with other sectors of the economy to create a win-win situation. It is essential for all of us to work together to alleviate poverty and its grave impact on living conditions that exist in rural India.

I congratulate Dr. Lourdes Poobala Rayen, the Dean of Arts and the Coordinator of Corporate Secretaryship for taking out an edited volume of the papers presented in the state level seminar organised by the Department of Corporate Secretaryship on the title 'Corporate Social Responsibility'. I am sure this book will help the students to understand the conceptual and different dimensions of Corporate Social Responsibility.

Rev. Dr. A. ALPHONSE MANICKAM, SJ
Principal

# Preface

Today, more and more companies are realizing that in order to stay productive, competitive, and relevant in a rapidly changing business world, they have to become socially responsible. In the last decade, globalization has blurred national borders, and technology has accelerated time and masked distance. Given this sea change in the corporate environment, companies want to increase their ability to manage their profits and risks, and to protect the reputation of their brands. Because of globalization, there is also fierce competition for skilled employees, investors, and consumer loyalty. How a company relates with its workers, its host communities, and the marketplace can greatly contribute to the sustainability of its business success.

The business community can make tremendous contributions in promoting good health and well being, especially if innovative CSR initiatives are undertaken in partnership with government and civil society. For decades, business has been engaged in charity, philanthropy, and civic activities including social investments in health. However, oftentimes these investments were less than strategic, and were not directed to real social change. Today, business understands that viewed through lenses of "doing well by doing good," CSR can be a revolutionary way of contributing to systemic social changes in which investments can produce lasting social benefits in the health arena.

The corporate India based in and around cities has been flourishing and marching ahead whereas rural India still remains desperately poor. The corporate India can play a key role in bridging this gap. Perhaps there is a fortune at the bottom of the pyramid for the corporate sector and it can only be mined if rural India is brought into the mainstream of development and not left behind. The concept of CSR applies equally to individuals and corporations as it does to the State. It is a joint and shared responsibility of civil society, activist groups, Government and corporate sector to create appropriate means and avenues for the marginalised and bring them to the mainstream. The success of CSR lies in practicing it as a core part of a company's development strategy.

This book presents the papers presented in the State level seminar organized by the department of Corporate Secretaryship, St.Xavier's College, Palayamkottai.

We are grateful to Shri Tilak Wasan, Director of Discovery Publishing House Pvt. Ltd, New Delhi for having come forward to publish this book.

Palayamkottai, **Dr. P. LOURDES POOBALA RAYEN**
November, 2011 **J.JEYA ANI**

# Contents

# List of Contributors

1. **Dr. A. Rangaswamy,** Department of Management Studies, Infant Jesus College of Engineering, Thoothukudi District.
2. **Ms. K.B. Sridevi** Assistant Professor, Department of Management Studies, Fatima College, Madurai.
3. **T. Samson Joe Dhinakaran,** Lecturer in Commerce (SF), St. John's College, Palayamkottai, Tirunelveli.
4. **Dr. C. Eugine Franco,** Associate Professor Department of Commerce, St. Xavier's College, Palayamkottai and **A. Arockia Mary,** M.Phil Research Scholar in Commerce.
5. **Dr. K. Krishnakumar,** Assistant Professor, Dept. of Commerce, Periyar University, Salem and **V. Selvam,** Ph.D Scholar.
6. **FX. Robert Bellarmine,** Associate Professor of Commerce, St.Xavier's college, Palayamkottai and **M.Shunmugam,** M.Phil, Research Scholar in Commerce.
7. **Dr. Lourdes Poobala Rayen,** Associate professor of Commerce, St. Xavier's College, Palayamkottai.
8. **T. Dhanabalan,** M.Phil scholar, Alagappa Institute of Management, Alagappa University, Karaikudi.
9. **J. Thilagan,** Lecturer, MBA Department, Panimalar Engineering College, Chennai.
10. **V. Sylviya Johnsi Bai,** Assistant Professor,and **J. Kamala Juliet Isaac,** St.John's College, Palayamkottai.
11. **P. Subbulakshmi,** Research Scholar in Commerce, St. Xavier's College, Palayamkottai.
12. **C. Steaphen Raj,** Research Scholar in Commerce,St Xavier's College, Palayamkottai.
13. **M. Susheela,** M.Phil Research Scholar in Commerce, **Dr.Lourdes Poobala Rayen,** Associate Professor Department of Commerc., St.Xavier's College, Palayamkottai.

14. **I.Lovisal Roselin,** M.Phil Research Scholar, St.Xavier's College, Palayamkottai.
15. **S. Saboor Siraj Nooriya,** M.Phil Research Scholar in Commerce, and **Dr. Lourdes Poobala Rayen,** Associate Professor of Commerce. St.Xavier's College, Palayamkottai.
16. **Rev. Dr. Selvanayakam,** Associate Professor Dept. of Commerce, St. Xavier's College, Palayamkottai and **S. Athilinga Senjith,** Research Scholar in Commerce.
17. **Dr. K. Maruthamuthu,** Assistant Professor of Commerce, Periyar University, Salem and **S. Boobalan,** Ph.D Scholar, Periyar University, Salem.
18. **Y.Sindhu,** M.Phil Research Scholar, St.Xavier's College (Autonomous), palayamkottai.
19. **Mrs. Dr.P.Rajeswari,** Assistant Professor, Head of Commerce the Department of Commerce and **MS.A.Sama**, Annai Hajira Women's College, Melapalayam.
20. **Mrs.Ponrani,** Assistant Professor, St.Johns College, Palayakmottai and **Dr.P.Lourdes Poobala Rayen,** Associate Professor, Department of Commerce.
21. **Ms.T.Swarnamughi,** Assistant Professor of Commerce, Sri Krishna Arts & Science,College, Coimbatore and **N.Nitesh Parsan,** B.Com, Sri Krishna Arts & Science College, Coimbatore.
22. **D.Jeyaraman,** Assistant Professor of Commerce, Sadakathullah Appa College and **P.Pandirajan,** B.com Sadakathullah Appa College, Tirunelveli.
23. **Ms. P.Aysha Banu**, Assistant Professor of Commerce, **P.Ramalingam,** B.Com.
24. **Ms.J.Jeya Ani,** Assistant Professor, Dept. of B.com Corporate Secretaryship, St. Xavier's College, Palayamkottai.
25. **FX.Robert Bellarmine,** Associate Professor, St.Xavier's College, Palayamkottai, and **S.Rajendran**, M.Phil Research Scholar, St.Xavier's College, Palayamkottai.
26. **M. Arockia G Ruban,** Assistant Professo, Department of Corporate Secretaryship, St. Xavier's College, Palayamkottai.
27. **Ms.K.Viswa Sarojini Devi,** Assistant Professor, St.Xavier's College, Palayamkottai.
28. **Mrs. P.Vasumathi,** Faculty Of Management Studies, Panimalar Engineering College, Chennai and **Ms. K. Nirmala Devi,** Faculty of Management Studies, Panimalar Engineering College, Chennai.
29. **A.Jebasheela Mary Margaret,** M.Phil Research Scholar, St. Xavier's College, Palayamkottai.

30. **Ms.P. Juliet,** M.Phil Research Scholar in Commerce, St. Xavier's College, Palayamkottai and **Dr. C. Eugine Franco** Associate Professor Department of Commerce, St. Xavier's College, Palayamkottai.
31. **Rev.Dr. Selvanayakam,** Associate Professor Department of Commerce, St. Xavier's College, Palayamkottai and **S. Muthu Rathin-am,** M.Phil Research Scholar in Commerce, St. Xavier's College, Palayamkottai.
32. **Ms. J.Jeya Ani,** Assistant Professor, Dept. of Corporate Secretaryship, St. Xavier's College, Palayamkottai and **Dr. Lourdes Poobala Rayen,** Associate Professor of Commerce, Dept. of Commerce, St. Xavier's College, Palayamkottai.
33. **K.Pandiyaraj**, Assistant Professor in Commerce, Rajapalayam Rajus'College, Rajapalayam and **M.Kanniraj,** B.Com, Rajapalayam Rajus'College, Rajapalayam.
34. **Ms. Christina Jeya Devi,** M.Phil Research Scholar, St. Xavier's College, Palayamkottai.
35. **Ms. P.Geetha,** Assistant Professor, St.John's College, Palayamkottai.
36. **R. Dhanalakshmi**, Dept. of Management Sciences, PSG College of Arts & Science, Coimbatore and **Anand Shankar Raja,** Dept. of Management Sciences, BBM, PSG College of Arts & Science, Coimbatore.
37. **Mrs.P.Priya,** Assistant Professor in Commerce, Sri Krishna Arts and Science College, Coimbatore, **Venkatesha Balaji** and **Manian,** B.Com, Sri Krishna Arts and Science College, Coimbatore.
38. **Dr.N.Magesvaran**, Head, Dept. of Commerce, Rajapalayam Rajus' College, Rajapalayam and **S.Karthik,** B.Com, Rajapalayam Rajus'College, Rajapalayam.
39. **J.Divya Merry Malar,** Lecturer, Muslim Arts College, Thiruvithancode, Kanyakumari District.
40. **M.Charlet Rose Mary Vijaya,** Assistant Professor, Dept. of Corporate Secretaryship, St. Xavier's College, Palayamkottai and **Dr. Lourdes Poobala Rayen,** Associate Professor, Dept. of Commerce, St. Xavier's College, Palayamkottai.
41. **Dr.B.Revathy,** Associate Professor, Department of Commerce, Manonmaniam Sundaranar University Tirunelveli and **K.S. Arockiasamy,** Assistant Professor, Department of B.Com Corporate Secretaryship, St. Xavier's college, Palayamkottai.
42. **Dr. C. Eugine Franco**, Associate Professor in Commerce, St. Xavier's College, Palayamkottai.
43. **Dr. M. Julias Ceasar,** Assistant Professor of Commerce, Dept. of Commerce, St. Xavier's College, Palayamkottai.
44. **F.X. Robert Bellarmine,** Assistant Professor, PG & Research Department of Commerce, St Xavier's College (Autonomous), Palayamkottai.

45. **J.Mexon P.Rayan**, Assistant Professor, Department of Corporate Secretaryship, St.Xavier's College, Palayamkottai.
46. **A.Oliver,** Assistant Professor in Commerce, St. Xavier's College, Palayamkottai.
47. **R.Ravindran,** Assistant Professor of Commerce, St. Xavier's College, Palayamkottai.
48. **S.Lawrence Leve,** Assistant Professor, Department of Business Administration, St.Joseph's College (Autonomous), Tiruchirappalli-620 002.
49. **R. Mareeswaran,** BCom and **B.Muthu Prabhu,** BCom, Sri Kaliswari College, Sivakasi.
50. **R.Jai Ganesh,** BCom, Sri Kaliswari College, Sivakasi.
51. **A.Nishani,** M.S.University, Tirunelveli and **N.Sudha,** M.S. University, Tirunelveli.
52. **V.Bergin Prince Bell,** BBA Noorul Islam College of Arts and Science, Kumara coil.and **A. Antony Britto** BBA, Noorul Islam College of Arts and Science, Kumara coil.
53. **R.Mayilammal,** M.Phil Research Scholar, M.S. University, Tirunelveli and **M.Rajalakshmi,** M.Phil Research Scholar, M.S. University, Tirunelveli.
54. **R.Janani,**.B.Com, Sri Kaliswari College, Sivakasi and **T.Gohila,** B.Com, Sri Kaliswari College, Sivakasi.
55. **V.Sudha,** B.Com, Sri Kaliswari College, Sivakasi and **M.Suhasini,**B.Com, Sri Kaliswari College, Sivakasi.
56. **K. Meena,** Bcom, Sri Kaliswari College, Sivakasi and **M.Murugeswari,** Bcom, Sri Kaliswari College, Sivakasi.
57. **M.Rajalakshmi,** M.Phil Research Scholar, Dept. of commerce, M.S. University, Tirunelveli and **R. Mayilammal,** M.Phil Research Scholar, Dept. of Commerce, M.S. University, Tirunelveli.
58. **P.Sudha**, M.Phil Scholar, Department of Commerce, Manonmaniam Sundaranar University, Tirunelveli and **B. Marilakshmi** M.Phil Scholar, Department of Commerce, Manonmaniam Sundaranar University, Tirunelveli.

# Prospects and Challenges of Corporate Social Responsibility in the New Emerging Scenario

Dr. A. Rangaswamy

## Introduction

The phrase "Social Responsibility" is widely used in the literature of sociology, anthropology economics, Politics and Business Management, H.R. Bowen has defined the concept of social responsibility as "obligation to pursue those policies, to make those decisions, or to follow these lines of action which are described in terms of the objective and values of our society". In the words of Kenneth Andrews, "By, Social responsibility we mean intelligent and objective concern for the welfare of society that restraints individual and corporate behaviour from ultimately destructive action has no matter how immediately profitable, and leads in the direction of positive conditions to human betterment variously as the latter may be defined."

## Corporate Social Responsibility

What is corporate social Responsibility? The definitions differ vastly according to the perception and sensitivity of the analyst. In United States, C.S.R has been defined traditionally more in terms of a philanthropic Model. Companies make profits unhindered except by fulfilling their duty to pay taxes. Then they donate a certain share of the profits to charitable causes.

The European model is much more focused on operating the core business in a socially responsible way, complemented by investment in communities for solid business reasons. It is believed that this model is more sustainable because of the following reasons.

(*a*) Social responsibility becomes an integral part of the wealth creation process – which if managed properly, should enhance the competitiveness of business and maximize the volume of wealth creation to society.

(*b*) When times get hard, there is the incentive to practice C.S.R. more and better – if it is a philanthropic exercise, which is peripheral to the main business.

But as with any process based on the Collective activities of communities, there is no "one size fits all".

### Impact of Social Responsibility on Profits

Classical writers felt that a business is functioning in a socially responsible way if it were using economic resources at its command efficiently and supplying goods and services required by the society at reasonable prices. If this was done, the business would get maximum profits and serve the best interests of the owners of the business. The classical, economists considered the concept of social responsibility contradictory to the operation of the private enterprise system. But this view is strongly condemned by the modern economists because of changed economic and social environment, consumer consciousness, emergence of strong education, increase in literary rate etc. it is often argued that expenditure on socially responsible activities may not lead to profits in the short-run, but will increase profitability in the long run.

### The Need for Social Responsibility

Modern business organizations have shown greater interest in social responsibility of business. According to keothe Davis, some of the major arguments for social responsibility are the following:

1. It is in the long-term interest of the firm with the highest goal as "Service to society" the company can increase its profit by satisfying all sections of the society.
2. It improves the public image of the firm. The arguments here are that a firm's profits depend partly on its public image which is enhanced when it supports social goals.
3. It increases the variety of the business system. If a Company wants to retain present economic and other powers in society, then it must be responsive to social needs of the day and should contribute its resources for the purpose.
4. It is necessary to avoid government regulation:

   It is believed that the company can avoid the problem of government regulation by voluntarily assuming social responsibilities which helps to reduce the need for new laws.
5. Socio-cultural norms require it Business leaders should not forget that their right to exist and flourish carries an Obligation to serve the society.

6. It is required for maintaining an orderly society.
7. It is in the shareholder's best interest.
8. Society should give business a chance to solve social problems that government has failed to solve.
9. Prevention of problem is better than cure. The business should do something to meet social needs before it is confronted with a situation when its own survival is endangered due to enormous social illnesses.

## Global Role of Social Responsibility

Over the last 10 years institutions that have grown in power and influence have been those which can operate effectively within global sphere of operations. Those institutions within are predominantly tied to the nation state have been finding themselves increasingly frustrated at their lack of ability to shape and manage events These include national-governments, policy, Judiciary and others.

## Models of Corporate Social Responsibility

Social scientists have formulated several theories that justify the importance of corporate engaged in promoting social welfare of the society in which they operate, these theories are:

1. Trusteeship Model.
2. The Social Entity Theory
3. The pluralistic Model.

The Trusteeship Model adopts a realistic perspective of the corporation as a social institution with a corporate personality. The Trusteeship model differs from the agency model in two ways. First, the fiduciary duty of the trustees is to sustain the corporation's assets including Shareholders wealth and the values of employees such as skills.

The social entity conception of the corporation regards the company not as a private association united by individual property rights, but as a public association constituted through political and legal processes as a social entity for pursuing collective goals with public objectives.

The pluralistic model supports the idea of multiple interests of stakeholders, rather than shareholder interest alone. It suggests that corporate governance should not move away from ownership right, but such rights should not be solely claimed by shareholders alone but by other stakeholders and employees.

## The Scope of Social Responsibitity

The scope of social responsibility is wide and could be considered in terms of different viewpoints, some of which are given below:

1. Protecting and promoting stakeholders interest.

2. Social concern and Promotion of common welfare programmes.
3. As an act of philanthropy.
4. Good corporate governance itself is a social responsibility.
5. Corporates in the vanguard of rendering social service.
6. Sponsoring social and charitable causes.
7. Corporations should supplement state efforts.
8. Social responsibility of corporates also lies in abiding by rules and regulations.
9. Ensuring ecological balance.
10. By focusing human elements.

## Social Responsibility and Indian Companies

Philanthropy is no longer limited to signing cheques for social causes and welfare programmes. The Commitment is getting much deeper as a large section of employees, including members of the top management, are now doing their sit for the cause close to their heart. The initiatives do not end with an odd blood donation. More Companies are joining hands with NGOs to set up labs, adopt Schools and Villages, educate kids and women in slums and start welfare programmes for Cancer and AIDS patients.

Indian industry is aggressive in its drive to being socially responsible. North Delhi Power Ltd. (NDPL), a joint venture of Tata Group and the Delhi government has joined hands to help out AIDS patients and improve awareness in industrial Areas of Naraina. A large number of Indian companies discharge their social responsibility functions that Indian Companies typically perform.

1. **Asian Paints** funded a large – scale community development project to enable farmers to use local resources effectively.
2. **BHEL**, has contributed to the development of the quality of life in rural areas, health care and family welfare, adult education etc.
3. **Brooke Bond** has been interested in animal welfare, providing veterinary services, and improvements in animal breeding.
4. **Colgate Palmolive** did pioneering work in the promotion of Sports, dental health, and small industry development.
5. **Escorts Ltd.** has worked for farm mechanization, agricultural development, health care, etc.
6. **Infosys Technologies** has helped through its Infosys Foundation schools in rural areas, acquire class rooms, libraries and buildings. It has also helped higher education and research.
7. **ITC Ltd** is socially active in the areas of agriculture, culture, sports and pollution control.
8. **SAIL** contributes to the sectors of agriculture, industry, education, health care, dairy, poultry, fisheries and protected water supply.

**TATA STEEL** has been a pioneer in discharging social responsibility and has made several contributions in areas such as community development, Social welfare tribal area development, agriculture and related activities, rural Industrialization, etc.

## Conclusion

The above analysis of the multidimensional work carried out by companies' show how corporates can do wonders if they pool their material and human resources to promote the welfare of the community. It is to be remembered that the Loyola Institute of Business Administration (LIBA) conferred on TVS motor company,, Ltd, the prestigious "Mother Theresa Award" for corporate citizen on March 31.2004.

## REFERENCES

1. Fr. PAUL De La Gueriviere, S.J and Fr. Louis Xavier, S.J., "Social Responsibility of Business" LIBA Publications (1996), Chennai.
2. Fernanad–A.C., "Corporate Governance" Pearsons Publications (2009) New Delhi.
3. Mittal. K.M., "Social Responsibilities of Business Concepts Areas and Progress". Chanakya, Publications, (1988) Delhi.
4. Sanjay Kumar Panda, "Corporate Social Responsibility in India Past, Present and Future" — The ICFAI University Press (2008) Agartala, India.

# Corporate Social Responsibility

## *A Plus Point to Prosper*

**Ms. K.B. Sridevi**

## Introduction

Corporate social responsibility, also called corporate conscience, citizenship, social performance, or sustainable responsible business, is a form of corporate self-regulation integrated into a business model. CSR policy functions as a built-in, self-regulating mechanism whereby business monitors and ensures its active compliance with the spirit of the law, ethical standards, and international norms. The goal of CSR is to embrace responsibility for the company's actions and encourage a positive impact through its activities on the environment, consumers, employees, communities, stakeholders and all other members of the public sphere. Furthermore, CSR-focused businesses would proactively promote the public interest by encouraging community growth and development, and voluntarily eliminating practices that harm the public sphere, regardless of legality. CSR is the deliberate inclusion of public interest into corporate decision-making, and the honouring of a triple bottom line: people, planet, profit.

**THE KEY DRIVERS FOR CSR:**

- *Enlightened self-interest* - creating a synergy of ethics, a cohesive society and a sustainable global economy where markets, labour and communities are able to function well together.
- *Social investment* - contributing to physical infrastructure and social capital is increasingly seen as a necessary part of doing business.
- *Transparency and trust* - business has low ratings of trust in public perception. There is increasing expectation that companies will be more open, more accountable and be prepared to report publicly on their performance in social and environmental arenas.

- *Increased public expectations of business* - globally companies are expected to do more than merely provide jobs and contribute to the economy through taxes and employment.
- *Ethical consumerism* - Consumers are becoming more aware of the environmental and social implications of their day-to-day consumer decisions and are therefore beginning to make purchasing decisions related to their environmental and ethical concerns.
- *Laws and regulations* - Another driver of CSR is the role of independent mediators, particularly the government, in ensuring that corporations are prevented from harming the broader social good, including people and the environment.

### Potential Business Benefits

The scale and nature of the benefits of CSR for an organization can vary depending on the nature of the enterprise, and are difficult to quantify. However, businesses may not be looking at short-run financial returns when developing their CSR strategy.

### Human Resources

A CSR programme can be an aid to recruitment and retention. Potential recruits often ask about a firm's CSR policy during an interview, and having a comprehensive policy can give an advantage. CSR can also help improve the perception of a company among its staff, particularly when staff can become involved through payroll giving, fundraising activities or community volunteering. Corporate Social Entrepreneurship, whereby CSR can also be driven by employees' personal values, in addition to the more obvious economic and governmental drivers.

### Risk Management

Managing risk is a central part of many corporate strategies. Reputations that take decades to build up can be ruined in hours through incidents such as corruption scandals or environmental accidents. These can also draw unwanted attention from regulators, courts, governments and media. Building a genuine culture of 'doing the right thing' within a corporation can offset these risks.

### Brand Differentiation

In crowded marketplaces, companies strive for a unique selling proposition that can separate them from the competition in the minds of consumers. CSR can play a role in building customer loyalty based on distinctive ethical values. Several major brands, such as The Co-operative Group, The Body Shop and American Apparel are built on ethical values. Business service organizations can benefit too from building a reputation for integrity and best practice.

### License to Operate

Corporations are keen to avoid interference in their business through taxation or regulations. By taking substantive voluntary steps, they can persuade governments and the wider public that they are taking issues such as health and safety, diversity, or the environment seriously as good corporate citizens with respect to labour standards and impacts on the environment.

## CORPORATE SOCIAL RESPONSIBILITY : INITIATIVES AND EXAMPLES

### SAP

"Here for Life" is a not-for-profit public benevolent organization focusing on education, awareness and research aimed at the prevention of youth suicide. The organization provides resources, education and school based life skills programs to help prevent suicide amongst young people. Through its charity sponsorship program SAP Australia supports "Here for Life" with monetary contributions, volunteering and staff involvement in the agency's programs.

### IBM

IBM - Japan's 'e-elder' initiative is a national program using training materials and other support from IBM Japan which will hire and train seniors as instructors for other seniors in an effort to help elder citizens more fully participate in a Web-based society.

### Microsoft

Microsoft works closely with international organizations such as the World Food Programme, Save the Children, and Mercy Corps to provide technology-based development assistance through the HEART (Humanitarian Empowerment and Response through Technology) program. More and more, global organizations rely on technology to improve the effectiveness of their humanitarian efforts around the world.

### Aptech Limited

Aptech Limited, a leading education player with a global presence, has played an extensive and sustained role in encouraging and fostering education throughout the country since inception. As a global player with complete solutions-providing capability, Aptech has a long history of participating in community activities. It has, in association with leading NGOs, provided computers at schools, education to the underprivileged and conducted training and awareness-camps.

Aptech students donated part of the proceeds from the sale of their art work to NGOs. To propagate education among all sections of the society throughout the country, especially the underprivileged, Aptech fosters tie-ups with leading NGOs throughout the country, including the Barrackpur-based NGO, Udayan, a residential school for children of leprosy patients in Barrackpur, established in 1970.The company strongly believes that education is an integral part of the country's social fabric and works towards supporting basic education and basic computer literacy amongst the underprivileged children in India.

### ICICI Bank Ltd

The Social Initiatives Group (SIG) of ICICI Bank Ltd works with a mission to build the capacities of the poorest to participate in the larger economy. The group identifies and supports initiatives designed to break the intergenerational cycle of poor health and nutrition ensure essential early childhood education and schooling as well as access to basic financial services. Thus, by promoting early child health, catalyzing universal elementary education and maximizing access to micro financial services, ICICI Bank believes that it can build the capacities of India's poor to participate in larger socio-economic processes and thereby spur the overall development of the country. The SIG locates cost effective and scalable initiatives and approaches that have the potential to address these gaps and supports research to understand their impact. This is undertaken in collaboration with research agencies, nongovernmental organizations (NGOs), companies, government departments, local stakeholders and international organizations.

### Infosys Technologies Limited

Infosys is actively involved in various community development programs. Infosys promoted, in 1996, the Infosys Foundation as a not-for-profit trust to which it contributes up to 1%PAT every year. Additionally, the Education and Research Department (E&R) at Infosys also works with employee volunteers on community development projects. Infosys leadership has set examples in the area of corporate citizenship and has involved itself actively in key national bodies. They have taken initiatives to work in the areas of Research and Education, Community Service, Rural Reach Programme, Employment, Welfare activities undertaken by the Infosys Foundation, Healthcare for the poor, Education and Arts & Culture.

### ITC Limited

ITC partnered the Indian farmer for close to a century. ITC is now engaged in elevating this partnership to a new paradigm by leveraging information technology through its trailblazing 'e-Choupal' initiative. ITC is significantly widening its farmer partnerships to embrace a host of value-adding activities: creating livelihoods by helping poor tribal make their wastelands productive; investing in rainwater harvesting to bring much-needed irrigation to parched dry lands; empowering rural women by helping them evolve into entrepreneurs; and providing infrastructural support to make schools exciting for village children. Through these rural partnerships, ITC touches the lives of nearly 3 million villagers across India.

### Hindustan Construction Company

HCC plays an active role in CSR initiatives in the fields of Health, Education, Disaster Management, and Environment. Disaster Resource Network DRN is a worldwide initiative, promoted by the World Economic Forum (WEF).Trained volunteers and equipment resources from Engineering Construction & Logistics companies will complement the existing efforts of Government, NGO's and International Organizations in disaster management. It was during the WEF annual meet that the massive earthquake struck Gujarat in January 2001. The need for a trained and effective participation from industry was first felt there. The members of Engineering and Logistics segment of WEF came together to establish this network. The idea was further strengthened during the 9/11 incident where again the industry participated in the relief operations. DRN Worldwide was formally launched in New York in January 2002. And shortly thereafter, DRN - India Initiative was launched.

### Larsen & Turbo (L & T) Limited

Considering that construction industry is the second largest employer in India after agriculture, employing about 32 million-strong workforce, L&T set out to regulate and promote Construction Vocational Training (CVT) in India by establishing a Construction Skills Training Institute (CSTI) on a 5.5 acre land, close to its Construction Division Headquarters at Manapakkam, Chennai. CSTI imparts, totally free of cost, basic training in formwork, carpentry, masonry, bar-bending, plumbing and sanitary, scaffolder and electrical wireman trades to a wide spectrum of the rural poor.

As a result of the good response it received in Chennai, CSTI set up a branch at Panvel, Mumbai, initially offering training in formwork, carpentry and masonry trades. The Manapakkam and Panvel facilities together provide training to about 300 candidates annually who are inducted after a process of selection, the minimum qualification being tenth standard. Since inception, these two units have produced about 2,000 skilled workmen in various trades, with about sixty percent of them being deployed to L&T's jobsites spread across the country. The success of this training-initiative demonstrates that adoption of systematic training techniques are bound to yield efficient and skilled personnel in the shortest possible time, and in the power to convert the potential of the Rural Youth in Construction and upgrading Rura Economy in a small way.

### Conclusion

CSR is titled to aid an organization's mission as well as a guide to what the company stands for and will uphold to its consumers. Development business ethics is one of the forms of applied ethics that examines ethical principles and moral or ethical problems that can arise in a business environment. ISO 26000 is the recognized international standard for CSR (currently a Draft International Standard). Public sector organizations (the United Nations for example) adhere to the triple bottom line. It is widely accepted that CSR adheres to similar principles but with no formal act of legislation. The UN has developed the Principles for Responsible Investment as guidelines for investing entities Corporate Social Responsibility (CSR) is becoming an increasingly important activity to businesses nationally and internationally. As globalization accelerates and large corporations serve as global providers, these corporations have progressively recognized the benefits of providing CSR programs in their various locations. CSR activities are now being undertaken throughout the globe.

## REFERENCES


1. Bansal, P.R. Roth (2000), "Why Companies Go Green: A model of Ecological Responsiveness", The Academy of Management Journal, Vol. 43, No. 4, pp. 717–736.
2. Bulkeley, H. (2001), "Governing Climate Change: The Politics and Risk Society", Transactions of the Institute of British Geographers, New Series, Vol. 26, No. 4, pp. 430–447.
3. Brand Strategy (2007), "10 key things to know about CSR". London, p. 47.
4. Feltus,C.; Petit, M.; Dubois, E.(2009), "Strengthening Employee's Responsibility to enhance governance of IT: COBIT RACI chart case study", ISBN 978-1-60558-787-5.
5. Fialka. J. (2006). "Politics & Economics: Big Businesses Have New Take on Warming; Some Companies Move From Opposition to Offering Proposals on Limiting Emissions". Wall Street Journal. p. A.4.
6. Grace, D., S. Cohen (2005), "Business Ethics: Australian Problems and Cases", Oxford University Press, ISBN 0195507940.
7. Pitts,C. (ed.), M. Kerr, R. Janda, & C. Pitts (2009), " Corporate Social Responsibility: A Legal Analysis", (Toronto: LexisNexis). ISBN 9780433451150.
8. Roux,M. (2007). "Climate conducive to corporate action: 1 All-round Country Edition". The Australian. Canberra, A.C.T., p. 14. online article.
9. Sun, William (2010), How to Govern Corporations So They Serve the Public Good: A Theory of Corporate Governance Emergence, New York: Edwin Mellen, ISBN 9780773438637.

# Role of Government and Private Institutions in Corporate Social Responsibility Development

T. Samson Joe Dhinakaran

## Introduction

Corporate Social Responsibility (CSR), can be described as, the continuous commitment by corporations towards the economic and social development of communities in which they operate. The concept of corporate social responsibility of large industrial groups has occupied a prominent place in the greater national discourse on economic issues since the pre-independence era in India. Gandhi described large business as 'trusts' of the 'wealth of the people' and thus emphasized on the larger social purpose that industrial wealth should serve in independent India. In the early days of the post-independence period, the Indian state under the heavy influence of Nehruvian socialism encouraged private industries to play an active role in the economic and social development of the backward sections of the society, while at the same time setup a mammoth public sector for serving larger societal interests. As Nehru's gentle socialism gave way to the more radical policies of nationalization and extensive state regulation of the Indira Gandhi era, industrial groups desperate to avoid the draconian state policies and regulations in economic affairs resorted to large scale corporate welfare programs to demonstrate that private wealth also played a important role in poverty alleviation and the socio-economic development of the nation and was not anti-people.

## INDIA'S TOP MOST PRIVATE CORPORATE SOCIAL RESPONSIBILITY

### TVS Motor Company Ltd.

- **Economic Development:** 38,340 families have a minimum income of

Rs. 4,000 per month. This has been made possible by helping the women to earn an additional income by way of income generation activities, increase in agriculture production and better livestock management. This income helps their families have both food and financial security.

- **Health:** Easy access to primary health care and adoption of proper sanitation, hygiene and nutrition has resulted in improved general health standards of the community. There has been no case of infant or maternal mortality in the project areas. Now, over 189 villages have access to safe drinking water. As against 70% of the women found anaemic 4 years ago, today the incidence of anemia is down to 11%. Only about 4% of the children are found malnourished.
- **Education:** There is 100% enrolment of children in schools. Average pass percentage of the government higher secondary schools in the project area is 72%. So far 10535 women members have become literate. They have basic reading skills up to class 2 levels.
- **Environment:** People segregate biodegradable and degradable garbage at their homes. Garbage is being collected by members of Self Help Groups. Biodegradable waste is converted to vermi compost. Over 27 tons of vermi compost is produced every month. Sale of vermi compost generates about Rs.1.08 lakhs per month. 10,900 individual toilets, 174 school toilets and 56 community toilets have been constructed and are being used. Over 1,12,000 hectares of degraded forests have been reforested. SST helped the people to earn an extra income from non-forest related activities. This has created awareness about safeguarding the forests.
- **Watershed Development:** Watershed development refers to the conservation, regeneration and the judicious use of natural (land, water, plants, animals) and human - within a particular watershed. Watershed management tries to bring about the best possible balance in the environment between natural resources on the one side, and human and other living beings on the other.

SST has taken up Micro Watershed Programs in Padavedu funded by Ford foundation. Irumbuli, Kothakondapalli and Saragapalli micro watershed development program have been funded by NABARD in Tiruvanamalai and Krishnagiri districts of Tamil Nadu.

Tata Motors is committed, in letter and spirit, to the improvement in the quality of life of people. Equally, Tata Motors believes in being proactive in achieving a balance between business growth and social and environment related needs. Hence, the company's business focus is both on personal and public transportation. Hence the company is itself working on or supporting development of alternate fuels, electric and hybrid vehicles, both for personal and public transportation. Whether in pursuing its business growth or meeting its responsibilities, Tata Motors intent is to contribute by "doing the right thing" as against merely being compliant by "not doing the wrong things."

- Boost to Brand Image
- Integrated Rural Development
- Technical and Vocational Training for Youth Members:
- Employment Opportunities for Empowering Women
- Direct Employment
- Partnering with the Public and the Social Sector
- Towards Community Development - MMV Trade Course at Sakwar
- Industry Partnerships
- Aid to NGOs
- Skill Upgradation
- Health Awareness

**Wipro Pvt. Ltd.**

Our commitment has never been limited to the IT initiatives we execute in our daily functions at Wipro. Over the years, we have developed a clear road to realize our vision of taking our success to other sections of society who struggle to care for their own basic needs.

- Wipro Cares
- Wipro Applying Thought in Schools
- Eco Eye
- Health
- Work-Life Balance

**RIL Pvt Ltd.**

Reliance Industry Ltd. has a long and strong tradition of supporting the larger communities that it connects with - from education, health, drinking water, large-scale development of employable skills, to assistance during natural calamities such as earthquakes and cyclones. The Reliance Foundation would address social development imperatives of India, specifically quality, formal and vocational eduation, affordable high-quality health care, meaningful rural development and urban renewal, and protection and promotion of India's priceless heritage of arts and culture.

- Education
- Community Health Care
- Community's Safety
- Rural Infrastructure Development
- Livelihood Support Programmes

- Relief Operations
- Wildlife and Animal Care
- Heritage Conservation
- Supporting Indian Culture
- Supporting Professional Organisations and NGOs
- Promoting Sports and Sportspersons
- Acknowledging and Supporting Talent
- Dhirubhai Ambani Foundation
- Dhirubhai Ambani International School (DAIS)

### Indian Oil

Indian Oil, corporate social responsibility (CSR) has been the cornerstone of success right from inception in the year 1964. Indian Oil's social responsibility programme, there is an Indian Oil Scholarship scheme, which provides for attractive scholarships to bright students selected on 'merit-cum-means' basis. As part of the scheme, special encouragement is being given to girl students, physically challenged students, and students from J & K as well as the Northeast States. Besides focusing primarily on the welfare of economically and socially deprived sections of society, Indian Oil also aims at developing techno-economically viable and environment-friendly products & services for the benefit of millions of its consumers, while at the same time ensuring the highest standards of safety and environment protection in its operations. Indian Oil has always been in the forefront in times of national emergencies. Indian oil people have time and again rallied to help victims of natural calamities, maintaining uninterrupted supply of petroleum products and contributing to relief and rehabilitation measures in cash and kind. Indian Oil has also set up the Indian Oil Foundation (IOF) as a non-profit trust to protect, preserve and promote national heritage monuments. Indian Oil is also committed to the Global Compact Programme of the United Nations and endeavors to abide by the 10 principles of the programme, some of which are already part of the Corporation's Vision and Mission statements. It is the firm resolves of Indian oil people to move beyond business, touch every heart and fuel a billion dreams.

### Life Insurance Corporation of India

LIC as a responsible Corporate Citizen has been fulfilling its social responsibilities from time to time. In fact, most of our investments are geared towards industrial growth, infrastructure growth and national development. LIC was contributing to Prime Ministers' National Relief Fund, Chief Ministers' Relief Funds of various states as also Rajiv Gandhi Foundation to help relief measures in case of calamities such as Earthquake, Tsunami etc. With a view to channelise our social responsibilities and give a formal shape to the same we have formed a Public Trust named 'LIC Golden Jubilee Foundation'.

The main objectives of the Golden Jubilee Foundation are:

- Relief of poverty or distress.
- Advancement of Education
- Medical Relief
- The advancement of any other object of general public utility.

The concept of corporate social responsibility (CSR) is not new to Indian companies. However, what is new is the way it has caught on with Corporates in India and the direct involvement of employees in implementation of these projects. The Golden Jubilee Foundation would provide a great avenue of fulfilling our social responsibility at the corporate level and our philanthropic needs at the individual level.

### Bharat Sanchar Nigam Limited (BSNL)

Bharat Sanchar Nigam Limited (BSNL), India's public sector telephone company has taken up a project to maintain and clean some long distance Rajdhani trains. BSNL will take care for up-gradation, cleaning and maintenance of these trains. This says the report, will also add on to (the company's) Corporate Social Responsibility activity. BSNL is using funds for PR in the name of Corporate Social Responsibility. While encouraging companies to become more responsible and undertake enhanced Corporate Social Responsibility the Ministry of Corporate Affairs and the Department of Public Enterprises should undertake a study of how money set aside for Corporate Social Responsibility is being spent. Merely making public announcements upgrading the annual Corporate Social Responsibility allotments will not ensure increased Corporate Social Responsibility activity.

### Bharat Heavy Electricals (BHEL)

Bharat Heavy Electricals (BHEL) seeks to collaborate with NGOs and social organizations to launch corporate social responsibility (CSR) projects in areas of environment protection, energy conservation, vocational training, infrastructure development and disaster management. The move is in line with government guidelines issued in April this year asking PSUs earning more than Rs 500crores to spend two per cent of annual profit on Corporate Social Responsibility activities. The guidelines also mandate PSUs to engage specialized agencies to implement activities identified under Corporate Social Responsibility. BHEL made a net profit of Rs 4,311crores during financial year ended March 31, 2010.

### Conclusion

The Corporate Social Responsibility initiatives have also seen greater people participation at all stages and tighter accountability standards. The issue of norms for corporate social responsibility seems to have been adequately dealt with by industry practices like benchmarking, Corporate Social Responsibility ratings and certification by different agencies. While the situation in the private sector seems satisfactory, there is fierce debate on the social role of the Indian public sector. There is a need for extensive research especially in form of empirical studies to address the questions related to this issue.

## REFERENCES

1. Asmus. P. (2003),"Corporate Social Responsibility [PDF document]", Retrieved from Lecture Notes Online Web site: http://www6.miami.edu/ethics/pdf_files/csr_guide.pdf
2. "Corporate Social Responsibility" (March 3, 2009),Retrieved August, 9, 2009, from http://www.iocl.com/Aboutus/corporatesocialresponsibility.asp
3. "Corporative social responsibility", Naukrihub, retrieved on 9th august 2009,http://www.naukrihub.com/hr-today/corporate-social-responsibility.html
4. "Crisis management", Retrieved August 8, 2009, from wikipedia: http://en.wikipedia.org/wiki/Crisis_management
5. "CSR: A brand building exercise for media houses?" *Kalinga Time,* Retrieved from http://kalingatimes.com/business_news/news2/20090729_CSR_A_brand_building_exercise_for_media_houses.html
6. Fauset. P. (2006). "What's wrong with Corporate Social Responsibility [PDF document]". Retrieved from Lecture Notes Online Web site:http://www.corporatewatch.org.uk/download.php?id=55

# Corporate Social Responsibility

## *Policies and Guidelines*

T. Samson Joe Dhinakaran

### Introduction

The 21st century is characterized by unprecedented challenges and opportunities, arising from globalization, the desire for inclusive development and the imperatives of climate change. Indian business, which is today viewed globally as a responsible component of the ascendancy of India, is poised now to take on a leadership role in the challenges of our times. It is recognized the world over that integrating social, environmental and ethical responsibilities into the governance of businesses ensures their long term success, competitiveness and sustainability. This approach also reaffirms the view that businesses are an integral part of society, and have a critical and active role to play in the sustenance and improvement of healthy ecosystems, in fostering social inclusiveness and equity, and in upholding the essentials of ethical practices and good governance. This also makes business sense as companies with effective CSR, have image of socially responsible companies, achieve sustainable growth in their operations in the long run and their products and services are preferred by the customers.

Indian entrepreneurs and business enterprises have a long tradition of working within the values that have defined our nation's character for millennia. India's ancient wisdom, which is still relevant today, inspires people to work for the larger objective of the well-being of all stakeholders. These sound and all-encompassing values are even more relevant in current times, as organizations grapple with the challenges of modern-day enterprise, the aspirations of stakeholders and of citizens eager to be active participants in economic growth and development.

CSR is not philanthropy and CSR activities are purely voluntary- what companies will like to do beyond any statutory requirement or obligation.

To provide companies with guidance in dealing with the abovementioned expectations, while working closely within the framework of national aspirations and policies, following Voluntary Guidelines for Corporate Social Responsibility have been developed.

While the guidelines have been prepared for the Indian context, Enterprises that have a trans-national presence would benefit from using these guidelines for their overseas operations as well. Since the guidelines are voluntary and not prepared in the nature of a prescriptive road-map, they are not intended for regulatory or contractual use.

While it is expected that more and more companies would make sincere efforts to consider compliance with these guidelines, there may be genuine reasons for some companies in not being able to adopt them completely. In such a case, it is expected that such companies may inform their stakeholders about the guidelines which the companies have not been able to follow either fully or partially. It is hoped that "India Inc." would respond to these guidelines with keen interest.

After considering the experience of adoption of these guidelines by Indian Corporate Sector and consideration of relevant feedback and other related issues, the Government may initiate the exercise for review of these guidelines for further improvement after one year.

### Corporate Social Responsibility

**Corporate Social Responsibility** also called corporate conscience, citizenship, social performance, or sustainable responsible business is a form of corporate self-regulation integrated into a business model. CSR policy functions as a built-in, self-regulating mechanism whereby business monitors and ensures its active compliance with the spirit of the law, ethical standards, and international norms. The goal of CSR is to embrace responsibility for the company's actions and encourage a positive impact through its activities on the environment, consumers, employees, communities, stakeholders and all other members of the public sphere. Furthermore, CSR-focused businesses would proactively promote the public interest by encouraging community growth and development, and voluntarily eliminating practices that harm the public sphere, regardless of legality. CSR is the deliberate inclusion of public interest into corporate decision-making, and the honouring of a triple bottom line: people, plant, profit.

The term "corporate social responsibility" came in to common use in the early 1970s, after many multinational corporations formed. The term stakeholder, meaning those on whom an organization's activities have an impact, was used to describe corporate owners beyond shareholders as a result of an influential book by R. Edward Freeman, Strategic management: a stakeholder approach in 1984.[2] Proponents argue that corporations make more long term profits by operating with a perspective, while critics argue that CSR distracts from the economic role of businesses. Others argue CSR is merely window-dressing, or an attempt to pre-empt the role of governments as a watchdog over powerful multinational corporations.

CSR is titled to aid an organization's mission as well as a guide to what the company stands for and will uphold to its consumers. Development business ethics is one of the forms of applied ethics that examines ethical principles and moral or ethical problems that can arise in a business environment. ISO 2600 is the recognized international standard for CSR (currently a Draft International Standard). Public sector organizations (the United Nations for example) adhere to the triple bottom line (TBL). It is widely accepted that CSR adheres to similar principles but with no formal act of legislation. The UN has developed the Principles for Responsible Investment as guidelines for investing entities.

### Corporate Social Responsibility -Indian Context

The 1990's have perhaps been the decade of profound change in India's economic paradigm and have significantly affected Corporate India. Structural adjustment has meant an increasing role for the corporate sector and freedom from controls-an opportunity of immense proportions. It has also meant competition, both from within and outside, and a breakdown of protections that the sector earlier enjoyed. As with every change, there are winners and losers. But it is undisputed that Corporate India will play, if it is not already doing so, a major role in the lives of all India. This cannot be ignored.

Corporate Social Responsibility (CSR), like many modern ideas, is not new to India. It is part of an ancient tradition, which is currently being practiced by some companies. It has been informed by ideas from the West through business collaboration between companies. Industrial associations, who have recognized that it is an essential part of business, have also promoted it. Socially responsible behaviour has two dimensions; one is the stakeholders who have a contractual relationship with the business e.g., employees shareholders, customers and so on. The other are those whose lives are impacted by the behaviour of the business. Of the latter, communities, particularly the most disadvantaged amongst them, are the most crucial.

Effective corporate social responsibility towards any community requires close interaction with current developmental thinking, which has been constantly evolving. Initially there was welfare and now there is empowerment. Basic needs are gradually becoming basic rights. These ideas seem to gain currency in the view that human development is the ultimate goal and economic.

### CSR Policy

Each business entity should formulate a CSR policy to guide its strategic planning and provide a roadmap for its CSR initiatives, which should be an integral part of overall business policy and aligned with its business goals. The policy should be framed with the participation of various level executives and should be approved by the Board. The CSR Policy should normally cover following core elements:

**1. Care for all Stakeholders:** The companies should respect the interests of, and be responsive towards all stakeholders, including shareholders, employees, customers, suppliers, project affected people, society at large etc. and create value for all of them. They should develop mechanism to actively engage with all stakeholders, inform them of inherent risks and mitigate them where they occur.

**2. Ethical Functioning:** Their governance systems should be underpinned by Ethics, Transparency and Accountability. They should not engage in business practices that are abusive, unfair, corrupt or anti-competitive.

**3. Respect for Workers' Rights and Welfare:** Companies should provide a workplace environment that is safe, hygienic and humane and which upholds the dignity of employees. They should provide all employees with access to training and development of necessary skills for career advancement, on an equal and non-discriminatory basis. They should uphold the freedom of association and the effective recognition of the right to collective bargaining of labour, have an effective grievance redressal system, should not employ child or forced labour and provide and maintain equality of opportunities without any discrimination on any grounds in recruitment and during employment.

**4. Respect for Human Rights**

1. The CSR policy of the business entity should provide for an implementation strategy which should include identification of projects/activities, setting measurable physical targets with timeframe, organizational mechanism and responsibilities, time schedules and monitoring. Companies may partner with local authorities, business associations and civil society/non-government organizations. They may influence the supply chain for CSR initiative and motivate employees for voluntary effort for social development. They may evolve a system of need assessment and impact assessment while undertaking CSR activities in a particular area. Independent evaluation May also be undertaken for selected projects/activities from time to time.
2. Companies should allocate specific amount in their budgets for CSR activities. This amount may be related to profits after tax, cost of Planned CSR activities or any other suitable parameter.
3. To share experiences and network with other organizations, the company should engage with well established and recognized programmes/platforms which encourage responsible business

Practices and CSR activities. This would help companies to improve on their CSR strategies and effectively project the image of being socially responsible.

4. The companies should disseminate information on CSR policy, activities and progress in a structured manner to all their stakeholders and the public at large through their website, annual reports, and other communication media.

   Companies should respect human rights for all and avoid complicity With human rights abuses by them or by third party.

**5. Respect for Environment:** Companies should take measures to check and prevent pollution; recycle, manage and reduce waste, should manage natural resources in a sustainable manner and ensure optimal use of resources like land and water, should proactively respond to the challenges of climate change by adopting cleaner production methods, promoting efficient use of energy and environment friendly technologies.

**6. Activities for Social and Inclusive Development:** Depending upon their core competency and business interest, companies should undertake activities for economic and social development of communities and geographical areas, particularly in the vicinity of their operations. These could include: education, skill building for livelihood of people, health, cultural and social welfare etc., particularly targeting at disadvantaged sections of society

## IMPLEMENTATION GUIDANCE

### Conclusion

Corporate Social Responsibility is a necessary condition for achieving excellence, not a sufficient one. Good governance is a source of competitive advantage and critical to economic progress. The quintessence of Corporate Governance is transparency, accountability, investor protection, better compliance with statutory laws and regulations, value creation for shareholders as also for other stakeholders and societal value.

## REFERENCES

1. www.forbes.com
2. www.referenceforbusiness.com
3. www.justmeans.com
4. www.sheshunoff.com
5. www.csreurope.org

# Corporate Social Responsibility

## *A Multidimensional Approach*

**Dr. K. Krishnakumar**
**V. Selvam**

### Introduction

Corporate Social Responsibility (CSR) is a well known concept but not implemented well by most of the corporate. They are not known about the benefits of CSR as well as there is negative school of thoughts about the CSR initiatives. There are more challenges to initiate the CSR activities which are the major hurdles to the development of CSR activities. There are an array of CSR standards, and initiatives. Despite an ongoing effort to develop a global CSR guidance standard unhappiness about the "state of play" exists along the spectrum of stakeholders. Too much regulation, or uncertainty about its form and arrival time, may present concerns for corporations and other actors. There may be a temptation to focus on environmental risks and "solving" some of them by going "green," but this focus may not be enough to ensure a company's health. Ignoring non-green CSR issues leaves a company open to significant financial and reputation risks. This is definitely a case where going green can leave you in the red - management might suffer thinner coffers and embarrassment from a CSR oversight.

### Challenges of CSR Initiatives

Eventually key components of effective CSR programs include having sufficient capacity to provide support, and legally protected advice and counsel in order to implement and effectively sustain CSR programs and the companies and stakeholders they seek to protect.

The following are the key issues in the CSR initiatives:

• **Lack of community participation in CSR activities:** There is a lack of interest of the local community in participating and contributing to CSR activities of companies. This is largely attributable to the fact that there exists little or no knowledge about CSR within the local communities as no serious efforts have been made to spread awareness about CSR and instill confidence in the local communities about such initiatives. The situation is further aggravated by a lack of communication between the company and the community at the grassroots.

• **Need to build local capacities:** There is a need for capacity building of the local non-governmental organisations as there is serious dearth of trained and efficient organisations that can effectively contribute to the ongoing CSR activities initiated by companies. This seriously compromises scaling up of CSR initiatives and subsequently limits the scope of such activities.

• **Issues of transparency:** Lack of transparency is one of the key issues in the CSR initiatives. There is an expression by the companies that there exists lack of transparency on the part of the local implementing agencies as they do not make adequate efforts to disclose information on their programmes, audit issues, impact assessment and utilisation of funds.

• **Non-availability of well organised non-governmental organisations:** There is also non-availability of well organised nongovernmental organisations in remote and rural areas that can assess and identify real needs of the community and work along with companies to ensure successful implementation of CSR activities. This also builds the case for investing in local communities by way of building their capacities to undertake development projects at local levels.

• **Visibility factor:** The role of media in highlighting good cases of successful CSR initiatives is welcomed as it spreads good stories and sensitises the local population about various ongoing CSR initiatives of companies.

• **Narrow perception towards CSR initiatives:** Non-governmental organisations and Government agencies usually possess a narrow outlook towards the CSR initiatives of companies, often defining CSR initiatives more more donor-driven than local in approach. As a result, it find that hard to decide whether they should participate in such activities at all in medium and long run.

• **Non-availability of clear CSR guidelines:** There are no clear cut statutory guidelines or policy directives to give a definitive direction to CSR initiatives of companies. It is found that the scale of CSR initiatives of companies should depend upon their business size and profile. In other words, the bigger the company, the larger its CSR programme.

• **Lack of consensus on implementing CSR issues:** There is a lack of consensus amongst local agencies regarding CSR projects. This lack of consensus often results in duplication of activities by corporate houses in areas of their intervention. This results in a competitive spirit between local implementing agencies rather than building collaborative approaches on issues. This factor limits company's abilities to undertake impact assessment of their initiatives from time to time.

## DIMENSIONS OF CORPORATE SOCIAL RESPONSIBILITY

The CSR viewed as three dimensional approach and the three dimensions are economic, social and ecological dimension which means the CSR involvement into the particular category of dimension.

### Economic Dimension

The responsibility of companies is to make profits. Nevertheless consumers and public insist on more transparency and they want that companies take social responsibility as "Corporate Citizens". Because of globalisation the expression "Corporate Social Responsibility" means that companies have to take societal responsibility and beside making profit they have also to show a trustworthy engagement for the society. The economic dimension includes a fair competition, concrete aspects of Corporate Governance and also Supply Chain Management. The basis of fair competition is the truth about costs and legal methods and means. Illegal practices in order to reduce costs break not only the law; they also influence health and security of the workers. Corporate Governance is concerned with rules for the management and control of listed companies. Through transparency it should be reached to have a better trust into the companies. Successfully Supply Chain Managements means to find fields for cost reducing. CSR means to convince also suppliers that societal means are better than others.

### Social Dimension

The company can transform and create its own strategy. That means especially the treatment with their staff: how to combine family and job, what about continued education, jobs for elder people and handicapped people, health and security for their staff. Therefore it is important to take into consideration the rules of the ILO. Also important is to respect cultural differences and to pay attention to the rules of international human rights. To adapt the structure and development are necessary to solve these social problems.

### Ecological Dimension

The Ecological dimension includes all parts of the precautionary principal and the eco-efficiency. The challenges for companies are to use the production factors eco-efficient and to achieve the maximum profits and at the same time to offer the best use for consumers. The precautionary principle means for companies and their managers to take responsibility seriously for the following generations. Only if this happens the natural resources can be preservated and the societal stability can be assured under the aspect of economical success. Eco-efficiency combines economical and ecological interests and it is the basis for sustainability. Ecologically efficiency cannot be reached in a short period of time it requires therefore a consequent treatment and a long term commitment an all parts of a company and management levels. Many companies have therefore especially in the last decades a number of successful means created in order to use energy very efficient.

## BENEFITS OF CSR TO THE COMPANY

The various benefits that a company derives out of its CSR activities are:

- **Improved Financial Performance:** In the last decade, an increasing number of studies have been conducted to examine the CSR activities improving the financial performance of the firm. There are many studies showed that overall financial performance sample companies was significantly better than that of the remaining companies which are not involving the CSR initiatives.
- **Reduced Operating Costs:** Many initiatives aimed at improving environmental performance—such as reducing emissions of gases or reducing use of agrochemicals, recycling initiatives, in the human resources arena, flexible scheduling and other work life programs that result in reduced absenteeism and increased retention of employees often save companies' money through increased productivity and reduction of operating costs.
- **Enhanced Brand Image and Reputation and Increased Sales:** Customers often prefer brands and companies with good reputations in CSR-related areas and potentially large and growing market for the products and services of companies perceived to be socially responsible.
- **Improved Productivity and Quality:** Company efforts to improve working conditions, lessen environmental impacts or increase employee involvement in decision making often lead to increased productivity and reduced error rate.
- **Increased ability to attract and retain employees:** Companies perceived to have strong CSR commitments often find it easier to recruit and retain employees, resulting in a reduction in turnover and associated recruitment and training costs.
- **Easier access to Capital:** The growth of socially responsible investing means companies with strong CSR performance have increased access to capital that might not otherwise have been available.
- **Enhance Stakeholder Relations and Credibility:** Meeting rising expectations for disclosure and transparency can build trust, credibility, and create a useful dialogue with a range of important

stakeholders, from local community representatives to environmental groups to employees.

- **Increase Integration and Alignment:** Many companies have found the CSR reporting process provides a useful tool for assessing their social and environmental impacts, conducting gap analyses of their existing CSR policies and programs, and driving performance on key goals and targets.
- **Strengthen Internal Communications:** Reporting also serves an internal function which is to help educate and motivate employees at all levels of the organization and across different regions and business units about the CSR strategy and performance. While key factors, which have contributed to Increased CSR Activities, include globalization, loss of trust, civil society activism and institutional investor interest in CSR, some of the many current issues that have an impact on the process.

## Conclusion

A multidimensional approach that combines binding rules, incentives and voluntary initiatives offers an alternative vision. The implementation of this approach will be more beneficiary to the company, society as well as the economy. Binding rules at both the national and international level serve as foundations for such a multidimensional approach should effectively regulate at the national level. Bilateral fund multilateral donors should offer support for building up national regulation systems. There should be no doubt that developing country governments bear the main responsibility for upholding human rights and the rule of law in their territory.

## REFERENCES

1. Hemingway, C.A. (2005), 'Personal Values as a Catalyst for Corporate Social Entrepreneurship', Journal of Business Ethics, pp. 233-49.
2. Carroll, A.B. (1979), 'A Three-dimensional Conceptual Model of Corporate Social Performance', Academy of Management Review, pp. 497-505.
3. Business for Social Responsibility, "Overview of Corporate Social Responsibility," Better Management.com, 2005.
4. http://www.iso.org/sr
5. www.ethicsinbusiness.net/case-studies/the-social-responsibility-of-business-is-to-increase-its-profits.

# Corporate Social Responsibility is a Business Strategy

Fx. Robert Bellarmine
M. Shunmugam

## Introduction

Corporate social responsibility is a way of achieving commercial success. The way includes honour ethical value, respecting people community and natural environment. Corporate social responsibility has economical, legal, ethical and discretionary expectation that society has to organized a scheme at a given point of time. Every organization wants to sustain in their field. In order to sustain, the company integrates social and environment concerns in their business operation. They want to maintain the relationship with society so that organization frames CSR policy. CSR policy is closely linked with principle of sustainability.

## Social Environment

We can classify the social environment into two categories.

- Internal Environment.
- External Environment.

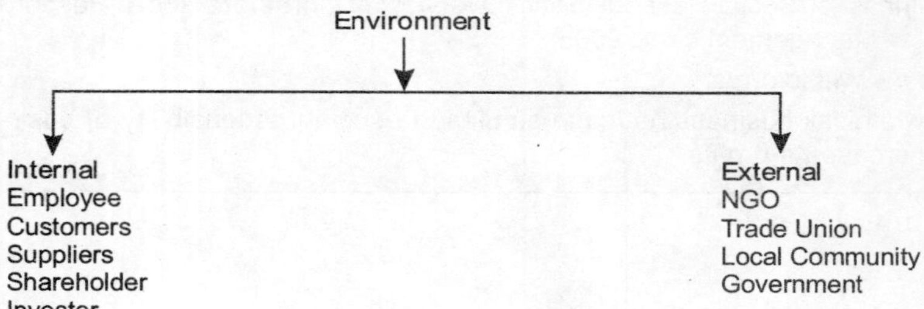


If the company has satisfied the above two environments need, then only the company can sustain and maintain the growth. When an organization frames the CSR policy they must consider above two factors the organization has response to provide service to the society where it is operating.

### Corporate Social Responsibility Towards Shareholders

Every organization must give attention to the shareholders expectation, because the share holders are the owners of the organization. They expect reasonable return to their investment. We can classify the shareholders into two types one is majority shareholders, and another one is minority share holders. Corporate wants to pay special care to minority shareholders, provide information properly to the shareholders and promote good governance through internal accountability and transparency.

### Corporate Social Responsibility Towards Labour

Corporate needs to provide safety measures for training programs, health treatments and also create awareness among the labours about their health. Our farmer Prime Minister **Jawaharlal Nehru** rightly said that "providing training is cost – but without training is much cost".

Every organization provide social security measures , quality of work life and fair wages to the worker which is possible only when the business man is willing to accept a voluntary ceiling on his own profit. Selection, training, promotion are given without any discrimination on ground of sex, race, religion and physical appearance. A business man should provide freedom self respect to employees.

### Corporate Social Responsibility Towards Suppliers

The organization allows the suppliers to study the details about production before entering into contract and allow them for a trail investment.

### Corporate Social Responsibility Towards Consumers

The customer expectations of that organization will produce goods and services that are needed and desired and it will be offered in reasonable price.

Organization offer better quality goods and service by developing new skills innovation and techniques by locating factory and market at a proper place and by rationalizing the use of capital and labour.

### Corporate Social Responsibility Towards Government

Government and local communities are expecting something from organization which is situated in their area. Example: Implementing Government schemes. Planting plastic free country, save nature, Afforest ration, providing education, properly disposing the wastage, Health awareness scan, provide free medical treatment.

Shunning active participation and direct identification with any political party. Provide direction to the economic and business life of community to bring about harmony between the limited enterprises and wider social interest of community.

### Argument for CSR

- The rise of the modern corporation created and continues to create many social problems. Therefore, the corporate world should assume responsibility for addressing these problems.
- In the long run, it is incorporations best interest to assume social responsibilities. It will increase the chances that they will have in future and reduce the chances of increased governmental regulation.
- Large Corporation have huge reserves of human and financial capital. They should devote at least some of their resources to addressing social issues.

### Arguments against CSR

- Taking on social and moral issues is not economically feasible.
- Corporations should focus on earning a profit for their shareholders and leave social issues to others.
- Assuming social responsibilities places those corporations doing so; at a competitive disadvantage relative to those who do not.
- Those who are most capable should address social issues. Those in the corporate world are not equipped to deal with social problems.

### Benefits of CSR Concept

Contribution of CSR is important and provides a number of benefits to both the community and business. Contributing to and supporting CSR does not have to be costly or time consuming and more and more businesses active in their local communities are seeing significant benefits from their involvement;

1. **Company benefits:**
   - Improved financial performance;
   - Lower operating costs;
   - Enhanced brand image and reputation;
   - Increased sales and customer loyalty;
   - Greater productivity and quality;
   - More ability to attract and retain employees;
   - Reduced regulatory oversight;
   - Access to capital;
   - Workforce diversity;
   - Product safety and decreased liability;
   - Reduce Labour turnover;
   - Increased recognition.
   - Increased staff morale and skills development.

**2. Benefits to the Community and the General Public**

- Developed relationships with the local community, partners and claims;
- Charitable contributions;
- Employee volunteer program;
- Corporate involvement in community education, employment and homelessness program;
- Product safety and quality.

**3. Environmental Benefits**

- Greater material recyclability;
- Better product durability and functionality;
- Greater use of renewable resources;
- Integration of environmental management tools into business plans, including life-cycle assessment and costing, environmental management standards, and eco-labelling.

Nevertheless, many companies continue to overlook CSR in the supply chain - for example by importing and retailing timber that has been illegally harvested. While governments can impose embargos and penalties on offending companies, the organizations themselves can make a commitment to sustainability by being more discerning in their choice of suppliers.

### Indian Context

In India, CSR has evolved to encompass employees, customers, stakeholders and sustainable development or corporate citizenship. The spectrum of CSR includes a number of areas as human rights, safety at work, consumer protection, climate protection and caring for the environment, and sustainable management of natural resource.

For instance TATA Motors provides desks, benches, chairs, table cupboards, electrical fittings and educational and sports material to various primary schools in Singur. The company has also planned similar programs to upgrade schools infrastructure and also planning to set up a computer laboratory in one of the high schools similarly, TVS electronics was involved in CSR during the Tsunami to provide relief measures to the victims.

### In Southern Tamil Nadu

The **sterilite** industry in Tuticorin has been providing education to poor people those who are living in where it is situated and they have been providing infrastructural facilities to the villages for their development

*Dharangadhara* chemical works in Arumuganeri has been running a school for their worker children.

In Tirunelveli *India Cements* is running a Polytechnic College where it is situated.

*Red - egg* info at Nagercoil conducts a seminar and rally on plastic free environment to public has adapted a village.

## Conclusion

In this corporate world the company wants to sustain and develop their product in the market. Only with the help of adapting new CSR policies and strategies in their organization, the concept of corporate social responsibility is now firmly rooted on the global business agenda. But in order to move from theory to concrete action, many obstacles need to be overcome.

## REFERENCES

1. www.indusby player.com/corporate_social_responsibility.php
2. www.reference forbusiness.com/management/comp-de/corporate socialres ponsibility.html
3. www. naukrihub.com/hr_today/corporate_social_responsibility.html

# Global Trends of Corporate Social Responsibility and Its Indian Situation

Dr. Lourdes Poobala Aryen

Business depends on the society for the needed inputs like money, men and skills. Business also depends on the society for market where products may be sold to their buyers. Thus, business depends on society for existence, sustenance and encouragement. Every decision the business man takes and every action he contemplates have social implications. Be it deciding on diversification, expansion, opening of a new branch, closer of an existing branch or replacement of men by machines, the society is affected in one way or the other. Even routine matters like over time and night shifts, sub contracting, and laying off employees due to load shedding have a social impact. Whether the issue is significant or not, the business man should keep his social obligations in mind before contemplating any action.

Social responsibility of business is not new to our country. In the olden days whenever there was a famine, the leading business men of the area would literally throw open their godowns and their treasure chests to provide food and other assistance to the needy. The history of every region of this country is replete with stories of the magnificent manner in which business men rose to the occasion in times of calamity. Even in ordinary times it was the business men who looked after the welfare of the destitute, wells and ponds wherever water was difficult to get. So to accept the social responsibility is no more than rededicating ourselves to the cherished values of our ancestors in the field of business.

CSR is a built-in, self-regulating mechanism whereby business monitors and ensures its active compliance with the spirit of the law, ethical standards, and international norms. The goal of CSR is to embrace responsibility for the company's actions and encourage a positive impact through its activities on the environment, consumers, employees, communities, stakeholders and all other members of the public sphere. Furthermore, CSR-focused businesses would proactively promote the public interest by encouraging community growth and development, and voluntarily eliminating practices that harm the public sphere, regardless of legality. CSR is the deliberate inclusion of public interest into corporate decision-making, and the honouring of a triple bottom line: people, planet, profit.

Proponents argue that corporations make more long term profits by operating with a perspective, while critics argue that CSR distracts from the economic role of businesses. Others argue CSR is merely window-dressing, or an attempt to pre-empt the role of governments as a watchdog over powerful multinational corporations.

CSR is titled to aid an organization's mission as well as a guide to what the company stands for and will uphold to its consumers. Development business ethics is one of the forms of applied ethics that examines ethical principles and moral or ethical problems that can arise in a business environment. ISO 26000 is the recognized international standard for CSR. The scale and nature of the benefits of CSR for an organization can vary depending on the nature of the enterprise, and are difficult to quantify, though there is a large body of literature exhorting business to adopt measures beyond financial ones. It was found a correlation between social/ environmental performance and financial performance. However, businesses may not be looking at short-run financial returns when developing their CSR strategy.

The definition of CSR used within an organization can vary from the strict "stakeholder impacts" will often include charitable efforts and volunteering. CSR may be based within the human resources, business development or public relations departments of an organisation, or may be given a separate unit reporting to the CEO or in some cases directly to the board. Some companies may implement CSR-type values without a clearly defined team or programme.

### Human Resources

A CSR programme can be an aid to recruitment and retention, particularly within the competitive graduate student market. Potential recruits often ask about a firm's CSR policy during an interview, and having a comprehensive policy can give an advantage. CSR can also help improve the perception of a company among its staff, particularly when staff can become involved through payroll giving, fundraising activities or community volunteering. CSR can also be driven by employees' personal values, in addition to the more obvious economic and governmental drivers.

### Risk Management

Managing risk is a central part of many corporate strategies. Reputations that take decades to build up can be ruined in hours through incidents such as corruption scandals or environmental accidents. These can also draw unwanted attention from regulators, courts, governments and media. Building a genuine culture of 'doing the right thing' within a corporation can offset these risks.

### Brand Differentiation

In crowded marketplaces, companies strive for a unique selling proposition that can separate them from the competition in the minds of consumers. CSR can play a role in building customer loyalty based on distinctive ethical values. Several major brands, such as The Co-operative Group, The Body Shop and American Apparel are built on ethical values. Business service organizations can benefit too from building a reputation for integrity and best practice.

### License to Operate

Corporations are keen to avoid interference in their business through taxation or regulations. By taking substantive voluntary steps, they can persuade governments and the wider public that they are taking issues such as health and safety, diversity, or the environment seriously as good corporate citizens with respect to labour standards and impacts on the environment.

### Criticism and Concerns

While there is a lot of appreciation of the idea of the social responsibilities of the business, there are also people who argue that social involvement of business has certain negative aspects. The Critics of CSR as well as proponents debate a number of concerns related to it. These include CSR's relationship to the fundamental purpose and nature of business and questionable motives for engaging in CSR, including concerns about insincerity and hypocrisy.

### Nature of Business

Milton Friedman and others have argued that a corporation's purpose is to maximize returns to its shareholders, and are only responsible to their shareholders and not to society as a whole. Although they accept that corporations should obey the laws of the countries within which they work, they assert that corporations have no other obligation to society. Some people perceive CSR as incongruent with the very nature and purpose of business, and indeed a hindrance to free trade.

### Motives

Some critics believe that CSR programs are undertaken by companies such as British American Tobacco (BAT), the petroleum giant BP (well-known for its high-profile advertising campaigns on environmental aspects of its operations), and McDonald's to distract the public from ethical questions posed by their core operations. They argue that some corporations start CSR programs for the commercial benefit they enjoy through raising their reputation with the public or with government. They suggest that corporations which exist solely to maximize profits are unable to advance the interests of society as a whole.

Another concern is that sometimes companies claim to promote CSR and be committed to sustainable development but simultaneously engaging in harmful business practices. For example, since the 1970s, the McDonald's Corporation's association with Ronald McDonald House has been viewed as CSR and relationship marketing. More recently, as CSR has become main stream, the company has beefed up its CSR programs related to its labour, environmental and other practices.

Critics concerned with corporate hypocrisy and insincerity generally suggest that better governmental and international regulation and enforcement, rather than voluntary measures, are necessary to ensure that companies behave in a socially responsible manner. Others, argue that CSR should be considered more as a corporate moral responsibility, and limit the reach of CSR by focusing more on direct impacts of the organization as viewed through a systems perspective to identify stakeholders.

### Ethical Consumerism

The rise in popularity of ethical consumerism over the last two decades can be linked to the rise of CSR. As global population increases, so does the pressure on limited natural resources required to meet rising consumer demand. Industrialization, in many developing countries, is booming as a result of both technology and globalization. Consumers are becoming more aware of the environmental and social implications of their day-to-day consumer decisions and are therefore beginning to make purchasing decisions related to their environmental and ethical concerns. However, this practice is far from consistent or universal.

### Globalization and Market Forces

As corporations pursue growth through globalization, they have encountered new challenges that impose limits to their growth and potential profits. Government regulations, environmental restrictions and varying standards of what constitutes "labour exploitation" are problems that can cost organizations millions of dollars. Some view ethical issues as simply a costly hindrance, while some companies use CSR methodologies as a strategic tactic to gain public support for their presence in global markets, helping them sustain a competitive advantage by using their social contributions to provide a subconscious level of advertising. Global competition places a particular pressure on multinational corporations to examine not only their own labour practices, but those of their entire supply chain, from a CSR perspective.

## Social Awareness and Education

The role among corporate stakeholders is to work collectively to pressure corporations that are changing. Shareholders and investors themselves, through socially responsible investing are exerting pressure on corporations to behave responsibly. Non-governmental organizations are also taking an increasing role, leveraging the power of the media and the Internet to increase their scrutiny and collective activism around corporate behavior. Through education and dialogue, the development of community in holding businesses responsible for their actions is growing.

## Ethics Training

The rise of ethics training inside corporations, some of it required by government regulation, is another driver credited with changing the behavior and culture of corporations. The aim of such training is to help employees make ethical decisions when the answers are unclear. The most direct benefit is reducing the likelihood of "dirty hands," fines and damaged reputations for breaching laws or moral norms. Organizations also see secondary benefit in increasing employee loyalty and pride in the organization.

Increasingly, companies are becoming interested in processes that can add visibility to their CSR policies and activities. One method that is gaining increasing popularity is the use of well-grounded training programs, where CSR is a major issue, and business simulations can play a part in this. Corporate social responsibility, what a company does to in trying to benefit society, versus corporate moral responsibility (CMR), what a company should morally do, are both important topics to consider when looking at ethics in CSR.

## Laws and Regulation

Another driver of CSR is the role of independent mediators, particularly the government, in ensuring that corporations are prevented from harming the broader social good, including people and the environment. CSR critics argue that governments should set the agenda for social responsibility by the way of laws and regulation that will allow a business to conduct them responsibly.

The issues surrounding government regulation pose several problems. Regulation in itself is unable to cover every aspect in detail of a corporation's operations. This leads to burdensome legal processes bogged down in interpretations of the law and debatable grey areas. Critics of CSR also point out that organizations pay taxes to government to ensure that society and the environment are not adversely affected by business activities.

Information on the companies' policies for CSR or socially responsible investments (SRI), information on how such policies are implemented in practice, and information on what results have been obtained so far and managements expectations for the future with regard to CSR/SRI is still voluntary, but if a company has no policy on this it must state its positioning on CSR in their annual financial report.

### Crises and their Consequences

Often it takes a crisis to precipitate attention to CSR. For example the lead poisoning paint used by toy giant Mattel, which required a recall of millions of toys globally and caused the company to initiate new risk management and quality control processes. In another example, Magellan Metals in the West Australian town of Esperance was responsible for lead contamination killing thousands of birds in the area. The company had to cease business immediately and work with independent regulatory bodies to execute a cleanup. Odwalla also experienced a crisis with sales dropping 90%, and the company's stock price dropping 34% due to several cases of E.Coli spread through Odwalla apple juice. The company ordered a recall of all apple or carrot juice products and introduced a new process called "flash pasteurization" as well as maintaining lines of communication constantly open with customers.

### Stakeholder Priorities

Increasingly, corporations are motivated to become more socially responsible because their most important stakeholders expect them to understand and address the social and community issues that are relevant to them. Understanding what causes are important to employees is usually the first priority because of the many interrelated business benefits that can be derived from increased employee engagement (i.e. more loyalty, improved recruitment, increased retention, higher productivity, and so on). Key external stakeholders include customers, consumers, investors (particularly institutional investors), and communities in the areas where the corporation operates its facilities, regulators, academics, and the media.

### The Indian Situation

The Indian business sector presents a mixed picture as far as social responsibilities is concerned. J.R.D. Tata who was instrumental in conducting the first social audit in India and perhaps in the world, was of the opinion that while on the side of production of growth of efficiency, Indian industry on the whole, did remarkably well, usually against odds and in spite of crippling infrastructural shortages unknown in advanced countries, on the distributional side, however, its record was often poor and, in some respects, dismal, judged by the size of the black-market, the volume of black money and the general corruption that pervaded our economic life.

True, many a time the imperfections on the distribution side mostly hoarding and black marketing-mercilessly gouge the unfortunate customer. "All though it is the trader rather than the manufacturer who is mainly responsible for such diversion of goods and for the resulting heavy burden imposed on the consumer, the fact remains that, to that extent, corporate management of even of large Indian industries has, perhaps unavoidably, failed in the important obligation of ensuring that their goods reach the consumer at fair prices." It is high time the producer realized that his responsibility does not end with producing goods and services; he should ensure that whatever is produced reached the ultimate consumer in time and at reasonable prices.

It is gratifying to note that a number of leading companies in India have shown recognition of the social responsibility of the corporate sector. The business community has been instrumental in setting up hundreds of institutions of public services, schools, colleges, management institutes, dispensaries, technological institutes, research institutes (medical, scientific and technological), libraries, dharmshalas, cultural institutions, institutes for the dumb, deaf and museums and places of religions worships. Some of the leading enterprises have extended welfare measures like health and medical facilities to the people of the surrounding villages. Many business men have risen up to the occasion to help the victims of droughts, floods, earth quakes and other natural calamities.

One of the important externalities of industrialization is the serious ecological damage it has inflicted. The problem of environmental pollution caused by industries is very serious in number of places in our country. Though some enterprises have taken pollution abatement measures, many – both in the private and public sectors-continue to be major offenders against the environment. Infact, some of the public sector enterprises are notorious for their irresponsibility in this matter.

As J.R.D.Tata has rightly pointed out, high standards of behaviour and the discharge of social obligations should be expected of or demanded from, not only business and industry but from all economic groups in the country whose actions have an impact on the public wheel. This applies in particular trade unions which, both in India and abroad, have, in recent years, acquired and often misused enormous economic powers, exceeded only by the government's own. The millions of man-days of production lost in India every year owing to labour unrest and the violent form which such unrest has taken in many cases, clearly indicate the need for a new approach to trade unionism and a recognition of the social obligations.

The participation of labour in the management has been suggested as a remedy for many a causes of industrial unrest. While it is a welcome suggestion, it should be ensure that the "collaboration" between labour and capital does not become instrumental in exploiting society. The social responsibility of the business is usually advocated for the private sector presumably on the assumption that the public sector is socially quite responsible. But the fact remains that the public sector in India has yet to prove that it is more responsive to society than the private sector. In some cases, in fact, the record of the public sector is more dismal than that of the private. As far as the pollution of the environment is concerned, the public sector is as guilty as the private.

Many public sector enterprises in India have undoubtedly failed to discharge their primary responsibilities-increase in the productivity and production, efficiency in the provision of the services, etc. This is reflected in the mounting losses of many public enterprises. Some may argue that the public sector is not, and should not be, profit motivated. But gone are the days of such philosophy. It has been clearly laid down that the public sector should generate surplus to finance our future development programmes. The huge losses incurred by the Indian public sector are not the result of any charity; they are the inevitable outcome of inefficiency, irresponsibility and mismanagement at various levels. The failure of the public sector in discharging its primary duties has made the plight of the common man worse than it would have been for it resulted in shortages, higher prices and more taxes. There is also a very wide gap between the sweet expectations from the public distribution system designed to save the common man from the clutches of the "unscrupulous private sector" and the bitter experiences of the way the public distribution system functions. The least said about the efficiency of the service of the public sector transport undertakings the better. In our country the social audit is indeed, perhaps, more for the public sector than the private sector.

## REFERENCES


1. Francis Cheruneelam, Business Policy and Strategic Management, Himalaya Publishing House, Mumbai, pp. 54-60.
2. K.Aswathappa, G.Sundarsana Reddy, Business Environment for Strategic Management, Himalaya Publishing House, Mumbai, pp. 533-563.
3. Orlitzky, Marc; Frank L. Schmidt, Sara L. Rynes (2003). "Corporate Social and Financial Performance: A Meta-analysis" SAGE Publications, London, pp. 403-441.
4. "Corporate Social Responsibility and Ethical Careers". University of Edinburgh Careers Service. Retrieved 2008-03-07.
5. Bhattacharya, C.B., Sankar Sen and Daniel Korschun (2008), "Using Corporate Social Responsibility to Win the War for Talent," MIT Sloan Management Review, 49 (2), pp. 37-44.
6. Kytle, Beth; Paramveer Singh (2005). "Corporate Social Responsibility as Risk Management: A Model for Multinationals", pp. 3-7.
7. Paluszek, John "Ethics and Brand Value: Strategic Differentiation (April 6–7, 2005).
8. "Dr. Tantillo's 30-Second 'How To': How To Brand CSR The American Apparel Way" Marketing Doctor Blog. March 28, 2008.
9. Friedman, Milton "The Social Responsibility of Business is to Increase its Profits". *The New York Times Magazine*. 2008, pp. 03-07.
10. McDonald's Corporation CSR information Roux, M. (2007). "Climate Conducive to Corporate Action".
11. J.M.Tata, "A Mater of Expectation", The Economic Times, August, 3, 1980.

# Corporate Social Responsibility and its Implications in India

T. Dhanabalan

## Introduction

At present the world economy is chanting the word Globalization. In India both the population and unemployment are the great problem and it leads to poor standard of living of people by which poor people not able to fulfill the forecasting the demand of various segments within and outside the parameters of the country. Economic liberalization and structural reforms were planning to promote the integration of Indian economy with the Global economy.

Globalization has brought a challenge before the Indian corporate, now the Indian corporate are facing competition from the multinational corporate like Pepsi, Coke... this is a challenge and there is an opportunity. Globalization does not simply mean allowing foreign investment and technology in India. It also means, creating Indian companies on bar with the global standard in terms of both investment and trade.

Indian corporates are no longer limited by the modest size of the domestic capital market and can tap the huge global market through EURO – issues and sales to foreign institutional investors in India. Globalization al so offered more possibilities for India's greater participation in global trade. India does not have a fair share of the world's reserves in some natural resources, but we have cheap labour. Now we have access to international capital market. This may give the country a competitive advantage in international trade. Thus it is seen that Indian corporate have easy accessibility to the capital market .this has played a whole new set of capacities in the hands of consumers and business.

Now a day's consumer has:

(*i*) Enough purchasing power

(*ii*) Availability of range of products for consumers choice

(*iii*) Available plenty of information about anything

(*iv*) Easy interaction in placing and receiving orders

(*v*) Knowledge on the product and service comparison

These benefits have come in the way of consumers, because of continuous changes and developments in the society is becoming literate. This literacy of the society has paves a way to the develop a concept known as "corporate social responsibility".

## Reason

From July, 1991 India has supposed to take the country from a boundary economy to market economy. Economic democracy supports the free market to develop. But it is also explicit that market mechanism is inadequate to offer distributive justice recognizing this the east Asian economies built a frame work of institutions to promote the opportunities for the low privileged to share in the benefits of growth via support for small and medium enterprises ,housing and health services. The accent was not on direct income transfers specific commodities but on increasing opportunities. With the continuous development of market economy and consumer awareness, industries had to satisfy the consumers.

This leads to the promotion of quality management, standardization, customer relationship management, brand building, after sales service, value addition, consumer retention etc. Leads to large competition in the industrial scenario.

On analyzing the recent few years, it could be concluded that consumers and society are developed in various expectations. This various expectations are the social responsibility of the corporate world. It is revealed that every industry have a profit motive. The earlier concept of profit maximization has no longer in use and the sales maximization concept came to the corporate scenario. Invention of modern marketing tools has led to increased competition and development of individual not the society.

## Information and Details

In India, it is being clear that the ground realities like unemployment, availability of labours, corruption poverty, education etc... are not looked into practically. The feasibility of the government plans and projects are under scanner. Here the question that arises that this is a critical situation is it the responsibility only of the government?

According to the various academic experts, both the public and private sectors has to play major role. To create an increasing database of consumer, the concept of CSR need to be put in place.

CSR may have become a hot topic in some management circles for the recent past years, but for a significant proportion of ordinary employees it is totally unrelated one. This is because of CSR has not been made to understand down the line, Corporate social responsibility.

The term CSR can be understand by the three waves of CSR such as:

(*i*) Community commitment

(*ii*) Socially feasible production process

(*iii*) Socially accountable employee relations

If the above said three things are align well in all respect, It will help to corporate to reap the benefits. The benefits such as:

1. Attracting investments
2. Increased market share
3. Mobilizing and developing the organization's human capital
4. Reducing the risk

In general a business can survive, if the companies maintain good relationships with their entire stake holder. These relationships can be strengthen it will support to the organizations to fulfill the obligations of the society and stakeholders.

### Corporate's Responsibility Towards the Society Includes

(*a*) Supporting public policies and practices to promote human development;

(*b*) Supporting the activities like people health, standard of living, education to the society development;

(*c*) Supporting peace, security, diversity, and social integration;

(*d*) Promoting donations to education and social welfare.

By which the society as well as the business can develop mutually. While business is expected to create wealth and provide opportunity for employment, society is expected to provide a suitable environment to the business.

Society expects corporate make its contribution to the community, in the same way the corporate depends on the society in which it operates.

If a company or a business wants to implement the social responsibility successfully, it should first audit its all activities and capacities, so that it can add real value to its activities. They are:

(*a*) Setting the achievable goal

(*b*) Identify the real objective of the programs to be implement

(*c*) Clearly identify what not to support

(*d*) Allocate budgets sufficiently

(*e*) Appoint well qualified staffs for organizing and providing support (*f*) Establish systems for report evaluation, getting feedback and do the modification if necessary

(*g*) Information process and updated on regular

**Corporate's Responsibility Towards the Stake Holders**

| Expectations / Stakeholder | Primary | Secondary |
|---|---|---|
| Owners | Return on Investment | Added value |
| Employers | Payment in time | Work Satisfaction |
| Customers | Supplying goods and services | Quality |
| Financiers | Credit worthiness | Security |
| Suppliers | Proper payment | Maintain good relationship |
| Society | Safety and security | Contribution to the society |
| Government | Payment of tax and duties properly | Improving competitiveness |

## Corporate's Responsibility Towards the Stake Holders

Expectations Stakeholders Primary Secondary Owners Return on investment Added value Employers Payment in time Work Satisfaction Customers Supplying goods and services Quality Financiers Credit worthiness Security Suppliers Proper payment Maintain good Relationship Society Safety and security Contributions to the society Government Payment of tax and duties properly Improving competitiveness.

From which we can understand that, building CSR activities into the heart of business leads to higher productivity and profitability. While a few business leaders has been sufficiently convinced about the business benefits of CSR that they have embedded those activities through their organizations, the major still pay lip service to CSR. CSR is no longer bluffing up one's corporate reputation. It's about doing good business. Employee's made a greater contribution towards their organization if they saw it as being a more responsible employer and this in turn influenced their decision to remain with the employer. Conversely, a strong correlation exists between increased sales volume and the perceived quality of line management, corporate culture, employee commitment and customer retention. The company who placed CSR policy at the heart of their business, it gains most in terms of performance outcomes.

## Conclusion

If organizations maintain good relationship with their stakeholders, it paves a way to the promotion of organizations goodwill, Because, CSR can help to maintain and enhance repetitions. However lack of leadership from the top is still a barrier to locate CSR at core of the business and a state of affairs can be addressed with a leadership agenda to help business leaders relate to the stakeholders.

## REFERENCES


1. OECD Secretary General Donald Johnston 'Promoting Corporate Responsibility: The OECD Guidelines for Multinational Enterprises' International Investment Perspectives (2004).
2. Corporations and Market Advisory Committee, Corporate Social Responsibility Discussion Paper (November 2005).
3. Andrew Clarke, the Models of the Corporation and The Development of Corporate Governance (2005).
4. Kerrie Burnmeister, 'Corporate Responsibility – A Matter or Ethics or Strategy', Blake Waldron Dawson.
5. <http://www.bdw.com.au/publications/issues/articles/Issues1 Corp_Responsibility.pdf> at 11 June 2006.
6. <http://www.legalaffairs.org/issues/March- April 2006/argument_Stout_marapr06.msp> at 18 June 2006.
7. http://www.lexvidhi.com/article-details/csr-in-india-132.html.

# Corporate Social Responsibility

## *The Continuous Commitment Towards Success*

J. Thilagan

### Introduction

The business world today has no boundaries. The cross border trade, awareness about climatic changes and societal responsibilities has forced the organisations to adopt a holistic way of performing business activities with transparency and accountability. The societal obligations with focus on stakeholders have become continuous commitment of the organisations. According to the World Business Council for Sustainable Development (WBCSD), "Corporate Social Responsibility is the continuous commitment by business to behave ethically and contribute to economic developments while improving the quality of life of the work force and their families as well as the local community and society at large". The concept of Corporate Social Responsibility has two elements. On one hand it exhibits the ethical behaviour that an organisation delivers towards its internal and external stakeholders. On the other hand, it deals with the responsibility of the organisation towards the environment and society in which it operates.

### Corporate Social Responsibility : A Historical View

The concept of Corporate Social Responsibility is not a new one to India. The concept of helping poor was cited in much of the ancient literature. Thiruvalluvar has written about Social Responsibility and Business Ethics. He has given two lines answers to the moral values and ethics to be followed by business in uncompromising and incomparable terms.

> *"Even if gainful, keep away at once*
> *from acts that are unjust and devoid of equity"* *(Verse 113, Thirukkural)*

Ilangovadigal has dealt with the charity and serving the poor people by the character Manimegalai in his Silappadhikaram. The Philosopher Chanakya has dealt with moral code and responsibilities to be followed by the business firms in his *Arthashastra.* Bharathi has showed his anger about poverty and inequalities in society through his invaluable poems. From Bible, we can get definitions of business ethics which is to consider the sake of all stakeholders and to know the difference between actions that are right or wrong. Many of the words of Bible have a significant impact on business ethics, as the following examples show:

*"Do unto others as you would have them do to you"*

*"Thou shalt not bear false witness"*

The concept of *"Dana Dharma"* of Hindus, *"Zakaat"* of Muslims and *"Daashant"* by Sikhs are the concern about the poor & society and they can be applied to the present modern business practices.

Before the concept 'Corporate Social Responsibility' came in to existence, the major aim of business is towards profit maximisation. However, over the past few years, as a consequence of globalisation and ecological issues, the perception of the role of corporates has been altered.

The role of corporates is redefined in terms of stakeholders and towards society and environment. Their performance is evaluated whether it is in ethical and socially responsible manner. Corporate Social Responsibility is becoming a catchword for the businesses and they are shifting from purely economic to economic with social dimension. The term Corporate Social Responsibility is used to define the commitment of the organisation to its environment. Corporate Social Responsibility is a link to sustainable development. The integration of Social, Economic and Environment considerations has brought a new dimension to the business.

According to 'Altered images: the 2001 state of Corporate Responsibility in India Poll' a survey conducted by Tata Energy Research Institute (TERI), the evolution of Corporate Social Responsibility in India has followed a chronological evolution of four stages:

- **Ethical model:** The pressure on Indian Industrialists to demonstrate their commitment to social progress increased during the Independence movement, when Gandhi developed the notion of 'trusteeship', whereby the owners of property would voluntarily manage their wealth on behalf of the people. Gandhi's influence prompted various Indian companies to play active roles in nation building and promoting socio-economic development during the Twentieth century.
- **Statist model:** The second model of Corporate Social Responsibility emerged in India after independence, when India adopted the socialist and mixed economy framework. Elements of corporate

responsibility, especially those relating to community and worker relationships, were enshrined in labour law and management principles.

- **Liberal model:** This approach was encapsulated by the American economist Milton Friedman. According to this model, Corporate Social Responsibility is confined to its economic bottom line. It implies that it is sufficient for business to obey the law and generate wealth, which through taxation and private charitable choices can be directed to social ends.
- **Stakeholder model:** The rise of globalisation has made to realise that the business have certain societal roles to fulfill. Companies are increasingly expected to perform according to 'triple bottom line' of Economic, Social and Environmental performance.

### Impact of Globalisation on Corporate Social Responsibilities

Technological advancements in communication and transportation have made it easier for companies to market globally and easier for consumers to buy products and services from marketers of other countries. As an outcome of cross-border trade, multinational enterprises and global supply chains, there is an increased awareness on Corporate Social Responsibility with respect to stakeholders, environmental protection, health, safety and other things. Performing business activities with social and ethical considerations is slowly becoming compulsory. There is also a necessity to create sustainable global economy where markets, labour and communities are able to function well together.

The conceptualisation of Corporate Social Responsibility in India till 1990 was purely in terms of philanthropy or charity. Welfare programmes were taking place as a form of charity and not as a responsibility. The business organisation did not commit its resources fully behind any social welfare project. They just offered one time or periodical financial grants as an act of charity.

But the business organisations are expected to do more than just providing employment and contributing to the economy through taxes. The profit is generated from the society and it becomes an expectation what the business is going to give in return for the society. The post-liberalisation phase has experienced a fundamental shift from the philanthropy-based model to a stakeholder participated model. The change in the perspective of Corporate Social Responsibility is denoted by Tata steel as follows: *"over the years, the nature of the company's involvement with the community has undergone a change. It has moved away from charity and dependence to empowerment and partnership"*.

The globalisation has stimulated the organisations to make their vision and mission towards stakeholders, environment and society. The global companies contribute themselves to alleviate poverty and hunger. The role of business organisations is explained in terms of stakeholders, environment and society after globalisation. The corporates are considering Corporate Social Responsibility as a separate entity and devoting attention to it. Companies are increasingly sensitive about their societal role. The globalisation has made the companies to think and act globally. The world's climate change also has tremendous impact in the activities of business practices. The companies not only concentrate on the quality of the product, but also about the emotions and values that people have about the products and the social role of the company.

### Corporate Social Responsibility: The Rising Trends

Indian corporates are aware that their reputation is intrinsically connected with how well they consider the effects of their activities on those with whom they interact. The Corporate Social Responsibility is a strategic approach to succeed in the business endeavours. The Corporate Social Responsibility considers the interest of stakeholders, society and environment. The Corporate Social Responsibility can help to boost the employee morale in the organisation.

Over the last few years, the trend in Corporate Social Responsibility is changing from *charity* to *responsibility*. There has been an apparent transition from *'giving as an obligation or charity'* to *'giving as a strategy or responsibility'*. The Corporate Social Responsibility follows a top to bottom mechanism with the focus on stakeholders, thereby considering Corporate Social Responsibility as a comprehensive set of policies and practices that are integrated throughout the business operations. Several innovative programmes in Environmental protection, Health care, Education, Microfinance and other related areas are developed with the concern about the local cultural context and the needs of the people. Apart from money, expertise in terms of knowledge, dedication and human resource are needed to successfully implement the innovative programmes.

Companies which have adopted and followed the Corporate Social Responsibility in India are: BHEL, Tata group, Wipro, Ashok Leyland, ITC, Asian paints, Larsen & Toubro, Orchid chemicals and pharmaceuticals, Hero Honda etc. The contribution of these companies towards Corporate Social Responsibility encompasses various initiatives like Starting social trusts; Adopting villages; Training unemployed youth; Providing medical facilities; Community development activities; Anti-pollution measures etc.

The massive HIV/AIDS campaign of Ashok Leyland covers all its employees, the driver community and the immediate community around its units. It also offers medical and blood donation camps. It has training schools in Namakkal (Tamilnadu) and Burari (near New Delhi) to train drivers. Offering massive employment to the physically challenged people is a part of Social Responsibilities of Sakthi Masala. The key thrust areas that the

Trust of Orchid chemicals and pharmaceuticals works on are Education, Health, Self-employment, Community asset development and Youth development. The trust has adopted 12 villages and 5 panchayats and works continuously in implementing several welfare schemes. In the area of education, the Orchid trust undertakes several activities like sponsoring salaries of additional teachers in Government schools, providing financial support to economically backward students and infrastructure development of schools. Hero Honda foundation has adopted various villages located within the vicinity of the factory at Dharuhera, Haryana for integrated rural development. It includes, Installation of deep bore pumps for drinking water, Construction of metalled roads and connecting these villages to National Highway, Promotion of non-conventional energy sources by providing 50% subsidy on biogas plants. Other key projects taken up by the foundation include: school, hospital, vocational training school and rural health care. Infosys has adopted various villages and implementing societal offerings for the welfare of the poor. Tata steel denotes its Corporate Social Responsibility as *"the primary purpose of our business is to improve the quality of people's life. Tata steel will volunteer its resources to the extent it can reasonably afford, to sustain and improve healthy and prosperous environment and to improve the quality of life of the people of the area in which it operates"*.

## Sustainability Reporting

Sustainability Reporting (SR) is a value added tool for displaying an organisation's commitment with transparency and accountability towards its stakeholders. It helps to report on the social, environmental and economic impact of its activities along with the internal management activities and employee welfare system in a transparent manner. A sustainability report should provide a balanced and reasonable representation of the sustainability performance of a reporting organization – including both positive and negative contributions. Sustainability reports based on the Global Reporting Initiative (GRI) organisation's reporting framework, disclose the outcomes and results that occurred within the reporting period in the context of the organization's commitments, strategy, and management approach. Reports can be used for the following purposes:

*Benchmarking and assessing* sustainability performance with respect to laws, norms, codes, performance standards, and voluntary initiatives; *Demonstrating* how the organization influences and is influenced by expectations about sustainable development; and *Comparing the performance* within the organization and with other organizations over time.

## Corporate Citizenship

The organizations are continuously innovating strategies with social considerations and they are working hard to integrate Corporate Social Responsibility in to their core practices. The Corporate Social Responsibility holds organisations to a higher moral and ethical standard considering the overall interests of society in the operations of its day-to-day business. Under this utilitarian view, business would need to take responsibility for the impact of their activities on all parties that they would affect customers, shareholders, surrounding communities and the environment- in all aspects of their operations.

A new terminology that has been emerged in the business community today is Corporate Citizenship. Corporate Citizenship is defined by the Boston College Centre for Corporate Citizenship as *'the business strategy that shapes the values underpinning a company's mission and the choices made each day by its executives, managers and employees as they engage with the society'*. Corporate citizenship recognizes that businesses have a responsibility to respect the individuals, the community and the environment in a way that when devising or implementing any rightful business strategy they will abide by laws and regulations and adhere to high ethical standards. Individual citizens also have responsibilities and rights. Together with corporate citizens these entail a set of social values that provide a benchmark upon which they can perform their respective roles in harmony with the wider community, for mutual benefit.

Thus Corporate Citizenship, similar to Corporate Social Responsibility concept, is focusing on the membership of the corporates in the political, social and cultural community with a focus on enhancing social capital. Though the terminologies are different, the purpose of Corporate Social Responsibility and Corporate Citizenship both focus towards a same target.

## Conclusion

The post-liberalisation phase of Indian economy has transformed all the Corporate Social Responsibility related practices of the business organisations. The charity oriented approach has been replaced by the stakeholder oriented approach. The organisations offer financial resources, expertise, manpower and technological advancements in order to provide a host of services that are flexible to accommodate the needs of the target community. The United Nations Council, International Labour Organization (ILO) and Organisation for Economic Co-operation and Development (OECD) have developed guidelines and principles about social norms for businesses. The implementation of Corporate Social Responsibility policies can be analysed by Benchmarking and CSR ratings and certification is issued by various agencies. The successful implementation of Corporate Social Responsibility is about how organisations place their business ethics and strategies to balance commercial success and business growth with the improvement of stakeholder group. The Corporate Social Responsibility is a long term involvement towards the goal of the organisation. The global market, cross-border trade and climatic changes all together make organisations to innovate and implement advancements in Corporate Social Responsibility and make it as a continuous commitment.

## REFERENCES

1. Andrew Kakabadse and Nada Kakabadse (eds), *CSR in Practice: Delving Deep.*
2. C.A. Harwell Wells (2002-2003), 'The Cycles of Corporate Social Responsibility: An Historical Retrospective for the Twenty-first Century', 51 *University of Kansas Law Review* 77.
3. CA. Harwell Wells, The Cycles of CSR: Historical Retrospective for the 21st Century, (2002-2003) 51 Kansas Law Review 77.
4. Carmen Valor (2005), 'Corporate Social Responsibility and Corporate Citizenship: Towards Corporate Accountability', 110 (2) *Business and Society Review* 191.
5. Elisabet Garriga and Domenec Mele (2004) 'Corporate Social Responsibility Theories: Mapping the Territory', 53 *Journal of Business Ethics* 51.
6. Huge Alexander Grossman (2005) 'Redefining the Role of the Corporation: the Impact of Corporate Social Responsibility on Shareholder Primacy Theory' 10 *Deakin Law Review* 572.
7. John L. Campbell, Why Would Corporations Behave in Socially Responsible Ways? An Institutional Theory of CSR, (2007) 32-3 Academy of Management Review 946.
8. Lance Moir (2001), 'What Do We Mean by Corporate Social Responsibility', 1,2 *Corporate Governance* 16.
9. R. Collin Mangrum, In Search of Paradigm of CSR, (1983-1984), 17 Creighton Law Review 21.
10. Terry Collingsworth, "CSR" Unmasked, (2003-2004) 16 St. Thomas Law Review 669.
11. www.wbcsd.org.
12. www.teriin.org.
13. www.ashokleyland.com.
14. www.tatasteel.co.in.
15. www.orchidpharma.com.
16. www.sakthimasala.com.

# Corporate Social Responsibility in Emerging Areas in Association with Hero Honda Motors Ltd.

V. Sylviya Johnsi Bai
J. Kamala Juliet Isaac

## Introduction

Amongst the many dramatic changes that have taken place in the business world since the 1990s, the rise of the corporate social responsibility (CSR) agenda is certainly one of the most noteworthy. Social Responsibility of business refers to what business does over and above the statutory requirement for the benefit of the society. The word "responsibility" emphasizes that the business has some moral obligations towards the society. India is a fast growing economy and is booming with national and multinational firms. At the same time, the Indian land also faces social challenges like poverty, population growth, corruption, illiteracy just to name a few. Therefore it is all the more imperative for the Indian companies to be sensitized to CSR in the right perspective in order to facilitate and create an enabling environment for equitable partnership between the civil society and business

## Importance of CSR

- **Globalization** of markets, consumer preferences, financial flows. Globalization is having momentous effects on the economies of all countries and on corporation in most sectors.
- **Increasing intensity of competition:** The Global completion today has created more challenges and instability.
- **Technology:** Rapid technological changes are transferring the markets, enabling greater customization of production, & contributing to high labor displacement.
- **Shift from Industrial:** Economy to a knowledge & information based economy. Human capital has become more important resource.

- **Environmental challenges:** Caused by pollution & resources depletion, Business are called upon to play an important role in meeting these challenges.
- **Life style:** Changes, expectation on the part of employees, customers and communication as a whole changing

### The Important Emerging Areas of CSR

- Rural Development
- Health care
- Education
- Micro finance
- Child Welfare
- Disaster management
- Community Development
- Women Empowerment
- Environment Protection
- Infrastructural Development

### Dimensions of CSR

- Economic - responsibility to earn profit for owners.
- Legal - responsibility to comply with the law (society's codification of right and wrong).
- Ethical - not acting just for profit but doing what is right, just and fair.
- Voluntary and Philanthropic - promoting human welfare and goodwill.

### Hero Honda Motors Ltd.

Hero Honda Motors Ltd. is the world's largest manufacturer of two – wheelers, based in India. The company is a joint venture between India's Hero Group and Honda Motor Company, Japan that began in 1984. In 2001, the company achieved the coveted position of being the largest two-wheeler manufacturing company in India and the 'World No.1' two-wheeler company in terms of unit volume sales in a calendar year by a single company.

### 2009-10 Performance

Total unit sales of 46, 00,130 two-wheelers, and growth of 23.6 percent. Total net operating income of Rs. 15860.51 Crores, growth of 28.1 per cent. Net profit after tax at Rs. 2231.83 Crores, growth of 74.1 per cent. Final dividend of 1500% or Rs. 30 per share on face value of each share of Rs. 2 BIDTA margin for the year 17.4 percent. EPS of Rs. 111.77, growth of 74.1 percent.

## CSR activities undertaken by the Hero Honda Motors Ltd

### Stake Holder Engagement and Relationship

Hero Honda Motors takes considerable pride in its stakeholder relationships, especially ones developed at the grassroots. The Company believes it has managed to bring an economically and socially backward region in Dharuhera, Haryana, into the national economic mainstream. An Integrated Rural Development Centre has been set up on 40 acres of land along the Delhi-Jaipur Highway. The Centre-complete with wide approach roads, clean water, and education facilities for both adults and children-now nurtures a vibrant, educated and healthy community. The Foundation has adopted various villages located within vicinity of the Hero Honda factory at Dharuhera for integrated rural development. This includes:

- Installation of deep bore hand pumps to provide clean drinking water.
- Constructing metal led roads and connecting these villages to the National Highway.
- Renovating primary school buildings and providing hygienic water and toilet facilities.
- Ensuring a proper drainage system at each of these villages to prevent water-logging.
- Promoting non-conventional sources of energy by providing a 50 per cent subsidy on biogas plants.

### Other key projects taken up by the Foundation include:

### The Raman Munjal Vidya Mandir

The Raman Munjal Vidya Mandir Began with three classes (up to class II) and 55 students from nearby areas. It has now grown into a modern Senior Secondary, CBSE affiliated co-educational school with over 1200 students and 61 teachers. The school has a spacious playground, an ultra-modern laboratory, a well-equipped audio visual room, an activity room, a well-stocked library and a computer centre.

### Raman Munjal Memorial Hospital

Multi-specialty hospital equipped with the latest diagnostic and surgical technology. The Raman Munjal Memorial Hospital provides healthcare to the rural population in and around Dharuhera, and also caters to accident and trauma victims driving along the Delhi-Jaipur highway.

### Raman Munjal Sports Complex

The Raman Munjal Sports Complex has basketball courts, volleyball courts, and hockey and f0000ootball grounds are used by the local villagers. In the near future, sports academies are planned for volley ball and basket ball, in collaboration with National Sports Authority of India.

**Vocational Training Centre**

In order to help local rural people, especially women, Hero Honda has set up a Vocational Training Centre. So far 26 batches comprising of nearly 625 women have been trained in tailoring, embroidery and knitting. The Company has helped women trained at this centre to set up a production unit to stitch uniforms for Hero Honda employees. Interestingly, most of the women are now self-employed.

**Adult Literacy Mission**

This Scheme was launched on 21st September, 1999, covering the nearby villages of Malpura, Kapriwas and Sidhrawali. The project started with a modest enrolment of 36 adults. Hero Honda is now in the process of imparting Adult Literacy Capsules to another 100 adults by getting village heads and other prominent villagers to motivate illiterate adults.

**Marriages of Underprivileged girls**

Marriages are organized from time to time, particularly for girls from backward classes, by the Foundation by providing financial help and other support to the families.

**Rural Health Care**

Besides setting up a modern hospital, the Foundation also regularly provides doorstep health care services to the local community. Free health care and medical camps are now a regular feature in the Hero Group's community outreach program.

**Environment**

- For a number of years, Hero Honda has been one of India's most environmentally sustainable firms. The company believes that to create a sustainable enterprise, it is critical to strike the right balance between business, mankind and nature. The Company has ensured complete compliance with all applicable environmental regulations and practices.
- For its efforts, Hero Honda was awarded for Safety Performance and Best working condition and Canteen facilities in the plant by the Government of Haryana for 2007.
- The Company has also been nominated for the Green Manufacturer of the year under the TERI Corporate Award Scheme. A green vendor development program was launched on the World Environment Day June 5, 2007. A green charter was released giving specific guidelines to the vendors and suppliers. A total of 31 vendors were selected in the first phase and in all, 256 vendors will be covered and certified as green vendors over a period of 5 years. Each vendor will initiate EARN programs in the areas of pollution prevention, waste reduction,

water conservation, energy conservation and statutory compliances. Each vendor will be evaluated and certified cluster wise.

- During the year, an environmental plan to reduce hazardous waste from the pollution control facilities was developed. As much as 30% of sludge generated was reduced through a sludge decanter system.
- The company also increased the conversion rate of paint sludge into useful primer from 15 MT to 25MT per month. Hero Honda has also successfully developed primer from the waste paint sludge, which used to be incinerated earlier. This development has been demonstrated to the state authorities, and the Company is seeking authorization to use this practice on a regular basis. The converted primer has already been used on the products, which has passed al l quality parameters.
- To fulfill its commitment towards water conservation, a recycling plant of 400KL per day capacity with reverse osmosis technology has been installed which recycles the sewage effluent into the process at the Haridwar plant. A similar project has also under progress at the Dharuhera plant and this is likely to be completed in 2008.

**Community**

- Hero Honda Motors takes considerable pride in its community relationships, especially ones at the grassroots that have evolved over time. The Company has played a pivotal role in bringing an economically and socially backward region in Dharuhera, Haryana, into the national economic mainstream through direct interventions in education, healthcare, vocational training, creation of social and physical infrastructure, and environment management.
- Most of the group's social enterprises–including the Rural Development Centre—are planned and executed by the *Raman Kant Munjal Foundation*. To help local people, especially women, Hero Honda has set up a vocational training centre which runs a 6 months Diploma Course for Tailoring, Embroidery and carpet weaving, etc.
- During the year in review, the Centre was upgraded. It now trains 50 girls per batch up from 25 & the duration of the course was increased from six months to 9 months. The Centre has also been equipped with modern machines to prepare the girls for the Garment Export Industry, where placement is 100%.
- Also during the year, women from four villages near the factory at Dharuhera benefitted from food-processing courses conducted at the Centre. In February 2007, the Foundation had set up a computer training & learning centre in partnership with Microsoft. A total of 8 to 10 batches (boys and girls) are run simultaneously consisting of 18- 20 students per batch. Till date, close to 400 students have been

trained at the centre. To enhance the value of rural youth in the job market, a spoken English course was started during the year. Currently the course is being run in three Batches during the day. It is proposed to train approx 120 students per year. The Foundation will make an effort to place them with BPO/Call Centres, provided the students also have the requisite computer training.

- A vocational centre for boys is expected to start during 2008-09 and will run on the lines of an ITI. The centre will provide training in Fitter, Welding, Carpentry and Plumbing & Electrician Trades. It is planned to train approx. 50 students every year, and efforts will be made to accommodate them in group companies.
- The Foundation also runs an Adult Literacy Program, a marriage facilitation service for underprivileged girls, besides doorstep healthcare programs and medical camps for the local population. A graduate teacher from the targeted village is appointed to teach the elders. Approx 650 people have benefited from this scheme spread over 20 villages.
- In every CSR Project undertaken, the Foundation always involves either a local NGO preferably the village itself or panchayat members not only during execution but also for subsequent sustainability/ maintenance of project. In certain areas such as computer learning by rural youth Udyan Care, a reputed NGO has been made a partner in association with Microsoft. In Projects like Hygiene, Sanitation & Safe Drinking Water, Local Government Representatives such as Block Development Officers are also involved.

## Conclusion

As the world business environment is changing, the requirement for staying and succeeding in business is also changing. As a result large corporations are emphasizing the maintenance of strategic relationship with different section of the society, ecological & human fabric & therefore they are responsible in varying degree to all stakeholders.

In this paper we are discussing CSR activities which have been under taken b the Hero Hondo Motor Ltd for the betterment of the society. Hero Honda Motor Ltd has undertaken the various projects for the betterment of the society. And it is continuously putting efforts towards the fulfillment of corporate social responsibility. The Foundation runs an Adult Literacy Program, a marriage facilitation service for underprivileged girls, besides doorstep healthcare programs and medical camps for the local population. The Company has ensured complete compliance with all applicable environmental regulations and practices. We can conclude that Hero Honda Motor Ltd is giving its full support to those activities and programmes that are helpful for the society.

Corporate Social Responsibility as a determinant of market success: An exploratory analysis with special reference to MNCs in emerging markets Sandeep K. Krishnan Rakesh Balachandran Doctoral Student, Student, Post Graduate Programme Indian Institute of Management Ahmedabad Vastrapur Vastrapur.

## REFERENCES


1. Krishnan, S. (2001). Corporate social responsibility: How and why in India, Retrieved on August 14, 2004 from http://www.coolavenues.com/know/
2. www.herohonda.com/co_csr.htm.http://www.herohonda.com/invest_annual_reports.htm .
3. Annual Report '07-'08 pg 18/19/20.
4. Corporate social responsibility ASOCIO Policy paper June 2004.
5. Shah Anuup "Corporate social responsibility" Global issues Corporate social responsibility initiatives of companies in India paper presented by Dr. M.K. Ramakrishnsn & Reshma.
6. Michael E. Porter and Mark R. Kramer, "Strategy & Society: The Link between Competitive Advantage and Corporate Social Responsibility," *Harvard Business Review* (December 2006), p. 80.

# Corporate Social Responsibility

## *The Potential Benefits to Business Enterprise*

P. Subbulakshmi

## Introduction

Being socially responsible is increasingly important for modern organizations. As consumers become more demanding and investors become more sophisticated, corporate social responsibility (CSR) becomes increasingly significant for businesses that need to demonstrate responsiveness to social problems.

The extent to which an organization can benefit from corporate social responsibility varies depending primarily on the nature of the business. However, business literature has identified a strong correlation between social performance and financial performance. Research from the Institute for Business Ethics suggests that organizations that demonstrate corporate social responsibility are more likely to be commercially successful in the future. Besides, over 90 percent of the FTSE 100 companies have an explicit policy on ethics, while over 50 percent of the organizations surveyed in a 2007 study by 'Personnel Today' had an explicit policy on corporate social responsibility. Although organizations should not focus on profit when implementing socially responsible policies, the long-term business benefits associated to such practices are numerous.

Explicit policies on corporate social responsibility can be addressed to several departments within the organization. Usually, such practices encompass the activities of human resources, marketing, business development, or finance departments and the benefits derived are based on the strategies implemented.

## Corporate Social Responsibility

Corporate Social Responsibility (CSR), also referred to as corporate citizenship, sustainable development, good governance, and so on, has as many definitions as it has names. In the most simple and encompassing manner, however, it can be regarded as the inclusion of stakeholder (public) interest into the decision-making and conduct of corporations. Stakeholders consist of not only investors and consumers, but also employees, communities, government, special interest groups, and the public sphere as a whole. As CSR is often loosely defined, there is a great variance in the ways in which companies integrate CSR programs into their broader business models. Generally, companies strive to implement its CSR strategy through the means of a set of policies, programs, training, or practices which extends throughout its operations and beyond.

If CSR is pursued by corporations as their commitment to be accountable to the economy, society, and environment, then the question remains: why do they wish to do so at their own cost? The fact is, CSR follows the logic that a business which manages the impacts of its operations in such a way that minimizes the damage and maximizes the benefits will also stand to gain profit in the long term.

CSR schemes include education sessions in schools, recycling schemes at work, alternative transport methods to make sure workers can be as green as possible when getting to and from work and only dealing in fair trade products and services. All of these things can be undertaken by businesses of any size and made a success of by individuals, staff and entire communities and only by working together can CSR benefit businesses and actually increase profit margins as well as doing good.

The potential business benefits derived from the implementation of corporate social responsibility are the following:

**1. Risk Management:** Modern organizations implement risk management strategies to decrease or even eliminate the risk posed on the organization by a variety of practices associated to several potential threats. Risk management is of vital importance to many corporate strategies. Organizations that have made strong efforts over the years to build a good reputation and have spent a lot of money to maintain it through product development and customer loyalty strategies, may be ruined is seconds due to a corruption scandal (Enron scandal) or an environmental accident (Chernobyl disaster). Such incidents draw the attention of the media and may cause irrevocable damage to the reputation of a firm. The only way to anticipate such events is to embed social responsibility into organizational culture in order to offset such risks.

**2. Product differentiation:** Organizations that want to remain competitive and viable in today's marketplace need to offer differentiated products.

Through product differentiation, organizations aim at achieving a competitive advantage by increasing the perceived value of their products relative to the perceived value of the products of their competitors. Particularly, for organizations that implement socially responsible policies, product differentiation can satisfy the unmet needs of consumers offering both financial and business benefits to the firm. Firms that offer environmentally friendly products experience higher sales growth than firms that sell conventional products, and usually such products sell at a higher price. Besides, firms that offer unique value propositions to consumers differentiate their products in consumers' minds and contribute to building customer loyalty based solely on ethical values. Therefore, in the context of corporate social responsibility, organizations develop new products aiming, not only to become more competitive, but also to make a greater impact on society through their ethical practices.

**3. Marketing:** It is always important for an organisation to be looking for new customers and for the retention of their current customers. In some cases CSR activities provide ways of promoting the business and its products and services to its customers and other stakeholders.

In Annual Reports, which will go to all an organisation's stakeholders, including its key customers, mention will be made of its behaviour and activities in the community.

Products themselves can be used to showcase an organisation's responsible business practice, which in itself gives customers another reason to buy the product, as well as its price and availability. This would incorporate the logo of the organisation, together with details of the cause, which might be CSR. This, in itself, can help to improve customer and consumer loyalty.

**4. Employee motivation:** Organizations that are socially responsible are more likely to recruit and retain their human capital easier. A 2007 research by Kenexa Research Institute (KRI) that surveyed employees from six countries (USA, Brazil, China, India, UK, Germany), suggests that when employees have a positive view for the organization's CSR strategies, they are more willing to work for it, participate to its efforts, align with its culture and recommend it as the best place to work. Employee satisfaction deriving from corporate social responsibility leads to higher productivity, higher employee retention rate, better organizational performance, and ultimately, higher profitability.

**5. Stronger Financial Performance and Profitability:** Businesses can use CSR and corporate sustainability to produce direct benefits for the bottom line. For example, operational efficiencies can be achieved through reducing energy and materials as input factors for production. Wastes can also be reduced and materials can be recycled. These sorts of actions from eco-efficiency can produce concurrent environmental and economic benefits for the company and thereby contribute to stronger financial performance and more positive profitability. Operational efficiencies can be achieved in other facets of CSR such as streamlining the way that information is provided to the investment community as well as to other stakeholders that demand increased transparency. Managing potential risks and liabilities more effectively through CSR tools and perspectives can also reduce costs. Using corporate responsibility and sustainability approaches within business decision-making can result not only in reduced costs but can also lead to recognizing new market opportunities such as when new manufacturing processes are developed that can be expanded to other plants, regions or markets. There are various studies that have examined the relationship between CSR and corporate financial performance and most of the evidence suggests that the links are positive.

**6. Enhanced Employee Relations, Productivity and Innovation:** A key potential benefit from CSR initiatives involves establishing the conditions that can contribute to increasing the commitment and motivation of employees to become more innovative and productive. Companies that employ CSR related perspectives and tools tend to be businesses that provide the pre-conditions for increased loyalty and commitment from employees. These conditions can serve to help to recruit employees, retain employees, motivate employees to develop skills, and encourage employees to pursue learning to find innovative ways to not only reduce costs but to also spot and take advantage of new opportunities for maximizing benefits, reduce absenteeism, and may also translate into marginally less demands for higher wages.

**7. Stronger Relations within Communities through Stakeholder Engagement:** A key feature of CSR involves the way that a company engages, involves, and collaborates with its stakeholders including shareholders, employees, debt holders, suppliers, customers, communities, non-governmental organizations, and governments. To the extent that stakeholder engagement and collaboration involve maintaining an open dialogue, being prepared to form effective partnerships, and demonstrating transparency (through measuring, accounting, and reporting practices), the relationship between the business and the community in which it operates is likely to be more credible and trustworthy. This is a potentially important benefit for companies because it increases their "license to operate", enhances their prospects to be supported over the longer term by the community, and improves their capacity to be more sustainable. Companies can use stakeholder engagement to internalize society's needs, hopes, circumstances into their corporate views and decision-making. While there are many questions about how far a company's responsibilities extend into communities relative to the roles of governments and individual citizens, there is a strong argument that CSR can effectively improve a company's relations with communities and thereby produce some key features that will improve business prospects for its future.

**8. Improved Reputation and Branding:** A potential benefit of CSR is that it can improve a company's reputation and branding and this in turn improves the prospects for the company to be more effective in the way that it manages communications and marketing in efforts to attract new customers and increase market share. CSR as a concept with various tools can help a company to position itself in the marketplace as a company that is more responsible and more sustainable than its competitors.

**9. Economic Benefits:** Contrary to popular belief, giving back can provide a company with economic benefits. From government grants, higher customer satisfaction and loyalty, to greater partnerships with stakeholders and investors, the Curtain University study concluded that through corporate social responsibility, these non-financial benefits eventually led to economic gain.

**10. Human Resources:** A CSR programme can be an aid to recruitment and retention, particularly within the competitive graduate student market. Potential recruits often ask about a firm's CSR policy during an interview, and having a comprehensive policy can give an advantage. CSR can also help improve the perception of a company among its staff, particularly when staff can become involved through payroll giving, fundraising activities or community volunteering. See also Corporate Social Entrepreneurship, whereby CSR can also be driven by employees' personal values, in addition to the more obvious economic and governmental drivers.

## Conclusion

Conclusively, although the benefits of corporate social responsibility cannot be explicitly measured as they are primarily based on the nature of the business, they are numerous and they cannot be neglected. Particularly, in an era that the protection of the environment is imperative and global warming threatens human existence, social responsibility is the least organizations can demonstrate to provide an optimistic future. Besides, the opportunities offered for exhibiting responsiveness to social, economic, environmental and ethical issues are numerous. At the end of the day, it is to their long-term interest to undertake socially responsible initiatives.

## REFERENCES

1. www.csrforhr.com
2. ww.csr-review.net
3. Ask.com
4. www.helium.com
5. www.csrandmanagement.eu
6. en.wikipedia.org
7. www.angelfire.com

# The Challenge of Corporate Social Responsibility in India

C. Stephen Raj

## Introduction

Corporate social responsibility is not a new concept in India. However, what is new is the shift in focus from making profits to meeting societal challenges. Now-a-days, employees are actively participating in the social activities even on holidays. This is mainly because employees feel a sense of pride when they are involved in such activities. Moreover, companies are having dedicated departments for CSR.

Giving a universal definition of Corporate Social Responsibility is bit difficult as there is no common definition as such. However, there are few common threads that connect all the perspectives of CSR with each other; the dedication to serve the society being most important of them. Most ideal definition of Corporate Social Responsibility (CSR) has been given by World Business Council.

For Sustained Development which says, "Corporate Social Responsibility is the continuing commitment by business to behave ethically and contribute to economic development while improving the quality of life of the workforce and their families as well as of the local community and society at large".

Firms can no longer continue to exploit environmental resources and escape from their responsibility by acting as separate entities regardless of the interest of the society. Organizations, now, are realizing the need to shift their focus on the interest of society. The sense of being socially responsible has to come from within. CSR involves various voluntary efforts in which companies engage themselves in order to give something back to the society. It involves providing innovative solutions to societal and environmental challenges. Organizations generally believe that acting in a socially responsible manner will create value for them. The fact that an organization is committed to social causes, also gives employees a sense that the company would also be committed to the welfare of its employees as well.

In India, CSR has evolved to encompass employees, customers, stakeholders and sustainable development or corporate citizenship. The spectrum of CSR includes a number of areas as human rights, safety at work, consumer protection, climate protection and caring for the environment, and sustainable management of natural resources. From the perspective of employees, CSR activities include providing health and safety measures, preserving employee rights and discouraging discrimination at workplace. This helps in fostering a healthy environment within the company. For example, after 1945, TATA implemented social welfare provisions for its employees that have since become the legislative norm. From the perspectives of customers, CRS activities may include commitment to product quality, fair pricing policies, and so.

### Benefits Both Internally and Externally

Corporate social responsibility offers manifold benefits both internally and externally to the companies involved in various projects. Externally, it creates a positive image amongst the people for its company and earns a special respect amongst its peers. It creates short term employment opportunities by taking various projects like construction of parks, schools, etc. Working with keeping in view the interests of local community bring a wide range of business benefits. For example, for many businesses, local customers are an important source of sales. By improving the reputation, one may find it easier to recruit employees and retain them. Businesses have a wider impact on the environment also. Plantation and cultivation activities taken up by Intel India are a step towards the same. Recycling used products also acts as a step towards minimizing wastes.

Internally, it cultivates a sense of loyalty and trust amongst the employees in the organizational ethics. It improves operational efficiency of the company and is often accompanied by increases in quality and productivity. More importantly, it serves as a soothing diversion from the routine workplace practices and gives a feeling of satisfaction and a meaning to their lives. Employees feel more motivated and thus, are more productive. Apart from this, CSR helps ensure that the organization comply with regulatory requirements.

### Social Awareness and Education

The role among corporate stakeholders is to work collectively to pressure corporations that are changing. Shareholders and investors themselves, through socially responsible investing are exerting pressure on corporations to behave responsibly. Non-governmental organizations are also taking an increasing role, leveraging the power of the media and the Internet to increase their scrutiny and collective activism around corporate behavior. Through education and dialogue, the development of community in holding businesses responsible for their actions is growing.

### CSR Various Challenges

The survey elicited responses from participating organisations about various challenges facing CSR initiatives in different parts of the country. Responses obtained from the participating organisations have been collated and broadly categorised by the research team. These challenges are listed below:

#### Lack of Community Participation in CSR Activities

There is a lack of interest of the local community in participating and contributing to CSR activities of companies. This is largely attributable to the fact that there exists little or no knowledge about CSR within the local communities as no serious efforts have been made to spread awareness about CSR and instil confidence in the local communities about such initiatives. The situation is further aggravated by a lack of communication between the company and the community at the grassroots.

#### Need to Build Local Capacities

There is a need for capacity building of the local non-governmental organisations as there is serious dearth of trained and efficient organisations that can effectively contribute to the ongoing CSR activities initiated by companies. This seriously compromises scaling up of CSR initiatives and subsequently limits the scope of such activities.

#### Issues of Transparency

Lack of transparency is one of the key issues brought forth by the survey. There is an expression by the companies that there exists lack of transparency on the part of the local implementing agencies as they do not make adequate efforts to disclose information on their programmes, audit issues, impact assessment and utilisation of funds. This reported lack of transparency negatively impacts the process of trust building between companies and local communities, which is key to the success of any CSR initiative at the local level.

#### Non-availability of well Organised Non-governmental Organisations

It is also reported that there is non-availability of well organised nongovernmental organisations in remote and rural areas that can assess and identify real needs of the community and work along with companies to ensure successful implementation of CSR activities. This also builds the case for investing in local communities by way of building their capacities to undertake development projects at local levels.

### Visibility Factor

The role of media in highlighting good cases of successful CSR initiatives is welcomed as it spreads good stories and sensitises the local population about various ongoing CSR initiatives of companies. This apparent influence of gaining visibility and branding exercise of ten leads many non-governmental organisations to involve themselves in event-bAased programmes; in the process, they often miss out on meaningful grassroots interventions.

### Narrow Perception Towards CSR Initiatives

Non-governmental organisations and Government agencies usually possess a narrow outlook towards the CSR initiatives of companies, often defining CSR initiatives more as donor-driven than local in approach. As a result, they find it hard to decide whether they should participate in such activities at all in medium and long run.

### Non-availability of Clear CSR Guidelines

There are no clear cut statutory guidelines or policy directives to give a definitive direction to CSR initiatives of companies. It is found that the scale of CSR initiatives of companies should depend upon their business size and profile. In other words, the bigger the company, the larger its CSR programme.

### Lack of Consensus on Implementing CSR Issues

There is a lack ofconsensus amongst local agencies regarding CSR projects. This lack of consensus often results in duplication of activities by corporate houses in areas of their intervention. This results in a competitive spirit between local implementing agencies rather than building collaborative approaches on issues. This factor limits company's abilities to undertake impact assessment of their initiatives from time to time.

### Seven Levels of Consciousness

From the point of view of traditional perspective, profit making was the whole sole objective of the organization but in its more progressive form, the organizations have extended from profit making to a much broader platform which could be called as success. Richard Barrot Associates9, which is the leader in building value drivenorganizations, has developed seven levels of consciousness (2006). Accordingly:

- Level 1 is achieved by taking care of financial stability.
- Level 2 by focusing on relationships that support the organizations.
- Level 3 is achieved by emphasizing high performance systems and processes.
- Level 4 is accomplished by adaptability, continuous renewal and learning.
- Level 5 by having shared vision and shared set of values.
- Level 6 is achieved through strategic alliances and partnerships.

The highest level 7 can be realized by serving to humanity and planet. According to them, organizations must learn how to master every level of consciousness to be the most successful organization.

When we examine consciousness from the point of view of corporate responsibility, this framework needs to be modified. Although we are not questioning these seven levels but at the same time we are giving it different reading by interpreting this framework in the sense that success is integrally dependent upon corporate responsibility. Progressive organization should understand that success itself rests upon corporate responsibility. Therefore success itself needs to be reinterpreted and redefined in the true sense. This approach spells out a new paradigm of success.

## Challenges of Setting Standards of Corporate Responsibility

Coming to the issue of setting international standards the main problem is that the extant approaches are in the form of global principles of CSR. It can be said that they deal with the problem at a very general level. For instance, amongst the most important principles, namely, The Bellagion Principles, Caux Roundtable, Ceres Principles, The Global Sullivan Principles, The Minnesota Principles and The UN Global Compact, The Bellagion Principles alone have a 'Practical Focus'. However, setting standards implies not just measurability but the amenability of standards to become benchmarks and for them to be objective and universal.

## CSR in India

Long referred to as a company's soul food, corporate social responsibility is finally being taken seriously by Indian tech companies as they embark on a gamut of philanthropic activities. Through Infosys foundation and other initiatives, Narayan Murthy chairman and chief mentor of Infosys has always been on the forefront of philanthropic activities as a part of CSR. Mr. Narayan Murthy firmly underlines the significance of CSR: "for benefit of globalization and technology to reach the poor, the private sector, philanthropic institutes and individuals should cooperate and establish partnership with government institutions. This would lift millions of our people out of the poverty, provide them with opportunities and make them participate in the process and progress of globalization". While Murthy and Infosys are proactive on the CSR front, how do other tech companies stuck up?

The sad part is that CSR still has not taken off in India according to a recent survey by Mumbai based online organization Karmayog. The second edition of the research revealed that nearly half of the top companies do nothing in way of CSR.

For the Indian company whatever the CSR activities are happening are centered around education, rural upliftment and helping the physically challenged. Some of the CSR initiatives the major IT companies have undertaken are: (1) Education for all; (2) Community development.

## CSR and Globalization

Globalization has changed corporate social responsibility, the boundaries between domestic and foreign industry and between in-house and out-houses activities which had led corporate to view from both political and economic view. On one side multinational company have taken the role of state and thus they should behave responsibly and on the other hand they need to have corporate social behavior in order to protect their image.

Example: Wal-mart which sells it product at remarkable low price and at the same time its brand image is also protected.

## Conclusion

It can be concluded that in today's informative world where information are readily available to general public CSR has been an important part of any organization to be successful. Organization in present world cannot be successful without taking into account the social responsibility. CSR has been a vital component for any organization to have perpetual success and to create brand.Even though companies are taking serious efforts for the sustained development, some critics still are questioning the concept of CSR. There are people who claim that Corporate Social Responsibility underlies some ulterior motives while others consider it as a myth. Is CSR really a stalking horse for an anti-corporate agenda. The reality is that CSR is not a tactic for brand building; however, it creates an internal brand among its employees.

## REFERENCES

1. Asmus. P. (2003), "Corporate Social Responsibility [PDF document]", Retrieved from Lecture Notes Online Web site: http://www6.miami.edu/ethics/pdf_files/csr_guide.pdf
2. "Corporate Social Responsibility" (March 3, 2009), Retrieved August, 9, 2009, from http://www.iocl.com/Aboutus/corporatesocialresponsibility.aspx
3. "Corporative social responsibility", Naukrihub, retrieved on 9th august, 2009, http://www.naukrihub.com/hr-today/corporate-social-responsibility.html
4. EurAsia Bulletin Volume 10 No. 11&12 Nov-December 2006.
5. Brown, Tom J., Peter A. Dacin. "The Company and the Product: Corporate Associations and Consumer Product Responses." Journal of Marketing, Vol. 61, No. 1, (Jan., 1997).
6. www.pdffactory.com.

# Corporate Social Responsibility as a Business Strategy

M. Susheela
Dr. Lourdes Poobala Rayen

## Introduction

Every aspect of business has a social dimension. Corporate social responsibility encourages open and transparent business practices that are based on ethical values and respect for employees, communities and the environment. It is designed to deliver sustainable value to the society at a large, as well as to the shareholders.

The concept of corporate social responsibility was first mentioned in 1953in the publication 'Social Responsibilities of the Businessman' by William J. Bowen. However, the term CSR has became popular only in the 1990s, when the German Betapharm, a generic pharmaceutical company decided to implement CSR. The generic market is characterized by an interchangeability of products. In 1997 a halt in sales growth led the company to the realization that in the generic drugs market companies could not differentiate on price or quality. This was the prelude for the company to adopt CSR as an expression of the company's values and as a part of its corporate strategies. By using strategic and social commitment for families with chronically ill children, Betapharm took a strategic advantage.

Nowadays firms have started using CSR as a strategy to focus on new opportunities and respond to interrelated economic, societal and environmental demands in the marketplace. Many firms believe that this focus provides a clear competitive advantage and stimulates corporate innovation and creativity. A more strategic approach to CSR can help the organizations to grow their business, make a bigger impact on the issues, and help ensure long-term viability and a stellar corporate reputation. In times of increased risk, shifting roles and responsibilities the firms can make use of the CSR strategy.

Stakeholders are also increasingly aware of the importance and impact of corporate decisions upon society and the environment and hence most of the corporations are involving their stakeholders in their decision-making and addressing societal challenges .The stakeholders are given the opportunity to reward or punish the corporations. Hence corporations can be motivated to change their corporate behavior in response to the business situations, where they can follow CSR approach in order to satisfy their stakeholders.

Companies can adopt the CSR strategies to assure some long-term benefits. They are:

- Creating and maintaining a high reputation for the organization.
- Securing and maintaining strong relationships with stakeholders.
- Creating better, safer and more stimulating work culture.
- Increasing employees' commitment.
- Improving the efficiency of the business management.
- Increase the financial performance and profitability of the company.
- Protecting from boycott actions; making access to funding easier.
- Benefits from fiscal advantages and administrative facilitation.

## Drivers of Corporate Social Responsibility

The following are the drivers of corporate social responsibility:

**Share holders:** Some business organizations indulge in corruption, stealing of Intellectual Property Rights, financial scams and scandals or producing environmentally hazardous products for the customers. Instead they have to build goodwill and trust among the customers and shareholders.

**Employees:** Building an ethically responsible culture in organizations can reduce the chances of employees indulging on unfair practices within the organization by emphasizing on professionalism, transparency, socially responsible investments, effective communication, employee participation, fairness, and promotions, adequate compensation and personal development.

**Brand equity:** Customers associate a brand with a promise and built on deep relationships with consumers. Its value to consumers is that it provides emotional as wells as functional aspects and reduces the risk, saves time and provides reassurance on value for money. Predictable results are the promise of a brand. Corporate Social Responsibility can play a major role in building customer loyalty based on ethical values practiced in the organizations. Brand loyalty can be strengthened through: increasing continuity of purchase via such techniques as "frequent purchaser" programs, "members clubs", "continuity promotions", that create identification between the users of a brand and its users.

**Ethical marketing practices and social awareness:** Rapid industrialization in many developing countries has now opened avenues for International Trade. These policies should cover distributor relations, advertising standards, customer's service, pricing, product development and general ethical standards. Now in this global scenario, companies need to apply high standards of ethics and morality when making corporate decisions. Due to increasing awareness among customers regarding the malpractices in the market, the consumers are now more conscious about their rights.

**The environment consciousness:**

- Many organizations had started realizing the importance of environmental protection, as they are directly or indirectly contributing towards environmental protection. There are many issues regarding the environmental protection and particularly the issues which require immediate attention involve:
- Climate change
- Water conservation
- Air emission

**Energy conservation and global warming:** Agriculture in our country had significantly faced its downturn due to the climate changes which were primarily caused by burning of coal, oil and other fossil fuels. The world produces more carbon dioxide and other gases which are responsible for manmade global warming. Hence it becomes very important to identify new fuels which may cause comparatively less pollution. Many companies are on their way to identify new non-renewable resources to ensure energy conservation as well a step to control the global warming.

**Responsibility towards the government:** All the Business Organizations have to comply with the general law applicable in every country. Management policies, strategies, mission, should be in accordance to the rules and regulations of the legal environment and should follow fair trade practices. Organizations should pay taxes and other dues and discourage bribery, corruption, and biases in the departments.

## CSR as a Business Strategy

A visible attention must be paid towards social and environmental consequences of business rather than aiming at mere profit maximization. Most of the companies consider Social concern and business as two independent responsibilities. But many companies lose focus of how social responsibility could have been integrated with the long term business outcomes. Businesses across the world are so obsessed with the immediacy of results that they cannot sight the vast opportunity that discharging of social responsibility holds for the long term sustainability of the organizations. As a result, based on the maturity of strategic thinking in the company, CSR is being implemented in one or more of the following ways as shown here:

- CSR as reactive strategy.
- CSR as an image building exercise.
- CSR for improving operational efficiency.
- CSR as a source of competitive advantage.

### CSR as Reactive Strategy

Generally many companies use CSR as a reactive strategy for recovering from lost fortunes of the company by gaining the confidence of the communities in which they operate. But now companies have started adopting a "proactive approach" in case of CSR by estimating and analyzing the cost of not discharging the social responsibility and as a result they practice the minimum to pull on and thus minimizing their spending on this account. CSR is viewed by these companies as a cost and compulsion. This approach only obscures a business from identifying the real potential CSR holds with respect to their core business.

### CSR as Image Building Exercise

Today many companies view CSR as an opportunity for building their corporate image. Companies announce their plans for various kinds of social philanthropic activities in order to draw the attention of media and general public. In case a company develops a systematic and deliberate approach for maintaining the focus on social welfare activities, this will not only enhance its image in the immediate future but also help the company in building a positive reputation of societal concern. This will definitely help the company in its future business forays in the region.

### CSR for Improved Operating Efficiency

Some companies take care of environment and society for the reason that it not only helps in operating within the environmental norms set by statutory authorities but also reducing their costs by improving operating efficiency. If the companies are operating barely within the norms set by statutory authorities then they are said to be in compliance mode. When companies deliberately plan and move beyond the compliance mode, the organization needs to integrate CSR and its business goals, which results in improved productivity or operational efficiency and better environmental conditions that fosters better living conditions for future generations.

### CSR as Source of Competitive Advantage

The major challenge for any type of industry today is to identify the social issues that drive its competitiveness both now and in the future. Hence the business managers must first believe that social concern or CSR will be a source for business opportunities and competitive advantage. This integration then would pave way for all round sustainability and growth. In the due course of time, the issues relating to climate change and social responsibility in the area of operations will be critical factors for survival of businesses. Thus CSR has the potential to change the way business conducted through out the world.

## Conclusion

Interest of shareholders, providing necessary information about the company, telling certain measures in health, wealth, happiness of the employees, satisfying customers, avoiding illegal activities, paying taxes regularly as these are all create a "Goodwill" of the company to sustain in the competitive world.

Even though companies are taking serious effort for the sustained development some critics still are questioning the concept of CSR. There are people claim that CSR underlies some ulterior motives while others consider it as myth. The reality is that CSR is not a tactic for brand building however it creates an internal brand among employees. Indulging into activities that help society in one way or other only adds to the "Goodwill" of a company.

## REFERENCES

1. Sanjay K. Agarwal, Corporate Social Responsibility in India, Sage Publications Pvt. Ltd., New Delhi.

# Corporate Social Responsibility A Business Strategy

I. Lovisal Roselin

## Introduction

Corporate social responsibility is essentially a concept whereby companies integrate social and environmental concerns in their interaction with their stakeholders on a voluntary basis. This means not only fulfilling legal expectations, but also going beyond compliance and investing in human capital, the environment and relations with stake holders. The Term Corporate Social Responsibility (CSR) is imprecise and its application differs. CSR can not only refer to the compliance of human right standards, labour and social security arrangements, but also to fight against climate change, sustainable management of natural resources and consumer protection.

The concept of Corporate Social Responsibility was first mentioned in 1953 in the publication 'Social Responsibilities of the Businessman' by William J. Bowen. However, the term CSR became only popular in the 1990s, when the German Betapharm, a generic pharmaceutical company decided to implement CSR. The generic market is characterized by an interchangeability of products. In 1997 a halt in sales growth led the company to the realization that in the generic drugs market companies could not differentiate on price or quality. This was the prelude for companies to adopt CSR as an expression of the company's values and as a part of its corporate strategies. according to *Business for Social Responsibility* (BSR), corporate social responsibility is defined as "achieving commercial success in ways that honor ethical values and respect people, communities, and the natural environment."

## Energing Areas in CSR

Corporate social responsibility is no longer a trend just among large multinational companies operating in developed countries, more and more emerging market companies are seeking the value of committing to responsible business practices. A strong strategy and reputation as a responsible business can help these companies to build trust with local stake holders thereby establishing a local license to operate. Better way of approaching employee concerns, such as progressive labour relations, have also been shown to enhance productivity and reduce costs associated with recruitment & turnover. A visible commitment to CSR can help emerging firms to attract multinational partners, access international source of capital and reach the society well.

Corporate social responsibility practice area develops tool and business models and support companies directly in developing strategies and implementing projects in three broad areas.

1. Community development and stakeholder's engagement.
2. CSR strategy and communications.
3. Labour practices and human rights at work.

**1. Community Development and Stake holder Engagement:** The social responsibility team has gathered substantial expertise in Local Community Development and works with IFC (International Finance Corporation) clients to design programs with direct links to business needs and competencies, while also ensuring education and income generation activities for local communities and targets socially excluded groups such as rural populations, indigenous people and women.

### Products and Services

1. Stakeholder mapping and needs assessments.
2. Stakeholder capacity building.
3. Local community development planning.
4. Strategies for livelihood and income. Generation.

### CSR Strategy and Communication

An integrated CSR strategy combined with effective communications can play in creating reputational business value for a company. Companies that communicate well can also encourage greater uptake of CSR among peers and competitors. The social responsibility practice area thus helps business not only to understand and operationalize CSR in their core activities, but also to articulate their vision to stakeholders.

### Products and Services

1. Stakeholder mapping and needs assessments.
2. Stakeholder capacity building.
3. Local community development planning.
4. Strategies for livelihood and income. Generation.

### Labour Practices and Human Rights at Work

The social responsibility team works with the private sector and in partnership with international institutions and global NGOs to provide alternatives to child labour and to remedy discriminations in the workplace. In addition, the program is exploring the opportunity to help emerging market companies to understand and work with human rights.

### Regulations

CSR is normally seen as voluntarily going beyond local requirements, governments can "raise the bar" through stricter regulation. This can come in the form of laws, regulations, penalties, and associated measures to control aspects of business investment or operations. Governments at different levels can regulate the behaviour or practice of business by defining minimum standards for business performance embedded within the legal framework; establishing targets for business to achieve; setting up enforcers and inspectorates to oversee business conduct; promulgating codes or laws to confine undesirable business conduct; or imposing license of operation or mandatory environmental friendly industrial systems.

There is no unitary or binding international norm for CSR Coverage for companies. The Organization Ceres. Investors and Environmentalists for Sustainable Prosperity hopes for a greater engagement - as well as more transparency in reference to CSR. A Uniform reporting would besides reduce the possibility of "Green washing" (more about: »Green washing – The Dark Side of Corporate Social Responsibility(CSR)«). More about the Guidelines and Global Reporting Initiatives (GRI). Recent new about CSR here.

### Companies that Provides Services in India

- Tata consultancy services (TCS) has set up fully equipped computers training laboratory for children from the society for the welfare of the physically challenged and research centre in Pune for imparting basic computer knowledge.
- NIIT has launched a highly popular "hole-in-the-wall scheme where it places a computer on a public wall in urban rural areas so that nearby children can learn computers basic using the play – way method.
- Bharat electronics Ltd built cyclone proof houres for the victims of the super cyclone in with the help of the victims them solves so that the houres are built according to their needs.
- Ion exchange has founded a profitable venture for environmental protection through water treatment afforestation and organic farming.

### Conclusion

In the competitive world MNCs are playing a vital role towards corporate social responsibility strategies. They are focusing to the society their image getting tax benefits from the government the MNCs must extend their performance towards ensuring social justice.

In all areas of business operation and service, the business house must aim at providing quality goods, better service, proper measurement, reasonable project and a responsible response. These are the major factors of corporate social responsibility.

## REFERENCES

**Websites**

1. www.csr.weltweit.de
2. www.thesro.org
3. www.etuc.org/
4. www.corporate social responsibility.org

**Books**

5. "Corporate Governance 7th Edition"—The Institute of Company Secretaries of India.

# Emerging Areas in Corporate Social Responsibility

S. Saboor Siraj Nooriya
Dr. Lourdes Poobala Rayen

## Introduction

Every business has a responsible for our society. Based on the social responsibility only, the business is made. Because, "Consumer is the king of market"—the famous quote by Mahatma Gandhi. Each and every corporate must consider the consumer health and wealth. Then only, the business can sustain in the market.

## Corporate Social Responsibility (CSR)

Corporate Social Responsibility is a concept whereby organizations consider the interests of society by actively taking responsibility for the impact of their activities on customers, communities, employees, shareholders and the environment in all aspects of their operations. Corporate Social Responsibility include introducing best practices of human resource management, taking adequate care of health and safety of their workers, taking care not to pollute the local environment and natural resources.

## Responsible For Whom?

A corporation's business environment includes a large number of groups with interest in a business organization's activities. These groups are known as corporate stakeholders.

## Promoting Corporate Social Responsibility in Emerging Markets

- Corporate Social Responsibility (CSR) is no longer a trend just among large multinational companies operating in developed countries. More and more emerging market companies are seeing the value of committing to responsible business practices.

- A strong strategy and reputation as a responsible business can help these companies build trust with local stakeholders there by establishing a local license to operate.
- Better ways of approaching employee concerns such as progressive Labour relations, have also been shown to enhance productivity and reduce costs associated with recruitment and turnover.
- A visible commitment to CSR can help emerging market firms attract multinational partners, access international sources of capital and reach socially conscious consumers with their products and services. It also better positions International Finance Corporation (IFC) investments to make lasting contributions to local development.
- Recognizing a growing need for support in this area among client companies and the wider private sector, IFC works through its social responsibility practice area to make advice and tools available to help emerging market firms incorporate CSR into strategic business planning and communications processes.

### Helping to Grow Responsible Business

International Finance Corporations social responsibility practice area develops tools and business models and supports companies directly in developing strategies and implementing projects in three broad areas:

1. Development of local Community and stakeholder engagement.
2. CSR strategy and communications.
3. Human resource practices.

Each area of engagement is designed to improve business performance by addressing key CSR issues.

By demonstrating the business and the social benefits of CSR, the program aims to encourage companies throughout emerging markets into their business operations.

## DEVELOPMENT OF LOCAL COMMUNITY AND STAKEHOLDERS ENGAGEMENT

The social responsibility team has gathered substantial expertise in local community development and works with IFC clients to design programs with direct links to business needs and competencies, while also ensuring relevance to local development needs. Our work focuses on health, education, and income generation activities for local communities and targets socially excluded groups such as rural populations, indigenous people and women. The objective is to ensure that the stakeholders impacted by investments are empowered to participate in and benefit from the local community development efforts led by the private sector.

### CSR Strategy and Communications

International Finance Corporation (IFC) recognizes the important role that an integrated CSR strategy combined with effective communications can play in creating reputation and business value for a company.

The social responsibility practice area thus helps business to not only understand and operationalize CSR in their core activities, but also to articulate their vision to stakeholders.

### Human Resource Practices

In 2006 April, International Finance cooperation introduced a new performance standard on Labour and working conditions, based on international best practice, including the core Labour standards.

The social responsibility team works with the private sector and in partnership with international institutions and global NGOs to provide alternatives to child labour and to remedy discrimination in the workplace. In addition, the program is exploring the opportunities to help emerging markets companies understand and work with human rights issues associated with business operations and the workplace.

### Shining Examples In CSR

Companies are expected to continuously improve their social, environmental and financial performance. Those who favor social responsibility claim that because organizations create many of the problems that need to be addressed such as air and water pollution and resource depletion. They should play a major role in solving them. Many large businesses often have surplus revenues that could potentially be used to help solve social problems. For Example: IBM routinely donates surplus computers to schools.

### INFOSYS

Infosys technologies ltd came into existence 4th Dec 1996 with the objective of fulfilling the social responsibility of the company by supporting and encouraging the underprivileged society. In short span of time, they undertaken various initiatives in providing medical facilities, rural education to remote rural areas.

### WIPRO

Wipro, through the Azim premji foundation has dedicated itself to the cause of universalisation of elementary education in India and currently runs 1900 schools in various parts of India.

### YES Bank

YES bank is pioneering a business approach titled responsible banking which integrates sustainability and social responsibility with the larger philosophy of the bank.

### Hindustan Petroleum Corporation Ltd (HPCL)

HPCL has a social responsibility in the way of improving the quality of life through wide range of assistance programs in the areas of primary education, health care, provision of drinking water.

HPCL received the Bombay chamber "Good corporate citizen Award 2002-03 for its wide ranging initiatives in the field of social welfare works and other considering parameters like business performance, corporate interests, Employee welfare, Customer satisfaction and customer awareness.

### Conclusion

CSR is an important concept in the new emerging market. CSR means the company preserves and protects our social foundations, values and institutions.

A business should produce goods and services efficiently and leave the solution of social problems to concerned individuals and government agencies. So the company will obtain the goal through innovative solutions to the challenges of development. The economic growth is sustainable only if environmentally and socially sound and helps to improve the quality of life for those living in developing countries.

## REFERENCES

1. Rajeev ray, entrepreneurship. Oxford
2. www.socialdbo.com
3. www.ashgate.com
4. www.csrforhr.com

# Corporate Social Responsibility (CSR)

## *As a Best Business Strategy*

Rev. Dr. Selvanayakam
S. Athilinga Senjith

### Introduction

In the current globalized business world, there exist large multinational as well as small local business organizations. Irrespective of the nature of business organizations, they should be ethically bound to their stakeholders, such as customers, owners/investors, government, suppliers and competitors in order to ensure good will, which in turn assure maximum business growth rates. Organizations follow different strategies to ensure their ethics in order to achieve goodwill among their stakeholders. One of such strategies used is Corporate Social Responsibility (CSR). CSR consists of a wide-range activities and programs that improve the organization's social, environmental and local economic impact, their influence on society, social cohesion and human rights, and fair trade. Particularly CSR greatly focus on environmental protection and the well being of employees, the community and civil society in general, both now and in the future through which the organizations assure goodwill among their stake holders.

### Corporate Social Responsibility

Corporate Social Responsibility (CSR) is the voluntary role and contribution of the business community towards a better social and environmental development, apart from their investment to organizational development. CSR is generally seen as the business contribution to sustainable development which has been defined as "development that meets the needs of the present without compromising the ability of future generations to meet their own needs", and is generally understood as focusing on how to achieve the integration of economic, environmental, and social imperatives.

According to Canadian Centre of Philanthropy, "CSR is a set of management practices that ensure the company minimizes the negative impacts of its operations on the society while maximizing its positive impacts."

Nowadays business firms had started realizing importance of CSR as a tool for dominating the competitive scenario prevailing in the national as well as international market, for customer retention, and sustainable growth. Such firms also focus on customer-driven excellence in terms of high quality products and services at the same time providing value for money, treating employees and partners as valuable assets, agility, innovation in products and services, social responsibility, and to develop environmental friendly techniques of production, design, recycle industrial waste- products and conserve natural resources, forest conservation, and customer solutions for Sustainable Business Practices. The Business Organizations affect the employees, customers, suppliers, shareholders, the local community and the environment in various ways. Corporate social responsibility (CSR) allows business organizations to develop responsible attitude toward the society and the environment and to behave ethically and contribute to economic development of the nations.

Corporate sector has a major role to play in a developing country like ours. However majority of the companies have a limited or myopic approach to corporate social responsibility. CSR is about improving the general living standards of the community, raising educational standards and creating a positive impact on society. Usually CSR concentrates on the activities that typically address the aspects of a firm's behaviour (including its policies and practices) with respect to such key elements as; health and safety, environmental protection, human rights, human resource management practices, corporate governance, community development, consumer protection, labour protection, supplier relations, business ethics, and stakeholder rights.

Nowadays firms have started using CSR as a strategy to focus on new opportunities and respond to interrelated economic, societal and environmental demands in the marketplace. Many firms believe that this focus provides a clear competitive advantage and stimulates corporate innovation and creativity. A more strategic approach to CSR can help the organizations to grow their business, make a bigger impact on the issues, and help ensure long-term viability and a stellar corporate reputation. In times of increased risk, shifting roles and responsibilities the firms can make use of the CSR strategy.

Stakeholders are also increasingly aware of the importance and impact of corporate decisions upon society and the environment and hence most of the corporations are involving their stakeholders in their decision-making and addressing societal challenges. The stakeholders are given the opportunity to reward or punish the corporations. Hence corporations can be motivated to change their corporate behavior in response to the business situations, where they can follow CSR approach in order to satisfy their stakeholders.

Companies can adopt the CSR strategies to assure some long –term benefits. They are:

- Creating and maintaining a high reputation for the organization
- Securing and maintaining strong relationships with stakeholders
- Creating better, safer and more stimulating work culture
- Increasing employees' commitment
- Improving the efficiency of the business management
- Increase the financial performance and profitability of the company
- Protecting from boycott actions; making access to funding easier
- Benefits from fiscal advantages and administrative facilitation.

## Tuners of Corporate Social Responsibility

The following are the tuners of corporate social responsibility:

**Employees and shareholders:** Some business organizations indulge in corruption, stealing of Intellectual Property Rights, financial scams and scandals or producing environmentally hazardous products for the customers. Instead they have to build goodwill and trust among the customers and shareholders. Building an ethically responsible culture in organizations can reduce the chances of employees indulging on unfair practices within the organization by emphasizing on professionalism, transparency, socially responsible investments, effective communication, employee participation, fairness, and promotions, adequate compensation and personal development.

**Brand equity:** Customers associate a brand with a promise and built on deep relationships with consumers. Its value to consumers is that it provides emotional as wells as functional aspects and reduces the risk, saves time and provides reassurance on value for money. Predictable results are the promise of a brand. Corporate Social Responsibility can play a major role in building customer loyalty based on ethical values practiced in the organizations. Brand loyalty can be strengthened through: increasing continuity of purchase via such techniques as "frequent purchaser" programs, "members clubs", "continuity promotions", that create identification between the users of a brand and its users.

**Ethical marketing practices and social awareness:** Rapid industrialization in many developing countries has now opened avenues for International Trade. These policies should cover distributor relations, advertising standards, customer's service, pricing, product development and general ethical standards. Now in this global scenario, companies need to apply high standards of ethics and morality when making corporate decisions. Due to increasing awareness among customers regarding the malpractices in the market, the consumers are now more conscious about their rights.

### The Environment Consciousness

Many organizations had started realizing the importance of environmental protection, as they are directly or indirectly contributing towards environmental protection. There are many issues regarding the environmental protection and particularly the issues which require immediate attention involve climate change, water conservation, air emission and E-waste

Many organizations like Tata, Infosys, Federal Express, Mahindra and Mahindra, NTPC Ltd, TNPL Ltd, etc are involved in several initiatives that help to protect the environment including greenhouse gas reduction, renewable energy and noise reduction, recycling and using alternative fuels in its own transportation fleet.

**Energy conservation and global warming:** Agriculture in our country had significantly faced its downturn due to the climate changes which were primarily caused by burning of coal, oil and other fossil fuels. The world produces more carbon dioxide and other gases which are responsible for manmade global warming. Hence it becomes very important to identify new fuels which may cause comparatively less pollution. Many companies are on their way to identify new non-renewable resources to ensure energy conservation as well a step to control the global warming.

**Responsibility towards the government:** All the Business Organizations have to comply with the general law applicable in every country. Management policies, strategies, mission, should be in accordance to the rules and regulations of the legal environment and should follow fair trade practices. Organizations should pay taxes and other dues and discourage bribery, corruption, and biases in the departments.

### CSR as a Business Strategy

A visible attention must be paid towards social and environmental consequences of business rather than aiming at mere profit maximization. Most of the companies consider Social concern and business as two independent responsibilities. But many companies lose focus of how social responsibility could have been integrated with the long term business outcomes. Businesses across the world are so obsessed with the immediacy of results that they cannot sight the vast opportunity that discharging of social responsibility holds for the long term sustainability of the organizations. As a result, based on the maturity of strategic thinking in the company, CSR is being implemented in one or more of the following ways as shown here:

- Reactive approach
- Building and image
- Operating Efficiency
- Way of competitive benefits

### Reactive Approach

Generally many companies use CSR as a reactive strategy for recovering from lost fortunes of the company by gaining the confidence of the communities in which they operate. But now companies have started adopting a "proactive approach" in case of CSR by estimating and analyzing the cost of not discharging the social responsibility and as a result they practice the minimum to pull on and thus minimizing their spending on this account. CSR is viewed by these companies as a cost and compulsion. This approach only obscures a business from identifying the real potential CSR holds with respect to their core business.

### Building an Image

Today many companies view CSR as an opportunity for building their corporate image. Companies announce their plans for various kinds of social philanthropic activities in order to draw the attention of media and general public. In case a company develops a systematic and deliberate approach for maintaining the focus on social welfare activities, this will not only enhance its image in the immediate future but also help the company in building a positive reputation of societal concern. This will definitely help the company in its future business forays in the region.

### Operating Efficiency

Some companies take care of environment and society for the reason that it not only helps in operating within the environmental norms set by statutory authorities but also reducing their costs by improving operating efficiency. If the companies are operating barely with in the norms set by statutory authorities then they are said to be in compliance mode. When companies deliberately plan and move beyond the compliance mode, the organization needs to integrate CSR and its business goals, which results in improved productivity or operational efficiency and better environmental conditions that fosters better living conditions for future generations.

### Way of Competitive Benefits

The major challenge for any type of industry today is to identify the social issues that drive its competitiveness both now and in the future. Hence the business managers must first believe that social concern or CSR will be a source for business opportunities and competitive advantage. This integration then would pave way for all round sustainability and growth. In the due course of time, the issues relating to climate change and social responsibility in the area of operations will be critical factors for survival of businesses. Thus CSR has the potential to change the way business conducted throughout the world.

## Conclusion

Most of the companies throughout the world had accepted that business is not just for making money and this is evident through their involvement in various community developmental activities. Many Business firms had realized the importance of using business ethics as a tool for retaining customers and increasing its market share by highlighting the initiatives it has taken for providing a clean environment for the society. Also some companies started using the CSR as a strategy which aims at mutual development of company and the community simultaneously.

## REFERENCES

1. www.csrwire.com
2. www.scribd.com
3. bms.co.in/tag/csr
4. www.accsr.com.
5. www.csr-books.com
6. www.encyclopedia.com
7. www.earthscan.co.uk

# Tata Group—A Forerunner in Corporate Social Responsibility Initiatives

Dr. K. Maruthamuthu
S. Boobalan

## Introduction

In recent years, the concept of Corporate Social Responsibility (CSR) has growing much more. It is a fundamental duty of any kind of business to the society to discharge their liability to them to more benefits gained from the society. Social responsibility is a concept of giving back to the society what it gets from it. Most corporations in the world look upon to initiate the CSR activities, these activities are not just like a liability but it gives more benefits and opportunities to grow the business. In India, Tata group is the pioneer to initiate the CSR activities, and leading to the Indian corporate sector to take them as a Role model in initiating the CSR activities. Nowadays most of the Indian companies showing their interest to do the CSR activities; they should take the Tata group as a real role model to perform the CSR activities, because the efforts taken by Tata group in the CSR activities are remarkable to the Indian corporate sector.

## Corporate Social Responsibility—Meaning and Definition

Corporate Social Responsibility involved in a wide range of concepts, principles and it is the obligation of business concerns for the well-being people, the state and the environment in which they operates and they required to safeguard health of the society as well. The CSR is broadly defined as; it is concerned with which should maintain the relationship between the global corporations, the legislative authorities and the individual peoples in the society.

According to Dahl, "every large corporation should be thought of as a social enterprise; that is an entity whose existence and decisions can be justified insofar as they serve public or social purposes", The European Commission's Green paper defined CSR as, "concept whereby companies integrate social and environmental concerns in their business operations and in their interaction with their stakeholders on a voluntary basis" as they are increasingly aware that responsible behavior leads to sustainable business success. Generally speaking CSR is about how the business community maintains their business processes to produce largely a constructive impact on society. The CSR activities are not only the give up of benefits by the companies, but it is one of the ways to attain more benefits.

### Tata Group and CSR

Tata companies operate in seven business sectors: communications and information technology, engineering, materials, services, energy, consumer products and chemicals. They are, by and large, based in India and also have significant international operations. The total revenue of Tata companies, taken together, was more than Rs. 325,334 crore ($70.8 billion), with 64.8 per cent of this coming from business outside India, and they employ around 363,039 people worldwide. The Tata name has been renowned and respected in India for over 140 years for its adherence to high values and business ethics.

As a global benchmark for CSR and a pioneer of the concept in India, the Tata group has adopted social responsibility as one of its integral values and the group has made concerted efforts to link it with the group's overall strategy for achieving business excellence. The Tata group has been actively involved in facilitating the development of this concept in India by setting standards and benchmarks. The founder of Tata Group, Jamsetji N. Tata, viewed "In a free enterprise, the community is not just another stakeholder in business but is in fact the very purpose of its existence." The group has always been recognized as a value-driven organization and its values were imbibed from the founder of the group and his successors who took on the leadership of the group.

**Tribal's culture and income generation activities:** The Tata Steel taken vigorous efforts to develop the Tribal people's culture and their standard of living, for the very purpose it has set up the Tribal Culture Centre at a cost of Rs 35,00,000. This Centre showcases the tribal legacy of four major and five minor tribes of Jharkhand and Orissa and evokes a lot of interest amidst scholars, researchers and even laypersons. The company has assisted the tribal population by the formation of many Self Help Groups (SHGs) for generating their income. These groups provided with training, networking and assistance in marketing.

**Health care activities:** The Company runs a big general hospital with modern facilities to reach out to its employees as well economically less privileged citizens across the Jamshedpur city. It established the Jamshedpur

Blood Bank to provide safe blood to those in need and has very successfully promoted a culture of voluntary blood donations. At its out locations the Company has set up hospitals, which cater to the healthcare needs of people from the surrounding rural areas.

**Environmental activities:** Tata Steel is the first company in the country to be conferred ISO-14001 Certification for its main steel works and utility services in Jamshedpur. All its mines and collieries are also ISO-14001 Certified for environmental management. Tata Steel's collieries and mines which support the 'Save Forests' campaign are a benchmark in environment management, further augmenting its commitment in this field, and it has planted 1.5 million surviving trees as a part of the 'Green Millennium' campaign. It may be worth mentioning that Jamshedpur has the best tree cover in the country.

**Other activities:** They have run endowment Schemes to provide higher education for deserving Indians and over 3,500 Tata Scholarships have been awarded to the students whom really deserve the financial assistance. J.R.D. Tata institutionalized CSR in the 1970s and decided that the group shall be mindful of its social and moral responsibilities to the consumers, employees, shareholders, society and the local community for all its major companies. They have formed group resource under the TCCI (Tata Council for Community Initiatives) on corporate sustainability would work on developing a Tata model using technical inputs from the UNDP. It is one of the extreme efforts taken by the Tata group for the corporate social responsibility. The thrust area was rural development, which included community health, basic education and vocational training.

### Awards to Tata Group for CSR Activities

The company has received a number of awards in recognition of its CSR efforts. The Energy & Resources Institute Award conferred on it in recognition of corporate leadership for good corporate citizenship and sustainable initiatives to the Tata Steel, also it was conferred the Global Business Coalition Award for Business Excellence in the Community for HIV /AIDS. The Tata Refractories Limited (TRL) has received many coveted awards and recognitions for their efforts in environment management, and certified with ISO 14001:2004 (Environmental Management System).

The Prestigious Awards received by Tata Group for CSR activities:

- The Golden Peacock Environment Management Award received in the year 2002.
- The Greentech Environmental Excellence Silver Award received in the year 2004.
- Tata Steel's Ferro Alloy Plant at Joda was awarded the first prize in the category of Longest Accident Free Period for the year 2007.

- The Tata Group honoured by Odisha State Disaster Management Authority (recognised by the Government of Odisha) for relief operations conducted by Tata Relief Committee during the devastating floods of 2008.
- The company has received the prestigious Think Odisha Leadership Award 2008, for its Services to the Nation for the last hundred years of Corporate Social Responsibility
- The Tata Steel Hospital at Joda received the Pollution Control Excellence Award 2008 from Odisha State Pollution Control Board.
- In the year 2009 conferred the prestigious 'CSR Leadership Award'.
- Tata Steel Limited has been awarded the prestigious Golden Peacock Global Award for CSR for the same year.
- Tata Steel has also received the Business World-FICCI-SEDF Corporate Social Responsibility award 2009.
- Tata Steel's Corporate Social Responsibility (CSR) initiatives have earned the steel giant the UK trade & Investment (UKTI) India Business Award 2009.

The above awards received by the Tata group of companies are some of the evidence in the compassion of them in performing the CSR activities. This shows that their efforts are the best effort from the Indian Corporate Sector in this regard.

## Conclusion

As a pioneer of CSR initiatives, the Tata Group performing well to develop the society and it plays a best role model to Indian Corporate. Every company should acts with the socially responsible behavior, they might cease to make a product but their relationship with the people and the natural environment will help them grow over time. The key to success lies in matching public expectations and priorities, and in communicating involvement and achievements widely and effectively. Therefore, for a company to be successful, in the long run, it must contribute towards the well-being of the society and the environment. So the corporate sector should take the Tata group as a benchmark of CSR activities, and get involves dynamically in the societal development activities.

## REFERENCES

1. Dahl, R. (1912): "A Prelude to Corporate Reform" *Business and Society Review*, Spring, 17-23.
2. European Commission (EU, 2001): "Green Paper—Promoting a European Framework for Corporate Social Responsibility", COM (2001) 366 final, Brussels, Official Publications of the European Commission, July 2.

3. Sharma, A.K. & Talwar. B. (2002): "Insights from Practice Corporate Social Responsibility: Modern vis-a-vis Vedic approach", *Measuring Business Excellence*, Emerald Group Publishing Limited, Vol. 9, No.1, 2005, 35-45.
4. 'Visionaries,' CSR Initiatives of Tata Group, www.indianngos.com, December 2004.
5. 'Tata Champions,' Tata Group, www.indianngos.com, December 2004.
6. http://www.Tata.com/company/releases/inside.aspx?artid=AMzaeJoYELI=
7. http://www.livemint.com/2009/03/04161615/Tata-Steel-bags-Golden-Peacock.html
8. http://steelguru.com/csr/index/49/CSR_award_for_Tata_Steel.html
9. http://www.zeenews.com/news564877.html

# Corporate Social Responsibility

## *A Tools to Sustain A Business*

V. Sindhu

### Introduction

Business firms are realizing its importance as a tool for dominating the competitive scenario prevailing in the national as well as international market, for customer retention, and sustainable growth by projecting itself as firm which also focuses and motivational and leadership skills, customer-driven excellence in terms of high quality products and service at the same time providing value for money, organizational and personal learning through regular training programs, treating employees and partners as valuable assets, agility, innovation in products and services, social responsibility and to develop environmental friendly techniques of production, design, recycle industrial waste–product and conserve natural resources, forest conservation, and customer solutions for sustainable business practices.

The business organizations affect the employees, customers, suppliers, shareholder the local community and the environment in various ways. Corporate social responsibility (CSR) allows business organizations to develop responsible attitude toward the society and the environment and to behave ethically contribute to economic development of the nations.

### Corporate Social Responsibility

Corporate social responsibility also called corporate conscience, citizenship, social performance, or sustainable responsible business) is a form a corporate self regulation integrated in to a business model. CSR policy functions as a built-in-self-regulating mechanism whereby business monitors and ensures its active compliance with the spirit of the law, ethical standards and international norms.

The goal of CSR is to embrace responsibility for the company's actions and encourage a positive impact through its activities on the environment, consumers, employees, communities, stakeholders and all other members of the public sphere. Furthermore, CSR-focused businesses would proactively promote the public interest by encouraging community growth and development and voluntarily eliminating practices that harm interest into corporate decision-making and the honoring of a triple bottom line; people, planet, profit.

### Types of Social Responsibility in Business Organizations

(*a*) **Internal social responsibilities:** Shareholders and employees.

(*b*) **External social responsibilities:** Customers, government, suppliers, community and the environment.

### Social objectives

It refers to a company's objectives and its responsi-bilities towards its employee, shareholders, and the public at large.

### Economic Objectives

It refers to optimization of available resources for maximization of profits and to survive in the competition prevailing in the industry. sun is named as one of the world's most ethical companies. It leads the industry in offering a portfolio of eco responsible products and services that deliver powerful, sustainable, energy-efficient computing solutions that don't compromise on capacity and security.

Eco Responsibility initiative focus on includes efforts to shrink carbon emissions develop an alternative-energy strategy, and otherwi8se reduce the environmental impact of its operations.

### Competencies Required for Corporate Social Responsibility

Each organization is different from the other and they reason why one firm emerges as a leader among other firm in the industry is due to the core competencies that is exclusive to a particular firm. The competencies that differentiates a firm from its competitors include:

*Management skill* (including organization building, effective communication skills, quick decision-making, awareness of advanced technologies, it, innovation, creative problem solving skills, strategic awareness, motivation skills, leadership skills, handling disputes).

*People skills* (include adaptability and empathy, training, influencing without power, interpersonal skills, integrated, general awareness, self-development and learning, building partnerships, and team work).

*Technical skills* (including technical expertise, understanding impacts of policies on stakeholder, consultancy, selling the business case, understanding human rights and understanding sustainability).

The most important core competencies for managers involved with CSR in organizations constitute:

- Understanding society
- Building capacity
- Accountability
- Stakeholder relations
- Strategic view
- Harnessing diversity
- Environment consciousness
- High quality products and services
- Avoid false advertisement claims

Tata group has constantly stressed on 'leadership with trust', unity, integrity, excellence, responsibility, commitment toward national interest, proving good working environment for the employees, avoidance of conflicts of interest, and emphasis on corporate social responsibility which has become an integral part of the company's core mission and vision statement and to promote ethical conduct in all its operations, which gives it an edge of stability and sustainability in the prevailing competitive scenario. But times have changed. Business firms whose primary motive is profit only might get success initiatives for ethical consumerism, and build stronger and healthier global communities.

## DRIVERS OF CORPORATE SOCIAL RESPONSIBILITY

1. Employees and shareholders
2. Brand equity
3. Ethical marketing practices and social awareness
4. The environment consciousness
5. Energy conservation and global warming
6. Responsibility towards the government

**1. Employees and shareholders:** According to Schlesinger and Heskett (1991) increased employees satisfaction leads to employee competence which results in superior service delivery and customer satisfaction. It takes decades for business organizations to build goodwill and trust in the minds of customers and shareholders which can be ruined through incident such as corruption, piracy, stealing of intellectual property rights, financial scams and scandals or producing environmentally hazardous products for the customers. Building and ethically responsible culture in organizations can reduce the chances of employees indulging on unfair practice with in the organizations by emphasizing on professionalism, transparency, socially responsible investment, effective communications, employee participation, fairness, and promotions, adequate compensation and personal development.

Calipers (the California public retirement system), one of largest US pension funds, to safeguard the interest of its shareholder, that is US pensioners.

**2. Brand equity:** A brand is a symbol carrying with eat certain associations and image. Customers associate a brand with a promise and build and deep relationship with consumer. Its value to consumer is that it provides emotional as wells as functional aspect and reduce the risk, saves time and provides reassurance and value for money. Practicable results are the promise of a brand. Corporate social responsibility can play a major role of building customers loyalty based on ethical values practiced in the organizations. Brand loyalty can be strengthened through increasing continuity of purchase via search technique as "frequent purchaser" programs, "members club". "Continuity promotions", that create identification between uses of a brand and its users.

**3. Ethical marketing practiced and social awareness:** Ethical in business refers to moral standards of the people working in the organizations, and the application of right or wrong practices prevailing in the business firm,.

Ethics is importance in all types of organizations.

The elements of business ethics are:

- Values-moral beliefs held by individuals, organizations and society as a whole.
- Rights type on accessibility of claims of the individuals in the society.
- Duties-duties are obligations, roles and responsibility of the individuals in the society.

The Nanhi kali programme is deeply committed to the education of the girl child and the currently supports the school level educations of 31,000 underprivileged girls across the nation.

**4. The environment consciousness:** Mahindra groups formally announced the lunch of project mahindra Hariyali in which 1 million trees will be planted nation-wide by mahindra employees and other stakeholders including customers, vendors, dealers, etc., by October 2008 of these, 1,50,000 trees have already been planted by mahindra employees since September 2007. issues which require immediate attention involve:

1. Climate change.
2. Water conservations.
3. Air emission.
4. E-waste

Federal express is involved in several initiatives that help to protect the environment including greenhouse gas reduction, renewable energy and noise reduction, recycling and using alternative fuels in its own transportation fleet.

**5. Energy conservation and global warming:** Agricultural in India will be significantly affected by the climate change due to burning of coal, oil and other fossil fuels that produces carbon dioxide and other greenho9use gases responsible for man made global warming. The effects of warming are being observed in the form of decline in productivity of certain crops such as wheat. Against thais backdrop it is essential for the global community as a whole to stabilize the earth's climate by reducing the concentration of green house gases in the atmosphere. The Asia-pacific region showed the strongest level of support for more regulation, at 100%, compared to 86% in mainland Europe, 77% in the UK and 69% in the US. Despite this call for stronger action by governments, most companies already expect the impact of climate change regulation on industry to increase over the next few years. UTI Ventures invest $8 million in presco (pragmatic environmental solutions Co) with beam environmental solutions, a company involved in waste oil recycling and alternate energy systems. Google has created research group for initiating a project called renewable energy cheaper than coal is meant to help Google cut its energy cost and then to offer customers cheaper power.

**6. Responsibility towards the government:** All the business organizations have to comply with the general law applicable in every country. Management policies, strategies, mission, should be accordance to the rules and regulations of the legal environment and should follow fair trade practices. Organizations should pay taxes and other dues and discourage bribery, corruption, and biases in the departments.

## Conclusion

CSR is a necessary condition for achieving excellence, not a sufficient one. Good governance is a source of competitive advantage and critical to economic progress. The quintessence of corporate governance is transparency, accountability, investor protection, better compliance with statutory laws and regulations, value creation for shareholders as also for other stakeholder and social value.

The reality is that CSR is not a tactic for brand building; however, it creates an internal brand among its employees. Indulging into activities that help society in one way or the other only adds to the goodwill of a company.

## REFERENCES

**Website :**

1. www.indianmba.com
2. http://en.wikeipedia.org/
3. www.corporate social responsibility.org

**Book :**

4. "Corporate Governance 7th Edition"—The institute of company secretaries of India.

# Emerging Trends in Corporate Social Responsibility

## *Perspective and Experiences from Post-Liberalized India*

**Mrs. Dr. P. Rajeswari**
**Ms. A. Sama**

### Introduction

Corporate Social Responsibility (CSR), can be described as, the continuous commitment by corporations towards the economic and social development of communities in which they operate. The concept of corporate social responsibility of large industrial groups has occupied a prominent place in the greater national discourse on economic issues since the pre-independence era in India. Gandhi described large business as 'trusts' of the 'wealth of the people' and thus emphasized on the larger social purpose that industrial wealth should serve in independent India. In the early days of the post-independence period, the Indian state under the heavy influence of Nehruvian socialism encouraged private industries to play an active role in the economic and social development of the backward sections of the society, while at the same time setup a mammoth public sector for serving larger societal interests. As Nehru's gentle socialism gave way to the more radical policies of nationalization and extensive state regulation of the Indira Gandhi era, industrial groups desperate to avoid the draconian state policies and regulations in economic affairs resorted to large scale corporate welfare programs to demonstrate that private wealth also played a important role in poverty alleviation and the socio-economic development of the nation and was not anti-people.

An impeding crisis in Indian economy led the Rajiv Gandhi and Narashima Rao governments to dismantle the 'license raj and introduce much-needed economic reforms in the country, which marked the beginning of the economic liberalization and the free market economy in India. The major impact of these economic reforms has been the increased presence of transnational corporations in the country and transformation of Indian businesses into large global enterprises. In this scenario, there is an increased focus on the social role of these private enterprises by both the proponents and opponents of liberalization in India.

In this paper we analyze the fundamental changes in paradigm of corporate social responsibility and the new innovative practices being applied for its implementation in the last decade in India, in the context of the liberalization of the Indian economy. Our central argument in the paper is that the rise of private enterprise in the free market setup has radically transformed the perception and understanding that corporations have of their large role in society and consequently, there has been a revolution in implementation of corporate social responsibility programs at the ground level.

## From Philanthropy to Stake Holder Participation : The New Paradigm of Corporate Social Responsibility

The conceptualization of corporate social responsibility up till the 1990's was purely in terms of philanthropy or charity. Welfare programs or initiatives were introduced not as a duty or a responsibility but as a form of charity that was supposed to indicate the virtues of the company or the organization. Many industrial groups like the Tatas or Birlas setup charitable trusts that provided financial grants for various worthy causes. Although there were some cases where the corporation took up a more active role like the establishment of the Birla Institute of Technology, Pillani by the Birlas or setting up of primary schools by several major industrial groups for their workers 's children but even in these cases the approach was philanthropically. The problem with the this philanthropy–based model has several problems:

- The corporation does not commit its resources fully behind such a project and often confines itself to one-time or periodical financial grants.
- Since it is an act of charity, the corporation does not feel the need for community participation in the designing or management of such initiatives and people participation, if any, is restricted to limited implementation aspects reducing the efficiency and effectiveness of corporate social responsibility measures at the ground level.
- The lack of involvement from the primary resource provider i.e. the corporation leads to low levels of accountability and transparency at the implementation level. However the post-liberalization phase has seen a fundamental shift from this philanthropy-based model of corporate social responsibility to a stakeholder- participation based model. The change is evident in the statements about corporate social responsibility being made by India's leading industrial groups like the Tatas, "over the years, the nature of the company's involvement

with the community has undergone a change. It has moved away from charity and dependence to empowerment and partnership and the consistent transformation in their corporate social responsibility practices in the last decade. In the stakeholder model the community in which the corporation is present in is seen as a stakeholder in the company and therefore, the company has certain obligation and duties towards it like it has towards its other stakeholders (customers, employees, shareholders). It is a recognition of the fact that companies perform in non-financial arenas such as human rights, business ethics, environmental policies, corporate contributions, community development, corporate governance, and workplace issues and company should be held accountable for its 'triple bottom line' that includes social, environmental, and financial performance and not just the financial aspect.

The question that arises at this juncture is what the reasons for this shift are in the basic paradigm in corporate social responsibility in the post-liberalization era. John Samuel and Anil Sari have argued that this transformation has been the result of three reasons.

- Recognition of the importance of 'reputation capital' for capturing and sustaining markets. Therefore corporate social responsibility is basically a new business strategy to reduce investment risks and maximize profits by taking all the key stakeholders into confidence.
- The growing importance attached to the 'eco-social' stability i.e. social and environmental stability and sustainability is necessary for the survival of a free-market economy in the long run.
- The importance being attached to accountability, transparency and social and environmental investment as the key aspects of corporate governance in the era of globalization.

Others like S. Sailaja have attributed the shift in conceptualization to a simpler 'benefit' argument that basically implies that the stakeholder model has been adapted as it makes CSR programs more effective and efficient, the need for which is recognized by corporation who see multiple benefits like increased sales and customer loyalty, enhanced brand value and reputation, increased ability to attract and retain quality employees, investors & business partners, better productivity of workforce, cooperation with local communities, efficient operations resulting in improved financial performance, increased stock value, reduced litigation & environmental costs, better and faster governmental approvals, rewards, tax benefits that come from good CSR practices.

While both these arguments are pertinent, we would venture to supplement them by drawing attention to two other important reasons for the basic shift in the corporate social responsibility model. Firstly, the post-liberalization phase saw the increased presence of large transnational corporations like IBM in India which have highly developed corporate social responsibility initiatives based on the stakeholder participation model that were introduced in India by them. The success and effectiveness of these programs had a 'rub-off' effect on Indian enterprises, which were also operating in the same market, in their approach to corporate social responsibility initiatives. Secondly as Indian industry started competing in the developed markets of Europe, America and the Far East it had to comply with entry level norms like certification for responsible corporate practices like ISO 14000, SA 8000, AA 100 as well as compliance codes formulated by OECD and UN Global Compact which meant that they had to adapt new corporate social responsibility standards.

## The New Innovations in Implementing Corporate Social Responsibility : The Revolution at the Grass Roots Levels

With the shifting of the corporate social responsibility paradigm to a stakeholder centric approach, practices at the ground level have also undergone a radical transformation. In every aspect of corporate social responsibility measures the last decade has seen corporations innovating to increase efficiency, effectiveness and accountability. The focus has been on initiatives that are people-centric with active community participation at all levels. Further, the corporations themselves have moved away from the charitable initiatives like giving financial grants or sponsorships to providing products and services in a manner that would make a real difference in the target communities.

The first perceptible change has been the introduction of a host of innovative programs and schemes in several areas like education, healthcare, rural development, environment protection, protection of artistic and cultural heritage and disaster management that are customized to meet the specific needs of the target group and corporations devote not only financial resources but expertise, manpower, products and services for the successful implementation of these schemes:

- Lupin India Ltd, India's third largest manufacturer of pharmaceuticals has started a project for providing sustainable development in 154 villages across Rajasthan. The scheme instead of providing for piece-meal assistance that does not lead to effective alleviation of poverty or adequate development is designed as a holistic action plan that includes an Agricultural Income Generation Scheme, land cultivation and fruit plantation programs, fodder preservation schemes, sericulture and water-recycling programs, establishment of medical and educational centers, adult literacy programs and credit schemes.
- Cipla, another Indian pharma major has found a novel approach to fulfill its corporate social responsibility obligations by offerering to sell a cocktail of three anti-HIV drugs, Stavudine, Lamivudine and Nevirapine, to the Nobel Prize-winning voluntary agency Medicine

Sans Frontieres (MSF) at a rate of $350, and at $600 per patient per year to other NGOs over the world. This offer has to led to an significant decrease in the prices of these drugs worldwide increasing the accessibility of these drugs especially in the developing countries.

- Ranbaxy, one of India's major pharmaceutical firms operates seven mobile healthcare vans and two urban welfare centers that reach over a lakh people in various parts of northern and central India as part of its corporate social responsibility initiative.
- Tata Consultancy Services (TCS) has set up a fully-equipped computer training laboratory for children from the Society for the Welfare of the Physically Handicapped and Research Centre, in Pune for imparting basic computer knowledge. NIIT has launched a highly popular 'hole-in-the-wall' scheme where it places a computer on a public wall in urban and rural areas so that neighborhood children can learn computer basics using the play-way method.
- Bharat Electronics Ltd built cyclone proof houses for the victims of the super cyclone in with the help of the victims themselves so that the houses are built according to their needs.
- Ion Exchange has founded a profitable venture for environmental protection through water treatment, afforestation and organic farming

Along with innovation, corporations have worked hard at integrating corporate social responsibility into their core practices. There is now greater evaluation and stricter accountability and transparency norms for social initiatives along the lines of norm set for mainstream projects and ventures. Sudha Murthy of the Infosys Foundation, the social initiative arm of the IT major Infosys, explains the great efforts that corporation are going into ensure that the projects they are involved with are actually genuine and serve a purpose, "We get a lot of projects, so we do a round of elimination....make a shortlist, as to which are the good ones, after a lot of verification. Then we supervise the implementation part by visiting the area. But we have to work very hard, during all holidays, weekends and 18 hours every day,"[vi] Several organizations like Gas Authority of India Ltd. (GAIL) have introduced benchmarking exercises for their CSR activities and industry bodies like Confederation of Indian Industries and FICCI have introduced cross-sectoral programs, for the first time, in CSR related areas.

### Public Sector Enterprises, Corporate Social Responsibility and Liberalization

In our narrative so far, we have focused on the private sector and its greater societal obligations. India, also, has a large public sector with several huge corporations. The Indian public sector has had a long tradition of corporate social responsibility and the initiatives of corporations like the Oil and Natural Gas Commission (ONGC), Steel Authority of India Ltd (SAIL) and Gas Authority of India Ltd. (GAIL) have critical in the development of several backward regions of the country. Indian Airlines and Bharat Heavy Electronics have been widely acclaimed for their disaster management efforts.

The era of liberalization has led to the privatization of several public sector units and others being forced to make switch from being monopolies to being free market players with intense private competition. These dynamic process have raised several key questions related to the corporate social responsibility of the public sector:

- What should the social involvement levels of a company or corporation once it is privatized?
- Should public sector units continue to play the same social role as they did in the pre-independence era or is there a need to scale back their social responsibility initiatives?

These are questions that are central to the post-liberalization debate and need further analysis and research. Meanwhile the opponents of privatization have used an 'corporate social responsibility' argument for their cause, they argue that considering the vital importance of the social role played by the public sector in India, there should not be any privatization of these vital industries. Once again the lack of adequate research specifically empirical data restricts us from an objective examination of this issue.

## Conclusion

The new economic era in India i.e. the post-liberalization phase of the Indian economy was a catalyst for the radical transformation in the corporate social responsibility related practices in the country, The change was twofold: transformation of the conceptual understanding of corporate social responsibility and innovations at the implementation level. At the conceptual level, there was a fundamental transformation from the charity-oriented approach to the stakeholder-oriented approach where the target group was seen as stakeholder in the community whose well-being was integral to the long term success of the company. However, the real revolution occurred at the implementation stages whre companies have started committing manpower, expertise in addition to financial resources in order to provide a host of services, programs and schemes that are flexible enough to accommodate the needs of the target community. The CSR initiatives have also seen greater people participation at all stages and tighter accountability standards. The issue of norms for corporate social responsibility seems to have been adequately dealt with by industry practices like benchmarking, CSR ratings and certification by different agencies.

While the situation in the private sector seems satisfactory, there is fierce debate on the social role of the Indian public sector in the post-liberalization phase especially in the light of the twin processes of privatization and the dismantling of monopoly/quota regimes. There is a need for extensive research especially in form of empirical studies to address the questions related to this issue.

# Business Sustainability through Corporate Social Responsibility

**Mrs. Ponrani**
**Dr. P. Lourdes Poobala Rayen**

## Introduction

*"A million Dollar question is: Can any business organization exist in Isolation? No!.* No business firm can survive without its employees, factors of production, customers, suppliers, distributors, society, culture, and environment as a whole. A company manufactures a product or service by combining land, labor, capital and enterprise. But in the end it is the choice of the customers to buy or reject a product if it does not serve their purpose. In the last twenty years, there has been a sea change in the nature of the triangular relationships between companies, the state and the society. No longer can firms continue to act as independent entities regardless of the interest of the general public. The evolution of the relationship between companies and society has been one of the slow transformation from a philanthropic coexistence to one where the mutual interest of all the stakeholders is gaining paramount importance.

## COMPETENCIES REQUIRED FOR CORPORATE SOCIAL RESPONSIBILITY

### Management Skills

It includes organization building, effective communication skills, quick decision making, awareness of advanced technologies , Information technology, innovation, creative problem solving skills, strategic awareness, motivation skills, leadership skills, handling disputes etc.. The management skill is very useful to build the organization which would improve co-operation and coordination among the employees in the organization.

### People Skills

It includes adaptability and empathy, training, influencing without power, interpersonal skills, integrated, general awareness, self-development and learning, building partnerships and team work etc. Here we should say that the people skill would develop the personality of each and every person in the organization.

### Technical Skills

It includes technical expertise, understanding impacts of policies on stakeholder, consultancy, selling the business case, understanding human rights and understanding sustainability. The most important core competencies for managers involved with CSR in organizations constitute:

- Understanding society
- Building capacity
- Accountability
- Stakeholder relations
- Strategic view
- Harnessing diversity
- Environment consciousness
- High quality products and services
- Avoid false advertisement claims

### Types of Social Responsibility

There are two types of social responsibility. They are as follows:

- **Internal social responsibility:** It implies the responsibility towards share holders and employees. Every organization has the responsibility to render the service for the benefit of share holders and employees. The responsibility towards share holders is to make them wealth through the organization's market value's stability. The responsibility towards the employee is to make the payment of salary at the correct time.
- **External social responsibility:** It implies the responsibility towards customers, Government, Suppliers, Community and the Environment. The customers should have satisfied with the quality and price and the service. It is also an important factor for business' sustainability. The responsibility towards government is to pay taxes at the correct time. We have to file our return on the due date. The duty towards suppliers is to settle the amount at the correct time.

### Sustainability of Business

Sustainability is an economic, social, and ecological concept. It is intended to be a means of configuring civilization and human activity so that society and its members are able to meet their needs and express their greatest potential in the present, while preserving biodiversity and natural ecosystems, and planning and acting for the ability to maintain these ideals indefinitely. All firms need introspect that their existence is impossible without the involvement of the society and it is their duty to adopt ethical consumerism and to provide clean healthy environment for all the future generations to come.

### Types of Sustainability

There are four types of sustainability. They are as follows:

- Human sustainability
- Economic sustainability
- social sustainability
- Environmental sustainability

### Human Sustainability

The very basic need of human sustainability is good reproductive health and safe childbearing. Those that reproduce have the responsibility of caring for their children, giving them access to proper education, and promoting their health and wellness. At some point, the children should have enough skills and knowledge such that they can sustain their own way of life. It is at that point that they become considered as productive human capital as well as individuals that can go through the process of reproduction and rearing. As long as this process is maintained at a rate that all human systems can support, human sustainability should be no cause for concern.

### Economic Sustainability

In simple terms, economic sustainability is having a set amount of capital for a certain period. Those who consume that capital must also conserve it so that they will continue to enjoy it towards the end of the specified period. This means that we must preserve all our resources as we consume them so that human beings in the future can enjoy them as well. To achieve this, we must regenerate our resources at a rate that is equal to or faster than our consumption.

### Social Sustainability

Social capital is an important aspect of sustainability because it is through communities and civil societies that humankind can easily and inexpensively work together. Without proper levels of social capital, it can easily deplete and violence as well as mistrust can take over. When that happens, societies and everything else that depends on them will be destroyed. Through proper maintenance of and adherence to laws, rules and values that societies have developed for the common good, social sustainability can be achieved.

## Environmental Sustainability

Environmental sustainability is important because it involves natural resources that human beings need for economic or manufactured capital. Materials taken from nature are used for solutions that address human needs. If nature is depleted faster than it can regenerate, human beings will be left without raw materials. Further more, environmental sustainability also involves ensuring that waste emissions are at volumes that nature can handle. If not, all humans and other living things on Earth can be harmed to the point of extinction.

## "CSR" Tool for Business Sustainability

In the ancient days there is no competition in the business as now. Because the system of monopoly is exists in the business. So the businessmen do not have heavy competition among them. But now-a-days this is not possible, because we have very heavy competition in the field of business. We have to struggle more for keeping our business stable for ever. To keep our organization sustainable, we have to do various kinds of activities. The activities which are done by an organization should be in the favour of society.

## Survey

A survey is taken by me among the various business men. Only 20 samplings are taken. Some of the business men are support the social responsibility of the business. Some business men are not support this concept. Because they said that this concept is not very successful in practice. The report derived from the survey is as follows:

As per the survey, the business men can divide in to three categories. They are:

1. Supporters
2. Semi supporters
3. Not supporters.

This table will helps us to understand the result of survey.

**Social activity a tool for business sustainability**

| Total. No. of. Business man | supporters | Semi- supporters | Not- supporters |
|---|---|---|---|
| 20 | 4 | 7 | 9 |

The result of the survey shows that there is no awareness about the social responsibility of the business. The business men should know about this. If the business men have no awareness about the social responsibility, well known personnel may be employed by them. We come to know that

1. only 20% the business man has the awareness about the corporate social responsibility.
2. 45% of the business man has no awareness about the corporate social responsibility.

**Limitations**

- Corporate social responsibility is a main feature of a developing firm. For example a firm can conduct a blood donation camp as social responsibility activity.
- But now-a-days the social responsibility activities done by a firm are for the only objective of advertise themselves not for service motive.
- We are individual, so we expect more benefit from an organization for the benefits of individual. Individual may expect high rate of dividend from an organization. But this is not a social responsibility of an organization.
- This will not be the factor which would determine the sustainability of the business. If an organization does any activity for the benefit of the society then the particular activity will determine the sustainability of the business.
- The customers are not interested to know the activities done by an organization. The customers purchase the goods and service of an organization when they like the products or service.
- When the customers are interested to know about every organization very well then only this system will become success.
- For example we can purchase goods from co-operative society, but purchased from departmental stores. But we are purchased goods from departmental stores.

**Cases**

- Nandi Kali programmed is deeply committed to the education of the girl child and currently supports the school level education of 31,000 underprivileged girls across the nation.
- National Thermal Power Corporation (NTPC) Limited has been awarded Business world FICCI-SEDF Corporate Social Responsibility Award for its continued efforts in integrating CSR into its core business operation.

NTPC Limited has decided to allocate **0.5%** of distributable profit annually for its "Research and Development Fund for Sustainable Energy," for undertaking research activities in development of green and pollution free technologies. The efforts towards ethical business operations by NTPC has earned profit after tax for the year 2007-08 to be around Rs. 7,415crores as compared to Rs. 6,865crores during the year 2006-07, an increase of 8.01% over previous year.

- Other organization which are involved in the corporate social responsibility activity as follows
- Pepsi & co

- Internet search giant Google
- banking majors HSBC
- BMW
- Oracle Corp
- Mahindra & Mahindra Limited
- Tata Tea Limited

## Conclusion

From this we come to know that the sustainability of a business depends upon the corporate social responsibility. Eco- friendly products and solutions accessible and reporting on the progress in Annual Corporate Social Responsibility Report. The business must accommodate itself to the various changes taking place in the environment. The scope of Business is to optimize the allocation of scarce natural resources thereby decreasing the costs and enhancing the productivity of the organization, for the benefit of the society. Customers also ready to support the organizations which are done social beneficiary activities. So if an organization wants to exist forever it should involve in social responsibility activities.

# Emerging Areas in Corporate Social Responsibility

Ms. T. Swarnamughi
N. Nitesh Parsan

## Introduction

In the last twenty years, there has been a sea change in the nature of the triangular relationship between companies, the state and the society. No longer can firms continue to act as independent entities regardless of the interest of the general public. The evolution of the relationship between companies and society has been one of slow transformation from a philanthropic coexistence to one where the mutual interest of all the stakeholders is gaining paramount importance. Companies are beginning to realise the fact that in order to gain strategic initiative and to ensure continued existence, business practices may have to be moulded from the normal practice of solely focusing on profits to factor in public goodwill and responsible business etiquettes(Reynard and Forstater, 2002). An examination of some of the factors which have led to the development of the concept of corporate social responsibility (CSR) would be ideal starting ground for the conceptual development of suitable corporate business practices for emerging markets. The business environment has undergone vast changes in the recent years in terms of both the nature of competition and the wave of globalization that has been sweeping across markets. Companies are expanding their boundaries from the country of their origin to the evolving markets in the developing countries which have been sometimes referred to as emerging markets. The current trend of globalization has brought a realisation among the firms that in order to compete effectively in a competitive environment; they need clearly defined business practices with a sound focus on the public interest in the markets (Gray, 2001). The increase in competition among the multinational companies to gain first mover advantage in various developing countries by establishing goodwill relationships with both the state and the civil society is ample testimony to this transformation. Secondly, in most of the emerging markets, the state still holds the key to business success because of the existence of trade and business regulations restricting the freedom of multinational companies to incorporate their previously successful business doctrines which have been tried and tested in the developed nations. The state with its duty of protecting the interests of the general public would naturally be inclined to give preference to companies which take care of the interests of all the stakeholders. Thirdly, emerging markets have been identified as a source of immense talent with the rising levels of education. For example, the expertise of India in churning out software professionals and China in manufacturing has now become internationally renowned. In order to draw from this vast talent pool coming up in developing countries, companies need to gain a foothold in these markets by establishing sound business practices addressing social and cultural concerns of the people. It has been observed that consumers consider switching to another company's products and services, speak out against the company to family/friends, refuse to invest in that company's stock, refuse to work at the company and boycott the company's products and services in case of negative corporate citizenship behaviours (Edenkamp, 2002).

Last but not the least, firms all over the world is beginning to grasp the importance of intangible assets, be it brand name or employee morale. Only firms that have gained the goodwill of the general public and are ideal corporate citizens will be to develop these intangible assets into strategic advantages.

### Emerging Markets

The term 'emerging market' was originally coined by IFC to describe a fairly narrow list of middle-to-higher income economies among the developing countries, with stock markets in which foreigners could buy securities. The term's meaning has since been expanded to include more or less all developing countries. World Bank (2002) says that developing countries are those with a Gross National Income (GNI) per capita of $9,265 or less. The World Bank also classifies economies as low-income (GNI $755 or less), middle-income (GNI $756–9,265) and high-income (GNI $9,266 or more). Low-income and middle-income economies are sometimes referred to as developing countries.

The evolution of CSR in these developing economies shows widely varying results. Chambers, Chapple, Moon and Sullivan (2003) evaluate the extent of CSR penetration in seven Asian countries (India, Indonesia, Malaysia, the Philippines, Singapore, South Korea and Thailand). Many researchers have hypothesised that CSR in emerging economies is still in a very nascent stage and suitable mechanisms do not exist to ensure that companies practise CSR with anything other than a charitable outlook. Kemp(2001) states "There are numerous obstacles to achieving corporate responsibility, particularly in many developing countries where the institutions, standards and appeals system, which give life to CSR in North America and Europe, are relatively weak." Chambers, Chapple, Moon and Sullivan (2003) measure the extent of CSR penetration in the seven Asian companies and show that the mean value for the seven countries (even including industrially advanced Japan) is just 41 per cent compared to say a score of 98 per cent for a developed nation like the United Kingdom. However, there are exceptions to the mean scores. India for example had an average CSR penetration of 72 per cent compared to Indonesia's 24 per cent. The concept of CSR as visualized in the emerging markets and the developed countries have very different understanding.

### Dimensions of CSR and Relevance for Emerging Markets

The Green Paper (2001) by the Commission of the European Communities identifies two main dimensions of CSR, an internal dimension relating to practices internal to the company and an external dimension involving the external stakeholders.

### Internal Dimension

This relates to practices internal to the company which need to be modified to incorporate CSR practices.

#### (*a*) Human Resources Management

CSR can be successfully implemented in an organization through precise management of its own work force. The internal dimension of CSR includes elements like providing an environment for lifelong learning for employees, employee empowerment, better information flow, improving the balance between work, family, and leisure, diversified work force, profit sharing and share ownership schemes, concern for employability as well as job security among others. Active follow up and management of employees who are off work due to disabilities or injuries have also been shown to result in cost savings for the companies. Moulding of recruitment policies to include people from ethnic minorities, older workers, women and the long- term unemployed would be a significant step forward to incorporating CSR practices in Human Resources Management.

In the context of emerging markets, the availability of cheap labour is an encouraging factor for companies. Dawar and Chattopadhyay (2000) infer from their research that many times, emerging markets are able to provide cheap skilled and unskilled labour at wages which would be substantially cheaper than the normal cost of automation of the job positions. Developed markets have clearly moved towards heavily capital-intensive distribution with the introduction of electronic data interchanges, mechanized movement and monitoring of goods, and vending machines that replace salespeople. By contrast labour-intensive distribution remains economical in emerging markets. For example, in emerging markets, Coca-Cola has not invested in vending machines. These are too expensive relative to salespeople. Benjamin, Brandt and Glewwe (2000) report that in China, instead of vending machines, the company has experimented with a pushcart program in which salespeople dispense the company's drinks by the single-serve bottle. Similarly, in India, almost 10 per cent of Coca-Cola sales take place through fountains, where a salesperson dispenses drinks by the paper cup. Daily sales of as little as 100 cups justify the cost of the fountain and the person employed to dispense the drinks.

### (*b*) Work Safety and Health Measures

Worker safety and labour health have been documented to be having a direct impact on productivity of the labour force. Although legal measures exist in most nations on maintaining standards for ensuring worker safety and providing health benefits, recent trends have made it imperative for companies to adopt a proactive approach to this issue. In emerging markets having significant cost advantages in labour, outsourcing of labour and processes have led to the situation where companies not only need to maintain high safety levels in their own premises but also ensure that their suppliers and other connected parties comply with these principles. The increased focus on safety standards and employee welfare has led to the development of standards across industries. Mechanisms are being designed especially in emerging markets for measuring, documenting and communicating these qualities thereby saving time, work and costs in the purchasing process.

### (*c*) Adaptation to Change

A recent trend in the global business scenario has been the wide spread use of mergers and acquisitions for business expansion. Also downsizing has been used, often ineffectively, as a cost cutting measure by firms in their relentless push for profits. According to the Green Paper (2001) by the Commission of the European Communities "Restructuring in a socially responsible manner means to balance and take into consideration the interests and concerns of all those who are affected by the changes and decisions. In practice the process is often as important as the substance to the success of restructuring. In particular this involves seeking the participation and involvement of those affected through open information and consultation. Furthermore, restructuring needs to be well prepared by identifying major risks, calculating all the costs, direct and indirect, associated with alternative strategies and policies, and evaluating all of the alternatives which would reduce the need for redundancies." However, Bhattacharyya and Rahman (2003) point out that although most emerging economies have labour laws preventing labour retrenchment even in the event of declining sales, in practise lobbying with the bureaucracy and government is an aspect which firms cannot chose to ignore.

### (*d*) Management of Environmental Impacts

The importance of this aspect of CSR cannot be overemphasised. Optimization of resource utilization and reducing environmentally damaging effluents can reduce the environmental impact. This will also enable the firms to affect significant cost savings in energy bills and pollution costs. Many firms in emerging markets have had to face serious repercussions from the state and society for over exploitation of natural resources and disregard for environmental safety measures. Studies by Consultancy and Research for Environmental Management on practises of Dutch multinational companies in India (2004) highlight the importance attached by the companies to maintenance of environmental standards. Many multinational companies are realizing to their cost that early compliance with accepted standards will provide strategic advantages in the long run even though cost inefficient in the near future.

### External Dimension

This dimension relates to practices concerning external stakeholders. The significance of this dimension of CSR has come to the forefront with the advent of globalization leading to the development of international standards for business practices.

**(*a*) Local Communities:** The development of positive relations with the local community and thereby the accumulation of social capital is particularly relevant for non-local companies. These relations are being increasingly used by multinational companies to support the integration of their subsidiaries into various markets in which they are present. Deep understanding of the local community and social customs is an asset which can be utilized by the companies to gain strategic advantage.

In emerging markets, this is more relevant than ever because of the availability of

cheaper labour from the local communities. Companies would find it in their interest to substitute capital substitution with labour and reap the cost benefits. For example, Dawar and Chattopadhyay (2000) point out the instance of Whirlpool. "Whirlpool discovered that it was unable to sell its high priced, fully automatic machines in the emerging markets. It was only after it introduced twin-tub machines that were cheaper and utilized the consumers' labour rather than electronics to complete the entire washing cycle that sales took off. Interestingly, due to the fact that these machines had long disappeared in the developed markets, Whirlpool had to acquire the 'obsolete' technology from Korea."

**(*b*) Business Partners:** Building long term relationships of sound ethical foundation with suppliers, customers (and even competitors in rare occasions) will enable companies to meet customer expectations better while reducing complexity and costs. Companies should realise their CSR practices will be judged taking into account the practices of their partners and suppliers throughout the supply chain. The effect of corporate social responsibility activities will not remain limited to the company itself, but will also touch upon their economic partners.

Companies in emerging markets actually take on additional CSR responsibilities because of the existence of outsourcing opportunities in the form of suppliers and outsourcing agents. Also as part of their social responsibility companies are expected to provide high quality products and services, which meet customer expectations in a manner reflecting the company's concern for the environment and the local conditions. Thus in emerging markets, consumer based business strategies would enable companies to build long lasting relationships with consumers based on trust.

### (c) Human Rights

According to Robbins (2000), "Companies operating in countries where human rights are regularly violated may experience a climate of civil instability and corruption that makes for uneasy relations with government officials, employees, local communities and shareholders." Amnesty International states:" Companies have a direct responsibility to ensure the protection of human rights in their own operations. They also have a responsibility to use their influence to mitigate the violation of human rights by governments, the forces of law and order or opposition groups in the countries in which they operate." The Caux Round Table Principles state that companies have a responsibility to respect human rights and democratic institutions; and promote them wherever practical.

In the context of emerging markets, operations of companies should not impinge on the land rights of the local community. In particular, the company needs to make sure that people are not forcibly removed from their homes and their livelihoods are not endangered. There is the growing need to develop proper consultative processes with local groups protesting against projects or operations in which they are involved. Firms also need to build confidence in the local community that people (including union members) participating in peaceful protests against company operations are not intimidated, arrested or in any other way threatened. Also, companies can take steps to ensure forced labour is not used in their own, or their suppliers' operations. According to Robbins (2000), there are reports of Gulags or prison labour camps in China producing products that are then sold locally or exported. An example of foreign companies benefiting from the ruling regime's abuse of its people is the building of the gas pipeline in Burma. Numerous reports tell of the use of forced labour on a grand scale. Companies need to ensure that human rights principles are withheld in all their operations and related activities in emerging markets.

**Conclusion**

Emerging markets like India have drawn the attention of large MNCs for the potential of market growth. These markets are untapped and give entirely new domain for operations. However, many MNCs also take the markets for granted and exploit the laxity in the norms of operations to their advantage. The lack of concern for the local community, the consumers and the environment by these corporations has created large scale public debate and action. It is important in this context to understand that the sustainable business growth is associated with care for the community and markets the corporations operate in. The negative publicity caused by the actions of MNCs has led to suspicion about their operations in the general public in these markets. The case of Coca Cola also proves without doubt that irresponsible corporate behaviour can have repercussion throughout their global markets.

# Corporate Social Responsibility in Emerging Markets

## *The Role of Multinational Corporations*

D. Jeyaraman
P. Pandirajan

### Introduction

Amongst the many dramatic changes that have taken place in the business world since the 1990s, the rise of the corporate social responsibility (CSR) agenda is certainly one of the most noteworthy. A recent special report in *The Economist* notes, "doing well by doing well" has become a popular business mantra. It implies that firms can be successful by acting in the broader interests of society as a whole even while they satisfy the narrow interests of shareholders.

In recent years, a diverse array of terms has appeared to express the idea that business needs to make positive contributions to societal good, amongst them 'corporate social responsibility,' 'corporate responsibility,' 'corporate citizenship,' etc. This paper uses 'corporate social responsibility (CSR)' and 'corporate responsibility (CR)' interchangeably. It adopts the acronym CSR rather than CR because the former is the more widely accepted term in academic and business literature. One should note, however, that with the word 'social' the term CSR may seem somewhat narrow and CR in this sense may be more encompassing and potentially more useful.

### Csr in Emerging Markets

For a long time the concept of CSR has been questioned in terms of its validity and usefulness for profit-making companies. Milton Friedman, for example, famously asserted that "the social responsibility of business is to increase its profits."[3] Although one can still hear "the business of business is business" type of argument, the question for today is no longer *whether* companies should practice CSR, but *what*, specifically, and *how*. Ultimately, the concept of CSR itself may disappear, as a corporate social agenda will be an integral part of business strategy in the 21st century.

If one adopts a strategic vision for CSR, a vision that recognises the interdependence between business and society, then it becomes clear that CSR can both help companies make money and promote societal welfare. Strategic CSR realises the dynamic interdependence and the importance of forming a community of interests amongst the firm and its various stakeholders in society. Conceived in this way, "CSR can be much more than a cost, a constraint, or a charitable deed—it can be a source of opportunity, innovation, and competitive advantage."

Emerging markets present both opportunities and risks for MNCs. On the one hand, the almost 2 billion consumers in emerging markets represent a huge market opportunity for MNCs. Indeed, the best way now to generate both profits and create societal value is to focus on emerging markets. On the other hand, MNCs operating in these countries face challenging and difficult security, environment, health, and other risks. Doing business in emerging markets will be difficult because many of them are characterized by either bad or weak public governance and administration, lack of public transparency, high levels of bribery and corruption, poor records on human rights, inadequate environmental, safety and labour standards and high levels of poverty and inequality. How can MNCs better practice CSR in such volatile circumstances?

Obviously it is important first to understand what CSR means in the context of emerging economies. CSR should be seen as a local, not a universal, concept. The historical and national context of communities, especially their corporate and societal governance frameworks and business-society relations impact on how CSR may be practised in these areas.

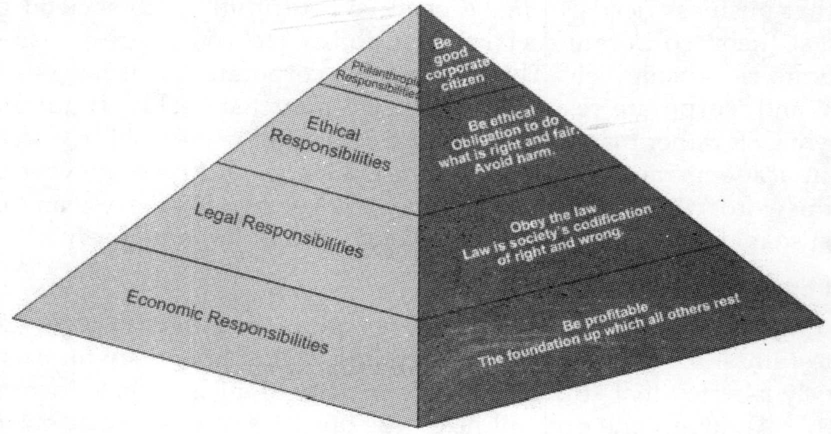


Carroll's CSR Pyramid

## Issues and Cases

These contextual issues need to be kept in mind when discussing CSR in emerging markets. In terms of specific issue areas that MNCs have to address, three are the most important. These are all areas where MNCs have encountered significant problems in the past, but also ones which can drive business innovation and create market opportunities.

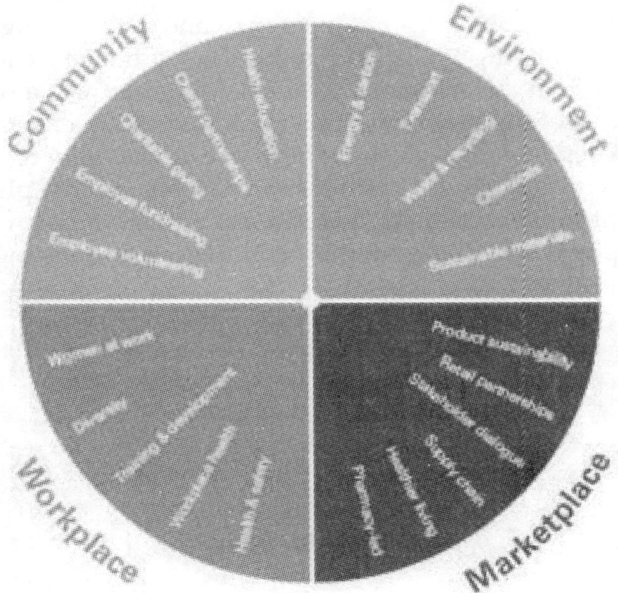


## Workplace

Workplace issues cover a wide and expanding array of topics, the Most prominent being labour standards. In addition to traditional human resource areas, workplace issues now include HIV/AIDS, work-life balance, diversity, sexual harassment, employee privacy, downsizing, and organisational development issues related to overall workplace culture and work processes.

### Nike

Nike's case in Southeast Asia in the 1990s illustrates how labour standards issues can damage a company's global image.7 At the same time it reveals the importance of the contextual variables for the meaning and practice of CSR. Nike in fact paid its workers in its Southeast Asian athletic footwear plants in accordance with local customs and practices. This is quite natural for MNCs: when a firm from a developed country does business in a less-developed one, it may establish a level of corporate virtue consistent with that of the host country. Yet this was exactly what opened Nike to charges of operating sweatshops.

### The Coca-Cola Company

Since 2002, and following a significant activist campaign, alongside a realisation that the economic viability of the business itself was threatened, the Coca-Cola Company in Africa in partnership with its bottling partners, has been implementing a programme to tackle HIV/AIDS in its workplaces across the continent.

With a clear and formal HIV/AIDS policy in place, the company recognises that HIV/AIDS is a public health emergency and acknowledges the role of the workplace in limiting the spread and effects of the epidemic. But it also realised early on that the company and its bottling partners alone would not be able to deliver a wide-ranging prevention and treatment programme for all its employees and associates. Therefore it decided to build strong partnerships with healthcare management organisations, pharmaceutical companies, medical treatment providers, and NGOs for prevention, awareness, orphan care, and voluntary counselling and testing.

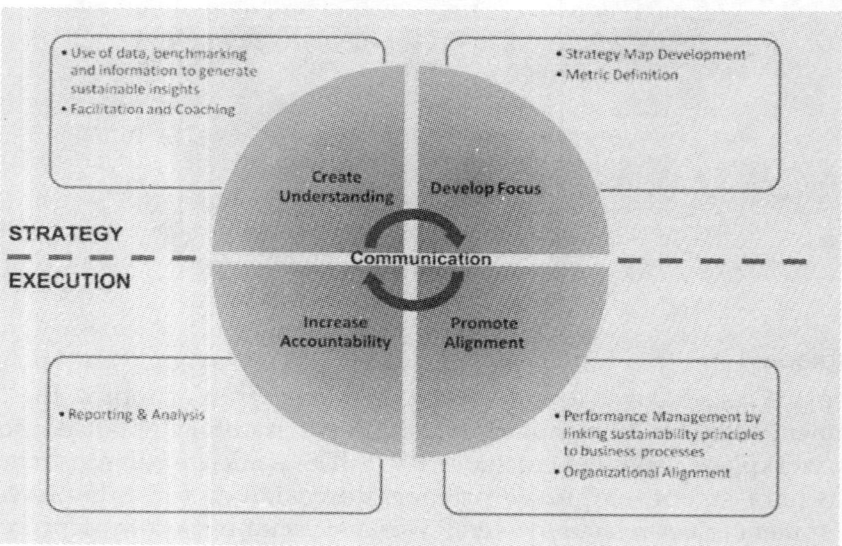


### Market Place

Marketplace issues extend across a wide range of business activities that define a company's relationship with its customers. These activities may be grouped into six categories: (1) integrity of product manufacturing and quality; (2) disclosure, labelling and packaging; (3) marketing and advertising; (4) selling practices; (5) pricing; and (6) distribution and access. Emerging issues include obesity and nutrition; integrity of the food chain, privacy and technology, drug pricing for the poor and elderly, marketing to children, heightened expectations for product safety, and extended product responsibility.

### HLL and Unilever

Unilever is a company that has traditionally been good at identifying new products and markets in low-income communities around the world. Here the example of its subsidiary, Hindustan Lever, Ltd. (HLL), is illustrative. For more than 50 years, HLL served a small elite population in India with the income to buy its products. Then in the 1990s HLL noted that an Indian firm, Nirma, was offering detergent products for poor consumers; in fact, Nirma had created an entirely new business system designed to meet the needs of under-served consumers, mostly from poor, rural areas.

With this stimulus, HLL drastically altered its traditional business model in 1995 to develop new products for rural markets. Its new detergent product, Wheel, was reformulated substantially to reduce the ratio of oil to water, responding to the fact that the poor often wash clothes in rivers and other public water systems. Most raw materials were sourced from local suppliers. Production, marketing, and distribution were all decentralised to leverage the large labour pool in rural India, quickly creating selling channels through the thousands of small outlets where poor people shop. HLL also changed the cost structure of its detergent business so it could introduce Wheel at a low price point. Today, rural markets account for more than half of HLL's total revenues—and profits.

This example demonstrates that low-income communities can be a very profitable market, especially if MNCs change their business models. HLL registered a 20 percent growth in revenues per year and a 25 percent growth in profits per year for 1993-1999. Its parent company, Unilever, has also benefited from its subsidiary's experience in India. Unilever used HLL's business principles to create a new detergent market among the poor in Brazil. But even more importantly, Unilever has adopted the low-income market as a corporate strategic priority. Indeed, by 2006, that market accounted for more than 20 percent of Unilever's sales on a global basis.

### The Environment

Although developed countries' economies have become more information and service intensive, globally, the unsustainable use of raw material and fossil energy has exploded during the past 50 years, with dire consequences for the world environment. Approximately 60% of the ecosystem services that support life on Earth—such as fresh water, oceans, soils, and climate—are being degraded or used unsustainably. In the past two decades, corporate environmental responsibility has evolved and expanded to cover substantially more than legal compliance, waste minimisation, and pollution prevention. Companies have embraced a variety of environmental initiatives while integrating environmental responsibility at all levels of their operations. Indeed, it is argued that companies need to go 'beyond greening' from today's pollution prevention and product stewardship towards tomorrow's clean technology and sustainability vision. Over the next decade or so, sustainable development will constitute one of the biggest opportunities in the history of commerce.

### General Motors

By the early 21st century, all major car companies had initiated clean technology (fuel cell or alternative) vehicle programmes. The most famous so far is perhaps Toyota's Prius, the hybrid electric/gasoline vehicle which has produced competitive advantage and environmental benefits. However, most of these programmes still envisioned the product in conventional terms: a heavy metal chassis and body with thousands of component parts. But in the early 21st century fuel cells were still many times more expensive to produce than internal-combustion engines. Thus, when a fuel cell (with an electric motor) is seen as a simple replacement for the internal-combustion engine, the result is an overpriced product that few consumers would ever consider buying.

### Conclusion

This paper has given an overview of the many issues surrounding CSR in emerging markets. It is meant to be suggestive, as a background briefing for more substantive and detailed discussions during the actual seminars. This project will now give an opportunity for a wide range of stakeholders to enter into the debate on CSR in emerging markets. The findings and insights it generates will inform the final paper of this project, due to be produced in summer 2008.

# Corporate Social Responsibility

## *A Role in Government Policy and Regulaion*

Ms. P. Aysha Banu
P. Ramalingam

## Introduction

"The important thing for business and society at large to understand is the limit to voluntary action, which is the point where government needs to intervene. If we are to live within the earth's capacity and share its resources equitably, economies must be transformed. That cannot be done by business alone."

This paper sets out to describe the role of Corporate Social Responsibility (CSR) in government policy and examine its relevance to a particular sector, the regulated utilities. Current theoretical and political debates and activities conducted at the national and international level, suggest a widespread interest shared by government, industry, civil society and non-governmental organizations (NGOs) regarding the role of government and business for the natural environment, social development and social inclusion.

## Corporate Social Responsibility

In the academic circles, some of Europe's leading business schools have teamed up with more than sixty multinationals to launch the European academy of business in society. In its own words, the academy was created as *"a response to calls from the public, as well as from managers, to better integrate the social responsibility aspect into business activities"* and has a mission to drive CSR into the mainstream of business practice. For the mission to be accomplished, the academy strives to undertake the following activities:

- To integrate the changing role of business in society into the core of business education;

- To deliver interdisciplinary research on CSR and create a global research bank on the role of business in society;
- To become Europe's training gateway to 'best-in-class' training practices and learning resources for businesses and corporate academies.

## Operational Definition of CSR—Compliance Plus, Best Practice and Cost-Benefit Analysis

CSR is developed around two main principles:

- The interests of the firm's stakeholders should be represented at the company board and the decision-making process of the firm;
- Since corporate law protects the interests of the firm's shareholders, a corporate socially responsible or 'corporate citizenship' stance would involve the formulation of decisions that go beyond legal requirements and exceed the law, 'compliance plus'.

Thus, the notion of CSR assumes corporate behaviour that goes beyond legal requirements. CSR is the detailed 'issues' which an organization may be taking into account when developing strategies and on which an organization exceeds its minimum required obligations to stakeholders.20 Traditionally, these issues are both internal and external to the organization i.e., employee welfare, working conditions, green issues, products etc. Today, the corporate social responsibility 'handbook' extends to human rights, workplace practices, globalisation practices, corporate power, environmental impact, corruption, community affairs and effective stakeholder dialogue (Cowe, Porritt, 2002). By meeting its legal obligations an organization should not necessarily assume socially responsible behaviour.

## The Role of Government

From the industrial revolution to recent years, social objectives have been almost entirely the responsibility of government. Social movements, NGO activity and pressure groups during the 70s and 80s led to the mobilization of public opinion demanding from corporations to demonstrate a socially responsible stance. Since the earlier twentieth century, European member states have developed legislation to control the relationship between employee and the firm, health and safety at work, issues of environmental interest, discrimination and equal opportunities at workplace. Across Europe, state owned companies were created to pursue commercial and social objectives, whereas private sector companies were allowed to pursue their commercial objectives almost exclusively.

Legislation, regulation and taxation have been the favorable tools employed by government to promote and protect social objectives. In the area of the environment, 'command and control' techniques have been favoured by the European Union since the 1970s whereas a shift towards 'shared responsibility' between government and industry is another favourable policy approach since the mid 1990s.

The Labour government has maintained the interest to 'bridge' public and private, social and financial objectives by drawing the private sector into the provision of social goods i.e., public-private partnerships. The government has taken steps to reinforce the responsibility of the private sector with regard to its social and environmental impact. A number of legislative measures have been passed to support sustainable development including the climate change levy, the community investment tax credit and the Pensions Act. The company law review (1998-2002) has rejected the concept of 'pluralism' which would have required directors to consider the interests of other stakeholders as well as pursuing the interests of shareholders, but the government's white paper, which incorporated the review's recommendations, has communicated the message that directors would be foolish to omit such matters.

Interestingly, recent published studies suggest that government may play a role to encourage and promote the social responsibility of business. As Table 1 shows, the World Bank has identified four principal public sector roles in relation to CSR that are mandating, facilitating, partnering and endorsing roles.

**Table 23.1 : Public Sector Roles Mandating**

| | 'Command and control' legislation | Regulators and inspectorates | Legal and fiscal penalties and rewards |
|---|---|---|---|
| Facilitating | 'Enabling' legislation | Creating incentives | Capacity building |
| Funding support | Raising awareness | Stimulating markets | — |
| Partnering | Combining resources | Stakeholder engagement | Dialogue |
| Endorsing | Political support | Publicity and praise | |

In the theory of the modern corporation it is argued that the government has a potential role to play towards promoting and enhancing corporate social responsibility.

Reich (1998) argues that the government should act as arbiter of business responsibility in society. The importance for society of relying on the good will and responsibility of executives rather than political forces is recognised. The argument, however, is that sometimes 'political decisions may be required to answer major questions' i.e., corporate social responsibility issues.

This view of government as arbiter of business responsibilities to society is reinforced by another argument that sees government as helping business to achieve corporate social responsibility though regulation, control and enforcement. This view is driven from experience in Scandinavia countries where the control/enforcement model is used to 'eliminate' the problem of cost externalisation.[57]

Five possible ways/models of avoiding cost externalisation are identified:

- Deregulation model: deregulation and viewing the company responsibility as directed towards the shareholders only;
- Corporatist model: providing management with more discretion to take non-profit goals into account;
- Control of management by an independent body: giving shareholders only an economic right but no voting right in the company and setting an independent body to control management;
- Non-shareholder interests representatives model: putting representatives for various non-shareholder interests on the company's board;
- Regulation and control/enforcement model: more regulation and control.

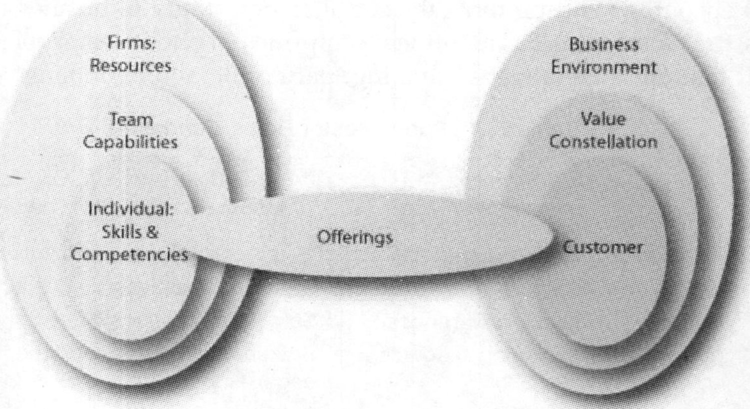


**Contrasting Models of the Corporation—A Schematic Overview**

According to the stakeholder model, *"all persons or groups with legitimate interests participating in an enterprises do so to obtain benefits and there is no prima facie priority of one set of interests and benefits over another"* (Donaldson, Preston, 1995, p68). Therefore, the arrows between the firm and its stakeholder constituents run in both directions.

As the authors Donaldson and Preston note (1995), the extent to which the stakeholder theory is understood to represent a challenging approach to conventional views varies greatly among market capitalist economies:

> "In America, for instance, shareholders have a comparatively big say in the running of the enterprises they own; workers have much less influence. In many European countries, shareholders have less say and workers more. In Japan, managers have been left alone to run their companies as they see fit, namely for the benefit of employees and of allied companies, as much as for shareholders" The Economist, 1993, p. 52.[59]

Nevertheless, the stakeholder model of the corporation is developed around theoretical concepts i.e., the meaning of property rights which are critical to the understanding of the purpose and role of corporations in society.

### Development of Corporate Social Responsibility (CSR)

The notion of corporate social responsibility made its appearance almost a hundred and fifty years ago. It emerged in the United States of America as a social and political reaction to the rapid growth of capitalism during the thirty years following the American civil war (1861-5).[24] Big companies, as we know them today, appeared in the United States in the 1870s. But as they grew, an 'anti-trust' movement against the 'robber barons', also grew.[25] McEwan (2001) explains that the rationale for the 'anti-trust' movement was "the new industrial trusts and corporations which had become too powerful, wasted resources, were politically dangerous and socially irresponsible"

In conclusion, the meaning of corporate social responsibility in the 1970s was associated with the excluded social costs of production and the hidden costs occurred by society as a result of business activities including:

- Industrial pollution and toxic waste;
- Racial and sexual discrimination;
- Political influence of powerful corporations;
- Invasion of employees' privacy;
- Deceptive information in marketing;
- Product safety;
- The price of technology, effects of pesticides, aerosols and nuclear power;
- Increasing concentration of wealth and income in fewer hands;
- Business crime (Nader et. al., 1974).

Alongside the 1970s events and the social and political movements, the statement by Milton Friedman on the social responsibility of business has been the starting point of academic discussion of corporate social responsibility.

### The New Meaning of Corporate Social Responsibility—The Theory of Modern Corporation

The classical view of business responsibility to society has been challenged by new arguments that made their appearance in the 1980s and have seen to contribute to the development of the 'theory of the modern corporation' (Bichta, 2000). These new arguments attach a new meaning to corporate social responsibility as they consider:

- A new stakeholder approach as opposed to the traditional view of promoting the exclusive interests of stockholders;
- Managerial values and discretion as being key promoters of socially responsible actions and the notion of organizational moral responsibility analogous to that of individuals;

- New aspects in corporate legitimacy;
- Alternatives to the traditional view of corporate governance;
- The role of an interventionist government in enhancing corporate social responsible behaviour (Bichta, 2000).

Each of these aspects are considered in turn.

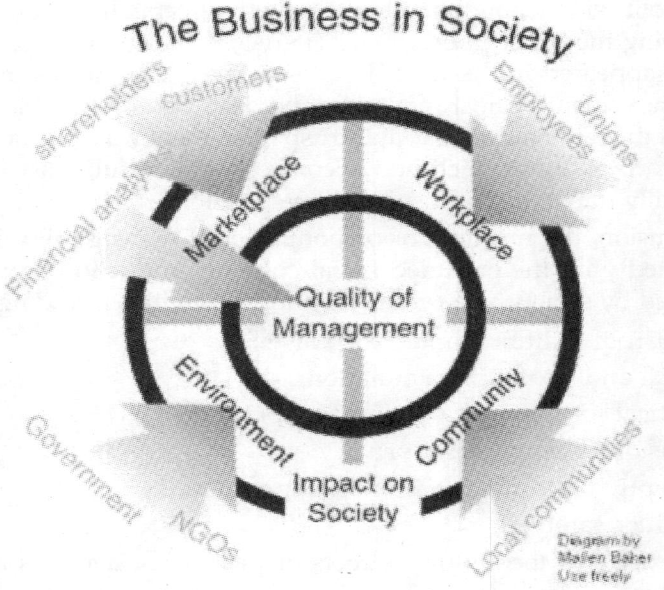


## The Stakeholder Theory

The central position of managerial capitalism has been challenged by the stakeholder theory of Modern Corporation. The stakeholder theory has made its appearance in the early eighties, and the pioneers of the theory have concentrated their arguments on three main aspects of the theory: a descriptive/empirical, an instrumental and a normative aspect.[37] Although in the management literature, the stakeholder theory corresponds to all three approaches, the discussion in the following paragraphs concentrates on the normative aspect as the underpinning basis of the stakeholder theory of modern corporation.

The stakeholder theory calls for a revitalization of the concept of managerial capitalism by replacing the notion that managers have a duty to stockholders with the concept those managers bear a fiduciary relationship to stakeholders. The stakeholder theory concentrates its focus on a particular question: "For whose benefit and at whose expense should the firm be managed"?

The structural mechanisms to facilitate the application of a stakeholder management concept are two:

- a stakeholder board of directors which will consist five stakeholder groups including employees, customers, suppliers, stockholders and community members;
- A revised and reformed 'corporate law' which requires corporations to be managed for the benefit of the stakeholders and allow these groups to participate in the decision-making of the firm given it will affect their welfare. For instance, some existing forms of law in this area are related to product liability and labour law.

## Conclusion

CSR assumes corporate behaviour that goes beyond legal requirements. CSR is the detailed 'issues' which an organization may be taking into account when developing strategies and on which an organization exceeds its minimum required obligations to stakeholders.[20] Traditionally, these issues are both internal and external to the organization i.e., employee welfare, working conditions, green issues, products etc. Today, the corporate social responsibility 'handbook' extends to human rights, workplace practices, globalisation practices, corporate power, environmental impact, corruption, community affairs and effective stakeholder dialogue.

# CSR as a Key to Deliver Sustainable Value to the Society

Ms. J. Jeya Ani

## Introduction

Social responsibility is fundamentally a philosophy about the relationship of business and society. It is a process of continuous improvement which begins small and expands overtime. It is inextricably linked to profitability as there can be no such responsibility without profits. Thus many companies use the strategy 'Corporate social responsibility'. It is becoming an increasingly important activity to businesses nationally and internationally. A strong corporate social responsibility programme is essential to sustainable businesses which need healthy economies, markets and communities.

## Corporate Social Responsibility

CSR is a built-in self regulating mechanism whereby business monitors and ensures its active compliance with the spirit of the law, ethical standards and international norms. It is often described as a voluntary responsibility above and beyond the demands of national legislation and which encompasses issues such as human rights, environmental responsibility and civic freedoms. The goal of CSR is to embrace responsibility for the company's actions and encourage a positive impact through its activities on the environment, consumers, employees, communities, stakeholders and public. Thus, it is an aid to organization's mission as well as guide to what the company stands for and will uphold to its consumers.

The challenges faced by today's business include the following.

(*i*) Globalisation of markets, consumer preferences, financial flows. Globalization is having momentous effects on the economies of all countries and on corporation in most sectors.

(*ii*) Increasing intensity of competition: The global completion today has created more challenges and instability.

(*iii*) Technology: Rapid technological changes are transferring the markets, enabling greater customization of production, and contributing to high labour displacement.

(*iv*) Shift from industrial economy to a knowledge and information based economy.

(*v*) Environmental changes caused by pollution & resources depletion, business are called upon to play an important role in meeting these challenges.

(*iv*) Lifestyle changes, expectation on the part of employees, consumers and communication as a whole changing.

Thus, business requires corporate social responsibility to face above challenges.

### Good Relations Lead to Profitability

The long-term survival of companies is partly dependent on maintaining relationships of trust. Deterioration of such relationships will jeopardize the ongoing development of the company. Experience shows that companies with an international outlook, which are open and adopt the long-term approach, are often best at maintaining relationships and hence at developing their operations. The ability to constantly go on improving products and processes is a basic prerequisite. Companies that want to keep developing have to be receptive to signals from and opinions expressed by the market, staff and the general public. Now that more and more customers—and stakeholders as well – are making demands of companies' ethical, social and environmental awareness, it is also natural for companies to be receptive to these issues and actively use them in their operations. Society's values and current levels of knowledge are reflected in companies' activities, and companies are judged according to current standards. Companies have always had to interpret society's moods or else go out of business. Companies have always had to adapt to fit in with values and norms. Then on top of these are the formal regulations that all companies, be they private and public, have to observe. It is very much in the interests of any company to be 'a good corporate citizen'. Companies that have a clear identity and clear business concepts often find it easier to handle and integrate ethical and social values and to take the environment into account. Having clear business objectives makes it easier to formulate and implement goals based on values and norms both within the company and among the general public. There are a number of reasons as to why companies should take ethical, social and environmental responsibility:

## Corporate Commitment to the Community

- Customer appreciation
- Brand reinforcement
- Support for new business
- Improvement in productivity
- Avoidance of business risk
- Creation of good-will towards politicians and other decision makers
- Creation of competitive advantage
- Support of recruiting
- Increase in company spirit and understanding of the business idea

## Corporates Towards Sustainable Development

A sustainable enterprise is one that contributes to sustainable development by delivering simultaneously economic, social and environmental benefits, the so-called triple bottom line.

Beyond this broad consensus on terminology, however, there remains disagreement among managers regarding the specific meaning of and motivation for enterprise-level sustainability. For some managers, it is a moral mandate; for others, a legal requirement. For still others, sustainability is perceived as a cost of doing business—a necessary evil to maintain legitimacy and right to operate. A few firms have begun to frame sustainability as a business opportunity, offering avenues for lowering cost and risk, or even growing revenues and market share through innovation. For most firms, the pursuit of enterprise sustainability remains difficult to reconcile with the objective of increasing shareholder value. Indeed, some have even advocated that creating a more sustainable world will require firms to sacrifice profits and shareholder value in favour of the public good. By starting with legal or moral arguments for firm actions, however, managers inevitably underestimate the strategic business opportunities associated with this important issue. To avoid this problem, managers need to directly link enterprise sustainability to the creation of shareholder value. The global challenges associated with sustainability, viewed through the appropriate set of business lenses, can help to identify strategies and practices that contribute to a more sustainable world and, simultaneously, drive shareholder value; this we define as the creation of sustainable value for the firm. The global challenges associated with sustainability, viewed through the appropriate set of business lenses, can help to identify strategies and practices that contribute to a more sustainable world and, simultaneously, drive shareholder value.

## Global Drivers of Sustainability

There are four sets of drivers related to global sustainability. A first set of drivers relates to increasing industrialization and its associated material consumption, pollution, and waste generation. Industrial activity has grown to the point where it may now be having irreversible effects on the global environment, including impacts on climate, biodiversity, and ecosystem function. While industrialization has produced tremendous economic benefits, it has also generated significant pollution burdens and continues to consume virgin materials, resources, and fossil fuels at an increasing rate. Resource efficiency and pollution prevention are therefore crucial to sustainable development. A second set of drivers relates to the proliferation and interconnection of civil society stakeholders. As the power of national governments has eroded in the wake of global trade regimes, nongovernmental organizations (NGOs) and other civil society groups have stepped into the breach, assuming the role of monitor and in some cases enforcer of social and environmental standards. At the same time, the spread of the Internet and information technology has enabled these groups to communicate with each other in ways that were unimaginable even a decade ago. Internet connected coalitions of NGOs are making it increasingly difficult for governments, corporations, or any large institutions to operate in secrecy. Sustainable development thus challenges firms to operate in a transparent, responsive manner due to a very well-informed, active stakeholder base.

A third set of drivers relates to emerging technologies that may provide potent, disruptive solutions that could render the basis of many of today's energy—and material-intensive industries obsolete. Genomics, biomimicry, nanotechnology, information technology, and renewable energy all hold the potential to drastically reduce the human footprint on the planet, making the problems of rapid industrialization all but obsolete. For example, bio- and nanotechnology create products and services at the molecular level, holding the potential to eliminate the concept of waste and pollution. Similarly, biomimicry represents an attempt to emulate nature's processes to create novel products and services without having to rely on brute force to hammer out goods from large stocks of virgin raw materials. Information technology and renewable energy are distributed in character, meaning that they can be applied in the most remote and small-scale settings imaginable, eliminating the need for centralized infrastructure and wire line distribution, both of which are environmentally destructive. Distributed technologies thus hold the potential to meet the needs of the billions of rural poor (who have thus far been largely ignored by global business) in a way that dramatically reduces environmental impact. Innovation and technological change are thus key to the pursuit of sustainable development. Finally, a fourth set of drivers relates to the increases in population, poverty, and inequity associated with globalization. While it took thousands of years for the human population to reach 1 billion, that number has swollen to over 6 billion in just the past two generations. Such rapid population growth has resulted in massive migration from rural areas to cities and growing inequities in income. Today, for example, over 4 billion people survive on less than $1500 per year, the minimum income needed to avoid serious deprivation. The combination of rising population and growing inequity is increasingly recognized as a prescription for accelerating social decay, political chaos, and terrorism. Social development and wealth creation on a massive scale, especially among the world's poorest 4 billion, therefore appear to be essential to sustainable development. However, such development must follow a fundamentally different course if it is not to result in ecological meltdown. In short, global sustainability is a complex, multi-dimensional concept that cannot be addressed by any single corporate action. Creating sustainable value thus requires that firms address each of the four broad sets of drivers. First, firms can create value by reducing the level of material consumption and pollution associated with rapid industrialization. Second, firms can create value by operating at greater levels of transparency and responsiveness, as driven by civil society. Third, firms can create value through the development of new, disruptive technologies that hold the potential to greatly shrink the size of the human footprint on the planet. Finally, firms can create value by meeting the needs of those at the bottom of the world income pyramid in a way that facilitates inclusive wealth creation and distribution.

### Growing Profits and Reducing Risk Through Pollution Prevention

The problems of material consumption, waste, and pollution associated with industrialization present an opportunity for firms to lower cost and risk through the development of skills and capabilities in pollution prevention and eco-efficiency. Pollution prevention is focused on improving the environmental efficiency of today's products and processes—that is, reducing waste and emissions from current operations. Less waste means better utilization of inputs, resulting in lower costs for raw materials and waste disposal. Effective pollution prevention requires extensive employee involvement, along with well-developed capabilities in continuous improvement and quality management. By deriving more saleable product or service per pound of input, pollution prevention can lead to lower costs and reduced risk. Environmental management systems (e.g., ISO 14000) built on total quality principles provide guidance for the development of systematic processes geared toward removing waste and lowering risk throughout a firm's operations. Programs that reduce waste and emissions through eco-efficiency have been widely adopted by firms over the past decade and include such notable cases as Dow Chemical's Waste Reduction Always Pays (WRAP) and Chevron's Save Money and Reduce Toxics (SMART). Additionally, pollution-prevention programs have proliferated at the industry level and receive a great deal of attention from regulatory bodies both in the United States as well as Europe as potential alternatives to command-control regulation. The well-publicized results of pioneering programs like 3M's

Pollution Prevention Pays (3P) illustrate the direct, bottom line benefits that can be realized through pollution prevention. Indeed, between 1975 and 1990, 3M reduced its total pollution by over 530,000 tons (a 50 per cent reduction in total emissions) and, according to company sources, saved over $500 million through lower raw material, compliance, disposal, and liability costs. In 1990, 3M embarked on 3P which sought to reduce the remaining waste and emissions by 90 per cent with the ultimate goal being zero pollution. Extensive empirical work has also now made it evident that, with the appropriate set of skills and capabilities (e.g., employee involvement, continuous improvement), firms pursuing pollution prevention and waste-reduction strategies actually do reduce cost and increase profits. Pollution prevention thus provides managers with the clearest, fastest way to increase shareholder value by growing the bottom line for existing businesses through reductions in cost and liability.

### Conclusion

As the world business environment is changing, the requirement for staying & succeeding in business is also changing. As a result large corporations are emphasizing the maintenance of strategic relationship with different section of the society. Hence the corporate social responsibility embraces multiple stakeholders and companies with good social & environmental records can alone perform better in the long run. It also helps the business firm to run its operations smoothly without any government interference.

## REFERENCES

1. Stiglitz, W. W. Norton, "*Globalization and Its Discontents*", New York, 2002.
2. The National Research Council, *Our Common Journey.* Washington, DC: National Academy Press, 1999.
3. *George Soros on Globalization,* New York: Public Affairs, 2002.
4. Elkington, J, "Towards the Sustainable Corporation: Win-win-win Business Strategies for Sustainable Development", 1994.
5. Holliday.C, "Sustainable Growth, the DuPont way. *Harvard Business Review,* 2001, 79(8): 129–132.
6. Drexler, E. 1986. *Engines of creation.* Garden City, NY: Anchor Press.
7. Corporate Social Responsibility—Doing the Most Good for your Company and your Cause, Philip Kotler and Nancy, John Wiley & Sons, NewJersy, 2008.

# Corporate Social Responsibility

S. Rajendran
FX. Robert Bellarmine

## Introduction

Corporate social responsibility is basically a concept whereby companies decide voluntarily to contribute to a better society and a cleaner environment. Corporate social responsibility is represented by the contributions undertaken by companies to society through its business activities and its social investment. This is also to connect the Concept of sustainable development to the company's level. Over the last years an increasing number of companies worldwide started promoting their Corporate Social Responsibility strategies because the customers, the public and the investors expect them to act sustainable as well as responsible. In most cases CSR is a result of a variety of social, environmental and economic pressures. The Term Corporate Social Responsibility is imprecise and its application differs. CSR can not only refer to the compliance of human right standards, labor and social security arrangements, but also to the fight against climate change, sustainable management of natural resources and consumer protection.

The concept of Corporate Social Responsibility was first mentioned 1953 in the publication 'Social Responsibilities of the Businessman' by William J. Bowen. However, the term CSR became only popular in the 1990s, when the German Betapharm, a generic pharmaceutical company decided to implement CSR. The generic market is characterized by an interchangeability of products. In 1997 a halt in sales growth led the company to the realization that in the generic drugs market companies could not differentiate on price or quality. This was the prelude for the company to adopt CSR as an expression of the company's values and as a part of its corporate strategies. By using strategic and social commitment for families with chronically ill children children,

Betapharm took a strategic advantage. In July 2001, the European Commission decided to launch a consultative paper on Corporate Social Responsibility with the title "Promoting a European Framework for Corporate Social Responsibility". This paper aimed to launch a debate on how the European Union could promote Corporate Social Responsibility at both the European and international level.

The paper further aimed to promote CSR practices, to ensure the credibility of CSR claims as well as to provide coherence in public policy on CSR.

### Definition of CSR

The definition of corporate social responsibility is not abstruse. According to *Business for Social Responsibility* (BSR), corporate social responsibility is defined as "achieving commercial success in ways that honor ethical values and respect people, communities, and the natural environment."

### Empirical Studies of CSR and Financial Performance

According to Margolis and Walsh (2002), one hundred twenty-two published studies between 1971 and 2001 empirically examined the relationship between corporate social responsibility and financial performance. The first study was published by Narver in 1971. Empirical studies of the relationship between CSR and financial performance comprise essentially two types. The first uses the event study methodology to assess the *short-run* financial impact (abnormal returns) when firms engage in either socially responsible or irresponsible acts. The results of these studies have been mixed. Wright and Ferris (1997) discovered a negative relationship; Posnikoff (1997) reported a positive relationship, while Welch and Wazzan (1999) found no relationship between CSR and financial performance. Other studies, discussed in McWilliams and Siegel (1997), are similarly inconsistent concerning the relationship between CSR and short run financial returns. The second type of study examines the relationship between some measure of corporate social performance (CSP) and measures of *long term* financial performance, by using accounting or financial measures of profitability.

The studies that explore the relationship between social responsibility and accounting-based performance measures have also produced mixed results. Cochran and Wood (1984) located a positive correlation between social responsibility and accounting performance after controlling for the age of assets. Aupperle, Carroll, and Hatfield (1985) detected no significant relation between CSP and a firm's risk adjusted return on assets. In contrast, Waddock and Graves (1997) found significant positive relationships between an index of CSP and performance measures, such as ROA in the following year. Studies using measures of return based on the stock market also indicate diverse results. Vance (1975) refutes previous research by Moskowitz by extending the time period for analysis from 6 months to 3 years, thereby producing results which contradict Moskowitz and which indicate a negative

CSP/CFP relationship. However, Alexander and Buchholz (1978) improved on Vance's analysis by evaluating stock market performance of an identical group of stocks on a risk adjusted basis, yielding an inconclusive result.

## MEASUREMENT PROBLEMS

### Measures of Corporate Social Responsibility

Determining how social and financial performances are connected is further complicated by the lack of consensus of measurement methodology as it relates to corporate social performance. In many cases, subjective indicators are used, such as a survey of business students (Heinz, 1976), or business faculty members (Moskowitz, 1972), or even the Fortune rankings (McGuire, J. B., A. Sundgren, and T. Schneeweis 1988; Akathaporn and McInnes, 1993; Preston and O'Bannon, 1997). Significantly, it is unclear exactly what these indicators measure. In other cases, researchers employ official corporate disclosures—annual reports to shareholders, CSR reports, or the like. Despite the popularity of these sources, there is no way to determine empirically whether the social performance data revealed by corporations are under-reported or over-reported. Few companies have their SCR reports externally verified. Thus, information about corporate social performance is open to questions about impression management and subjective bias. Still other studies use survey instruments (Aupperle, 1991) or behavioral and perceptual measures (Wokutch and McKinney, 1991). Waddock and Graves (1997) drew upon the Kinder Lydenberg Domini (KLD) rating system, where each company in the S& P 500 is rated on multiple attributes considered relevant to CSP. KLD uses a combination of surveys: financial statements, articles on companies in the popular press, academic journals (especially law journals), and government reports in order to assess CSP along eleven dimensions1. Based on this information, KLD constructed the Domini400 Social Index (DSI 400), the functional equivalent of the Standard and Poors 500 Index, for socially responsible firms.

### Measures of Financial Performance

Although measuring financial performance is considered a simpler task, it also has it specific complications. Here, too, there is little consensus about which measurement instrument to apply. Many researchers use market measures (Alexander and Buchholz, 1978; Vance, S. C., 1975), others put forth accounting measures (Waddock and Graves 1997; Cochran and Wood 1984) and some adopt both of these (McGuire, J.B., Sundgren, A., Schneeweis, T., 1988). The two measures, which represent different perspectives of how to evaluate a firm's financial performance, have different theoretical implications (Hillman and Keim, 2001) and each is subject to particular biases (McGuire, Schneeweis, & Hill, 1986). The use of different measures, needless to say, complicates the comparison of the results of different studies. In other words, accounting measures capture only historical aspects of firm performance (McGuire, Schneeweis, & Hill, 1986). They are subject, moreover, to bias from managerial manipulation and differences in accounting procedures (Branch, 1983; Brilloff, 1972). Market measures are forward looking and focus on market performance. They are less susceptible to different accounting procedures and represent the investor's 1Additional details on the KLD file and the social "screens" is presented in Waddock and Graves (1997) and Kinder and Domini (1997). evaluation of the ability of a firm to generate future economic earnings (McGuire, J. B.,A. Sundgren, and T. Schneeweis, 1988). But the stock-market-based measures of performance also yield obstacles (McGuire, Schneeweis, & Branch, 1986). According to Ullmann (1985), for example, the use of market measures suggests that an investor's valuation of firm's performance is a proper performance measure (McGuire, J. B.,Sundgren, A., Schneeweis, T., 1988).

## METHOD

### Measuring Corporate Social Responsibility and Financial Performance

In the current study, in order to measure CSR, we employ two measures. The first measure is the KLD rating data for the companies in the S& P 500. We convert the absolute KLD scores to scale, with 10 as a base. Any score lower than 10 shows that the CSR concerns about the company are more than its CSR strengths. As a second measure, we use the Domini 400 Social Index as a proxy. As in McWilliams, A., and D. Siegel (2000), our measure of CSP is a dummy variable, with a value of 1 if a firm is included in the DSI 400 in a given year (for having passed the "social screen") and 0 otherwise. In our study, firm financial performance is measured by accounting variables. The financial data used are return on assets (ROA), return on equity (ROE), and return on sales (ROS). The source of our data is the COMPUSTAT database. The survey covers the firms included in the S&P 500 index for the years 1996-2000.

### Stronger Financial Performance and Profitability

Businesses can use CSR and corporate sustainability to produce direct benefits for the bottom line. For example, operational efficiencies can be achieved through reducing energy and materials as input factors for production. Wastes can also be reduced and materials can be recycled. These sorts of actions from eco-efficiency can produce concurrent environmental and economic benefits for the company and thereby contribute to stronger financial performance and more positive profitability. Operational efficiencies can be achieved in other facets of CSR such as streamlining the way that information is provided to the investment community as well as to other stakeholders that demand increased transparency. Managing potential risks and liabilities more effectively through CSR tools and perspectives can also reduce costs. Using corporate responsibility and sustainability approaches within business decision-making can result not only in reduced costs but can also lead to recognizing new market opportunities such as when new manufacturing processes are developed that can be expanded to other plants, regions or markets. There are various studies that have examined the relationship between CSR and corporate financial performance and most of the evidence suggests that the links are positive.

### *CSR-Coverage*

There is no unitary or binding international norm for CSR Coverage for companies. Investors and Environmentalists for Sustainable Prosperity hope for a greater engagement—as well as more transparency in reference to CSR. A Uniform reporting would besides reduce the possibility of "Green washing" (more about: »Green washing—The Dark Side of Corporate Social Responsibility (CSR)»).

### CSR: A Cornerstone of our Enduring Success

At Indian Oil, corporate social responsibility (CSR) has been the cornerstone of success right from inception in the year 1964. The Corporation's objectives in this key performance area are enshrined in its Mission statement: "...to help enrich the quality of life of the community and preserve ecological balance and heritage through a strong environment conscience."

We at Indian Oil have defined a set of core values for ourselves—Care, Innovation, Passion and Trust—to guide us in all we do. We take pride in being able to claim all our countrymen as our customers. That's why, we coined the phrase, "Indian Oil – India Inspired", in our corporate campaigns. Public corporations like Indian Oil are essentially organs of society deploying significant public resources.

We, therefore, are aware of the need to work beyond financial considerations and put in that little extra to ensure that we are perceived not just as corporate behemoths that exist for profits, but as wholesome entities created for the good of the society and for improving the quality of life of the communities we serve.

### Human Resource

As a constructive partner in the communities in which it operates, Indian Oil has been taking concrete action to realize its social responsibility objectives, thereby building value for its shareholders and customers. The Corporation respects human rights, values its employees, and invests in innovative technologies and solutions for sustainable energy flow and economic growth. In the past five decades, Indian Oil has supported innumerable social and community initiatives in India. Touching the lives of millions of people positively by supporting environmental and health-care projects and social, cultural and educational programmes.

Besides focusing primarily on the welfare of economically and socially deprived sections of society, Indian Oil also aims at developing techno-economically viable and environment-friendly products & services for the benefit of millions of its consumers, while at the same time ensuring the highest standards of safety and environment protection in its operations.

### Business Case for CSR

Corporate social responsibility is about the integration of social, environmental, and economic considerations into the decision-making structures and processes of business. It is about using innovation to find creative and value-added solutions to societal and environmental challenges. It is about engaging shareholders and other stakeholders and collaborating with them to more effectively manage potential risks and build credibility and trust in society. It is about not only complying with the law in a due diligent way but also about taking account of society's needs and finding more effective ways to satisfy existing and anticipated demands in order to build more sustainable businesses. Ultimately, it is about delivering improved shareholder and debt holder value, providing enhanced goods and services for customers, building trust and credibility in the society in which the business operates, and becoming more sustainable over the longer term. Is there a business case for CSR?

While there are different ways to frame the benefits because they are interrelated, they generally include the following:

- stronger financial performance and profitability through operational efficiency gains.
- improved relations with the investment community and better access to capital.
- enhanced employee relations that yield better results respecting recruitment, motivation, retention, learning and innovation, and productivity.

- stronger relationships with communities and enhanced licence to operate.
- improved reputation and branding.

### Enhanced Employee Relations, Productivity

A key potential benefit from CSR initiatives involves establishing the conditions that can contribute to increasing the commitment and motivation of employees to become more innovative and productive. Companies that employ CSR related perspectives and tools tend to be businesses that provide the pre-conditions for increased loyalty and commitment from employees. These conditions can serve to help to recruit employees, retain employees, motivate employees to develop skills, and encourage employees to pursue learning to find innovative ways to not only reduce costs but to also spot and take advantage of new opportunities for maximizing benefits, reduce absenteeism, and may also translate into marginally less demands for higher wages.

### Improved Reputation and Branding

A potential benefit of CSR is that it can improve a company's reputation and branding and this in turn improves the prospects for the company to be more effective in the way that it manages communications and marketing in efforts to attract new customers and increase market share. CSR as a concept with various tools can help a company to position itself in the marketplace as a company that is more responsible and more sustainable than its competitors.

### A Word CSR as an Investment

CSR can be viewed by businesses as a form of investment that helps to differentiate a company and its goods and services. What then is the right way to look at CSR as an investment - particularly given that it frequently involves intangible and less quantifiable domains? The bottom line is that a prudent business may tend to regard CSR in the same way it treats most investment decisions. It would be inclined to use the same systematic approach to assess the anticipated benefits and related revenues relative to the costs that it employs for investment proposals. A rigorous and systematic approach to CSR investment is likely to yield the most positive results for both the business and society as it is likely to demonstrate the most efficient allocation of resources from the perspective of both the firm and society.

There are many different areas where a firm can invest to develop CSR attributes (e.g. human resource management, environmental protection, health and safety, community involvement, etc.). Investment decisions on CSR need to take account of various factors and parameters as well as the anticipated cost and benefit stream to be produced by the investment.

## Conclusion

Successful programmes on social responsibility rely heavily on enlightened people management practices. In this context HR department is assumed to be the coordinator of CSR activities in getting the employment relationship right which is a precondition for establishing effective relationships with external stakeholders and thus can orient the employees and the organization towards a socially responsible character. There is also an increasing trend in the corporate sector which has started leveraging upon employees and their management for exhibiting their commitment towards CSR. Armed with a strong and committed organizational culture reinforced by responsible Human Resource Management practices, the organizations can achieve heights of success by improved profitability, employee morale, customer satisfaction, legal compliance and societal approval for its existence. It is high time for all other organizations which have been paying only lip service to CSR that they must capitalize upon the existing Human Resource Department in framing such practices, procedures and policies that ensure the internalization of quality, ethics and excellence in the whole system. By doing this they can sensitize the employees and the whole organization towards CSR without adding any additional cost. To recapitulate it can be said that companies have increasingly felt the need to co-ordinate their CSR activities and demonstrate their commitment to social responsibility. But delivery, not rhetoric, is the key in developing the trust of external stakeholders for any organization and it cannot be done without beginning charity at home. To do that social responsibility needs to be embedded in an organization's culture to bring change in actions and attitudes in which Human Resource can play a significant role. Otherwise, CSR may run the risk of being categorized as shallow 'window-dressing'.

Even though companies are taking serious efforts for the sustained development, some critics still are questioning the concept of CSR. There are people who claim that Corporate Social Responsibility underlies some ulterior motives while others consider it as a myth. Is CSR really a stalking horse for an anti-corporate agenda? The reality is that CSR is not a tactic for brand building; however, it creates an internal brand among its employees. Indulging into activities that help society in one way or the other only adds to the goodwill of a company.

## REFERENCES

1. Corporate Governance 7th Edition—The institute of company secretaries of India

**Website**

www.csr and financial performance.com
www.etuc.org/
www.corporate social responsibility.org

# Corporate Social Responsibility As Business Strategy

M. Arockia G. Ruban

## Introduction

The 1990s have perhaps been the decade of profound change in India's economic paradigm and have significantly affected Corporate India. Structural adjustment has meant an increasing role for the corporate sector and freedom from controls-an opportunity of immense proportions. It has also meant competition, both from within and outside, and a breakdown of protections that the sector earlier enjoyed. As with every change, there are winners and losers. But it is undisputed that corporate India will play, if it is not already doing so, a major role in the lives of all Indians. This cannot be ignored.

Corporate Social Responsibility (CSR), particularly the corporate code of conduct, has been one of global business' preferred strategies for quelling popular discontent with corporate power. By "business strategy" mean organized responses, through organizations like the International Chamber of Commerce (ICC), to the threat public regulation poses to business's collective self-interest. Attention to CSR's historical development reveals it has flourished as discourse and practice at times when corporations became subject to intense public scrutiny. In this essay outline two periods of corporate crisis, and account for the role codes have played in quieting public concern over increasing corporate power

Recent global protest activity, from the streets of Seattle in 1999 to the fences of Cancun in 2003, has been largely impelled by the social, economic, and environmental 'externalities' associated with economic globalization (that is, inadequate wages, poor working conditions, deforestation, general environmental degradation). A solution to these externalities being increasingly forwarded by business organizations is private sector self-regulation. Self-regulation—more popularly known as Corporate Social Responsibility (CSR)—is presented as a way to balance the interests of business and society without expanding government intervention in the global market place. What exactly is Corporate Social Responsibility (CSR)? CSR is defined by Business for Social Responsibility, a global non-profit funded by corporations, as "achieving commercial success in ways that honor ethical values and respect people, communities, and the natural environment". According to Jeremy Moon, Professor of Corporate Social Responsibility at Nottingham University, Business social responsibility...refers to the voluntary contribution of finance, goods or services to community or governmental causes. It excludes activities directly related to firms' production and commerce. It also excludes activity required under legislation or government direction. The common thread that weaves through the various definitions of "Corporate Social Responsibility" is the voluntary nature of the good practices referenced. What makes CSR initiatives "socially responsible" is that they are not mandated by governmental or intergovernmental institutions—they are voluntarily pursued. The most celebrated mechanism in the CSR toolkit, and my focus in this study, is the corporate code of conduct. The Organization for Economic Co-operation and Development (OECD) defines corporate codes as "commitments voluntarily made by companies, associations, or other entities, which put forth standards and principles for the conduct of business activities in the marketplace". The consensus underlying these divergent findings is that, even if voluntary codes have potential, they are not currently addressing globalization's externalities in a sustained way. But if voluntary codes have not proven effective, or if there is at least no consensus on their effectiveness, why then are corporations, intergovernmental organizations like the UN, and even civil society so interested in them? That is the central question guiding this paper. I begin with the less obvious: unpacking civil society's investment in voluntary codes of conduct. For labor and social activists, corporate codes of conduct, even if voluntary, can strengthen efforts to hold corporations accountable. Simply put, condemning an organization for unethical behavior is easier when said organization has already and openly agreed that ethical behavior is virtuous. Bama Athreya of the International Labor Rights Fund concretizes this point in relation to her organization's campaign against Nike: "Let's face it, hypocrites are far more interesting than mere wrongdoers, and its been much easier to sensitize press and public to Nike's failure to implement its own code of conduct than to its failure to comply with Indonesian labor laws"

Most labour and social activists supportive of corporate codes of conduct are also mindful of their limits. For one, activists lack the resources to monitor the plethora of TNC activity spanning the globe. Thus, a strategic hope for activists is that voluntary corporate codes of conduct developed by individual companies, and international organizations like the UN and OECD, will nurture more regulation friendly environments both nationally and internationally. There are thus long-term (gateway to binding social regulation) and short-term (immediate improvements in corporate conduct) rationales for supporting voluntary codes of conduct. My aim in this paper, however, is to question whether the short-term gains provided by CSR and corporate codes are worth the costs. My argument is that the primary cost of supporting voluntary codes is the forestallment of precisely what global civil society hopes to gain through them: the binding regulation of transnational corporations. I argue that the primary reason for business's trenchant interest in corporate codes is that they are an effective means of quelling popular discontent with corporate power and the political change that discontent might impel. My research has convinced me to approach corporate codes of conduct less as exemplars of business ethics and more as effective business strategy. By "business strategy," mean organized responses, through organizations like the International Chamber of Commerce (ICC) and World Business Council for Sustainable Development (WBCSD), to the threat that public regulation (both domestic and international) poses to business's collective self-interest. Thus in simple terms, by unpacking why business is so invested in corporate codes of conduct, CSR aim to convince civil society organizations and concerned members of the business community to become disinterested. I support this aim with an historical analysis. Attention to the corporate code of conduct's historical development reveals that it has flourished as discourse and practice at times when corporations became subject to intense public scrutiny. In this paper I examine two recent periods of crisis for the business world – times when the threat of public regulation loomed large

## Corporate Social Responsibility

Corporate Social Responsibility (CSR), like many modern ideas, is not new in India. It is part of an ancient tradition, which is currently being practiced by some companies. It has been informed by ideas from the West through business collaborations between companies. Industry associations, who have recognized that it is an essential part of business, have also promoted it.

Socially responsible behaviour has two dimensions: one is the stakeholders who have a contractual relationship with the business, e.g., employees, shareholders, customers and so on. The other are those whose lives are impacted by the behaviour of the business. Of the latter, communities, particularly the most disadvantaged amongst them, are the most crucial.

Effective corporate social responsibility towards any community requires close interaction with current development thinking , which has been constantly evolving .initially there was welfare and now there is empowerment. Basic needs are gradually becoming basic rights. These ideas seem to gain currency in the view that human development is the ultimate goal and economic growth alone cannot ensure it. Whatever trickles down is not enough.

### In India context, CSR could Encompass

- All activities aimed at communities (be they philanthropic, social investment or commercial initiatives) that benefit them in a sustainable manner, however, a company that undertakes such activities but does not comply with business basics cannot be termed as socially responsible.
- Basic business practices and value chain that go beyond legal compliance to benefit the disadvantaged amongst the company's stakeholders, e.g, poor customers, marginalized producers (small/ marginal farmers or traditional craftpersons, for instance) and so on.
- Advocating for change in public policy and laws that benefit disadvantaged people.

### In India, CSR has its Origin Since Ages

The famous, Kural, the great book of Tiru Valluvar's verses is a treatise par excellence on the art of living. Kural has attracted the best of minds of the world down the ages. Raja Gopalachari's English version of Kural stipulates the following moral verses for discharge of social responsibilities. Apart from human beings, these aptly apply to corporate citizens:

- What good did the creatures of the earth do to the clouds that pour the rain? So indeed should you serve society, seeking no return;
- Good men put forth industry and produce wealth, not for themselves but for the use of society;
- Wealth is not to be earned for the purpose of self indulgence or for satisfaction of greed. Wealth should be treated as the citizens instrument for helpfulness but helpfulness combined with a sense of duty;
- There is no pleasure in this or in the other world equal to the joy of being helpful to those around you. Do not lose the opportunity for this rare pleasure;
- Man is born as a social being. He alone truly lives who functions as a social cooperator. He who does not recognize this duty is to be counted as one dead;
- Poverty does not stop the social cooperation of those who have a clear understanding of the duties of life. They continue their social service undeterred by adversity.

### CSR Surveys in India

A number of surveys have been conducted in India to understand what corporate social responsibility (CSR) means in the Indian context, what are the expectations of different stakeholders and the drivers and barriers facing companies.

The survey conducted by the Tata Energy Research Institute (TERI) called 'Altered Images: the 2001 State of Corporate Responsibility in India poll', traces back the history of CSR in India and identified four models. The 'ethical model' as suggested by Mahatma Gandhi, where companies voluntarily committed to public welfare and participated in national building. Then followed the 'statist model' post India's independence. Propounded by Pt. Jawaharlal Nehru this model calls for state ownership and legal requirements of CSR.

The 'liberal model' by Milton Friedman talks about CSR being limited to private owners or shareholders. And the latest is the 'stakeholder model' championed by R. Edward Freeman, which calls for companies to respond to all stakehoder's needs.

"Altered Images" surveyed workers, company executives and the public in the four metropolitan cities. Some of the main findings were:

- Environmental pollution was regarded with great concern by all groups.
- The main expectation of the companies by the public was that the companies provide good quality products at low prices treat employees well without discrimination, protect the environment, help bridge the gap between the rich and the poor , and help in social and economic development. Expectation however, different across regions.

**Global Business becomes Global Business**

Writing about the 1960 and 1970 period, Stephen Krasner notes how "The South has been able to take two legacies of the North—the organization of political units into soverei states and the structure of existing international organizations—and use them to disrupt, if not replace, market-oriented regimes over a wide range of issues" (1985, 124) The business response to this more global crisis was not perfectly coherent. A main line of tension, speaking generally, was between the money and productive capitalist fractions. To explain this difference, and the forging of a more global perspective for business, a theoretical digression is required. Capitalist Fractions and Karl Polanyi's Double Movement For political economists Henk Overbeek and Kees van der Pijl: "Fractions of total capital are aggregates of capitalist interests which crystallize around a particular function in the process of capital accumulation" (1993, 3). Money capital means, very simply, investors who buy and sell money (e.g. J.P. Morgan), while productive capital means capitalists who buy and sell product (e.g. General Motors), be it raw or processed. If your business is buying and selling money, you will want as much flexibility and freedom of movement for your product as possible; it is in your best interest to have barriers to investment removed—barriers that include burdensome social regulations and high taxes.

Productive capital has tended to be more parochially minded. It has historically sought barriers to trade-barriers meant to protect domestic industry from foreign producers. This barrier-seeking reached its peak in the US American context with the Smoot-Hawley tariffs in 1930. But tariffs have not been the only kind of protection productive capital has been inclined towards. Productive capital's literal boundedness, its spatial fixity exemplified by the factory, has put it in closer proximity to tangible factors of production, including human labor and raw materials (or the natural environment). This proximity has predisposed productive capital to the protection of the human labor and natural environs it relies upon, what appears to money capital as "nonmarket, non-value aspects of the productive process"

## Conclusion

The basic argument is that codes of conduct have been historically designed to forestall public regulation more than ensure responsible corporate behavior, and should thus be resisted. This argument is particularly targeted at Civil Society Organizations (CSOs) that see voluntary codes as gateways to more binding regulation. The first development I'd like to report, however, is that my argument is quickly losing its critical bite! A civil society consensus is already forming around the perspective supported here—that the self-regulation paradigm has not fulfilled its promise. The clearest marker of this fast forming consensus is the recent report published Eddie Yuen nicely captures the currently uneven, but increasingly generalized police response to 'antiglobalization' protestors. What made the 'drive for international regulation' so powerful in the 1960s and 70s was the impressive coalition between the international trade union movement, Western social activists and developing country governments. This social democratic coalition, broken in the 1980s, is reforming—the second development worth highlighting. I cannot claim trade union resurgence, but as aforementioned, the global justice movement is much larger and stronger than its earlier incarnations. The final development I'd like to report on is the compelling set of corporate responsibility Norms being compiled by the UN Sub-Commission on the Promotion. Finally this paper confirms Corporate Social Responsibility as a Business Strategy.

# Corporate Social Responsibility

## *As a Key to Deliver Sustainable Value to the Society*

**Ms. K. Viswa Sarojini Devi**

## Introduction

Every company or business usually starts out with its own set agenda, which differs from business to business. A lot of businesses exist simply to make money. There are others who seriously wish to provide a needed service to a community or to the world. Each of these businesses has a corporate responsibility to the public, its shareholders and the world it trades in.

In its most basic terms, corporate responsibility can come down to the ethics of a business. Each company has its own set of core values, but the company's values also touch everyone that the business deals with. Years ago, a company's corporate responsibility was dictated by its government. There were set laws that had to be adhered to regarding financial and social responsibility. Today, however, corporate responsibility has to take into account the world that we live in on a much wider scale. The public has become much more globally aware, and there are a number of groups that monitor corporations closely. These groups have the conditions of the world in mind. They think about the social issues of the world, such as labour laws and the exploitation of workers. They are also concerned with environmental issues, such as the rain forests disappearing. Corporations are now held accountable not just by the government, but also by the public. Corporate responsibility must now take into account how dealings with customers, shareholders and employees are seen by the world. Large global corporations know that people are watching them and that any wrongdoing will not go unnoticed. Therefore, it becomes necessary for each and every business concern to carry out its social responsibilities in one way or the other.

## Corporate Social Responsibility (CSR)

Corporate social responsibility is the integration of business practices into a company's business model that consider factors beyond profit, such as sustainability or a positive impact on the community. It is a commitment to improve community well-being through discretionary business practices and contributions of corporate resources. A key element of this definition is the word discretionary. We are not referring here to business activities that are marked by law of that are moral or ethical in nature and perhaps therefore expected. Rather, we are referring to a voluntary commitment a business makes in choosing and implementing these practices and making these contributions. Such a commitment must be demonstrated in order for a company to be described as socially responsible and will be fulfilled through the adoption of new business practices and/or contributions, either monetary or non-monetary. The term community well-being in this definition includes human conditions as well as environmental issues.

Others have offered several definitions of corporate social responsibility (CSR). One from the World Business Council for Sustainable Development reflects the council's focus on economic development in describing CSR as "business' commitment to contribute to sustainable economic development, working with employees, their families, the local community and society at large to improve their quality of life." The organization Business for Social Responsibility defines CSR as "operating a business in a manner that meets or exceeds the ethical, legal, commercial, and public expectations that society has of business." This definition is somewhat broader as it encompasses business decision making related to "ethical values, legal requirements, as well as respect for people, communities, and the environment."Corporate social initiatives are major activities undertaken by a corporation to support social causes and to fulfill commitments to corporate social responsibility. Causes most often supported through these initiatives are those that contribute to community health (e.g. AIDS prevention). Business corporations are created and survive only as a special privilege of the state. It is absurd to regard the corporation simply as an enterprise established for the sole purpose of allowing profit making. One has simply to ask: Why should citizens, through their government, grant special rights, powers, privileges, and protections to any firm except on the understanding that its activities are to fulfill their purposes? Corporations exist because we allow them to do so. Some companies make their corporate social responsibility efforts a primary element of the company brand.

## CSR in Developing Countries

Carroll's four-part pyramid construct in The Oxford Handbook of Corporate social responsibility can be useful to look at how CSR is manifested in a developing country context.

## CSR Pyramid for Developing Countries

Hence, in developing countries, economic responsibilities still get the most emphasis. It includes providing investment, creating jobs and paying taxes promptly. However, philanthropy is given second highest priority, followed by legal and then ethical responsibilities. Philonthropic responsibilities include setting aside funds for corporate social/community projects. Legal responsibilities constitute ensuring good relations with the government officials whereas ethical responsibilities include adopting various codes. But, it is not proposed that legal and ethical responsibilities should get such a low but rather that they do in practice.

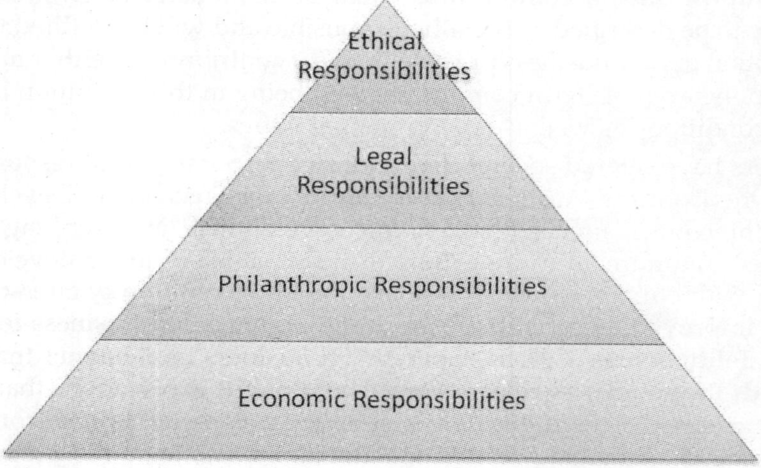


## Approaches to CSR

An approach for CSR that is becoming more widely accepted is community-based development approach. In this approach, corporations work with local communities to better themselves.For example, the Shell Foundation's involvement in the Flower Valley, South Africa. In Flower Valley they set up an Early Learning Centre to help educate the community's children as well as develop new skills for the adults. Marks and Spencer is also active in this community through the building of a trade network with the community - guaranteeing regular fair trade purchases.

A more common approach of CSR is philanthropy. This includes monetary donations and aid given to local organizations and impoverished communities in developing countries. Some organizations do not like this approach as it does not help build on the skills of the local people, whereas community-based development generally leads to more sustainable development.

Another approach to CSR is to incorporate the CSR strategy directly into the business strategy of an organization. For instance, procurement of Fair Trade tea and coffee has been adopted by various businesses including KPMG.

Its CSR manager commented, "Fair trade fits very strongly into our commitment to our communities."

Another approach is garnering increasing corporate responsibility interest. This is called Creating Shared Value, or CSV. The shared value model is based on the idea that corporate success and social welfare are interdependent. A business needs a healthy, educated workforce, sustainable resources and adept government to compete effectively.

Many approaches to CSR pit businesses against society, emphasizing the costs and limitations of compliance with externally imposed social and environmental standards. CSV acknowledges trade-offs between short-term profitability and social or environmental goals, but focuses more on the opportunities for competitive advantage from building a social value proposition into corporate strategy.

There are a number of ways in which the company can have a sustainable CSR , not depending on the mercurial dispositions of CEO's who themselves have ephemeral biographies within an organization. The mantra to sustainable CSR quite clearly is to relate it to fundamental principles of business ethics. CSR is truly take holder oriented and not just indiscriminate philanthropy.

### Corporate Social Responsibility Practices in India—A Preview

Not new to India, companies like TATA and BIRLA have been imbibing the case for social good in their operations for decades long before CSR become a popular cause.

At Indian Oil, corporate social responsibility (CSR) has been the cornerstone of success right from inception in the year 1964. The Corporation's objectives in this key performance area are enshrined in its Mission statement: "...to help enrich the quality of life of the community and preserve ecological balance and heritage through a strong environment conscience." As a constructive partner in the communities in which it operates, IndianOil has been taking concrete action to realise its social responsibility objectives, thereby building value for its shareholders and customers. The Corporation respects human rights, values its employees and invests in innovative technologies and solutions for sustainable energy flow and economic growth. In the past five decades, Indian Oil has supported innumerable social and community initiatives in India, touching the lives of millions of people positively by supporting environmental and health-care projects and social, cultural and educational programmes.

Besides focusing primarily on the welfare of economically and socially deprived sections of society, they also aims at developing techno-economically viable and environment-friendly products & services for the benefit of millions of its consumers, while at the same time ensuring the highest standards of safety and environment protection in its operations.

In spite of having such life size successful examples, CSR in India is in a very nascent stage. It is still one of the least understood initiatives in the Indian development sector. It is followed by a handful of public companies as dictated by the very basis of their existence, and by a few private companies, with international shareholding as this is the practice followed by them in their respective foreign country. Thus the situation is far from perfect as the emphasis is not on social good but rather on a policy that needs to be implemented.

## Survey on Corporate Social Responsibility (CSR) Practices

Times Foundation, in partnership with TNS India, has performed a great service for India in launching the first nationwide survey on corporate social responsibility practices. The survey results provide an important initial baseline from which a collective vision can be created and progress measured. The objective of the survey is to provide an understanding of the role played by corporate and public sector undertakings (PSUs) in CSR domain and their perceptions about it. The survey, carried out by TNS India on behalf of Times Foundation, used online administration of questionnaire and covered 11 PSUs, 39 private national agencies and 32 private multinationals. The organisations covered were from various sectors including information technology, insurance, automobile, cement, paper & pulp, construction, petrochemicals, metal, media, pharmaceutical, sugar, mining and other important sectoral industries. About 90 per cent of the 82 organisations—all the 11 PSUs, four-fifth of the private national agencies (85 per cent) and 94 per cent of the private multinationals—are involved in various CSR initiatives.

The involvement of the corporate sector in CSR seems to have picked up after 1991 as 64 per cent of the participating organisations started CSR during 1991-2005. About two-third of the private multinational agencies (70 per cent) and private national agencies (67 per cent) initiated CSR during this period, and one-third of the PSUs too started their CSR programmes during this period.

A quarter of the organisations surveyed felt the government was not doing much in facilitating CSR initiatives. However, half the respondents mentioned the role of the Government in helping with the project implementation. About 70 per cent of the organisations surveyed stated that they have separate allocation of funds towards CSR projects.

Some of the challenges faced by the companies in implementing CSR programmes pertain to community participation and capacity building within the organisation as well as those of NGOs that they tie up with. Especially in the rural areas, companies face the problem of lack of well-organised civil society groups that could identify the real needs of the society and work to address them. Lack of transparency too is a problem they face. Companies also identified the problem of having no way of scientifically researching and gathering evidence on the impact of their CSR initiatives on the communities they target and work for. Without knowing the impact of their programmes, they felt it was difficult to tailor the programmes according to the needs of the people they were meant for. The suggestions put forth by the participating organisations to make CSR initiatives more effective and useful include spreading awareness about CSR among the general public so as to generate project demand and effective partnership between all stakeholders including corporates, community, employees, and the Government. They also felt that the introduction of CSR in the SME sector would help more organisations to reach out to remote areas. The priority areas that the respondents felt ought to be covered under CSR initiatives include education (82%), environment (81%), health (81%), women empowerment (63%), livelihood promotion (62%), sanitation (61%), microfinance (60%), HIV/AIDS (54 per cent), child care (55%), slum improvement (50%), disaster management (44%) and agricultural development (29 per cent).Resource pooling, adopting best practices, risk analysis and mapping of CSR initiatives were some of the suggestions offered by the participating firms and organisations. The respondents also recommended accreditation of CSR initiatives by an independent agency and making CSR a part of the curriculum at management schools, colleges and universities. Integration of CSR into the DNA of business, active role played by media in highlighting CSR success stories, top management commitment, streamlining of CSR with stringent monitoring and CSR-friendly laws were other important recommendations put forward by participating organizations.

## Conclusion

Many companies have a social conscience, treat employees fairly and try to do the best for their shareholders while trying to be socially responsible. There are, however, many other corporations who see nothing wrong with employing third world country workers to make their products. Many corporations have been forced into taking corporate responsibility. They know that it does not make good business sense to be seen as a company that is damaging the world that we live in. Huge penalties and fines also await corporations that break ethical and environmental laws. According to a recent CSR survey in India, social responsibility is not the exclusive concern of the government.

Corporate responsibility has a huge impact not only on the local community, but also on the world. Its effects are social, economic and environmental. Bad and good corporate responsibility has effects that reach from the worker in the third world country to the air that we breathe.

Recent reports stated that major investors are now more likely to invest in a corporation that has shown corporate responsibility. Investors are aware of the customer's strength of opinion regarding unethical companies. The customer is now in a better position to shape corporate responsibility than ever before. In total, corporate social responsibility is a constructive, practical and effective way to deliver sustainable value to the society.

## REFERENCES

1. The Oxford handbook of corporate social responsibility, Andrew Crane, Oxford University Press, 2008.
2. Corporate Social Responsibility—Doing the most good for your company and your cause, Philip Kotler and Nancy, John Wiley &Sons, NewJersy, 2008.
3. Orlitzky, Marc; Frank L. Schmidt, Sara L. Rynes (2003). "Corporate Social and Financial Performance: A Meta-analysis" (PDF). Organization Studies (London: SAGE Publications) 24 (3): 403–441. doi:10.1177/0170840603024003910.
4. Corporate social responsibility, concepts and cases. C V Baxi, Ajit Prasad. Excel Books, New Delhi 2005, reprint 2009.

# Corporate Governance

## *Role of Management and Directors*

Mrs. P. Vasumathi
Ms. K. Nirmala Devi

### Introduction

Corporate governance is more than an effective legal process; it must also embrace the aim of fulfilling the purpose of the organization and achieving its goals. The aim of effective corporate governance should be to create a business that can sustain success over the long run. Primary actions in the cycle of corporate governance encompass the board's hiring an appropriate CEO and then delegating the responsibility for managing the business to him or her. To fulfill its responsibilities, however, the board must remain active in the affairs of the enterprise.

### Board Relationships

An active board of directors engages in numerous relationships, both internally and externally. Several of these relationships, which are major determinants of the board's relative effectiveness, are discussed below.

### Relationship Between Individual Members

While the individual relationships between board members very, with some naturally closer than others, effective boards are characterized by the respect and trust their members demonstrate for one another. It is not usual for members of strong boards to develop personal as well as professional friendships. The ability of boards to function effectively as a group, however, is often severely disrupted when cliques form or when one or more directors are not trusted or respected because of suspect motives or dysfunctional behavior. Nominating committees must keep in mind the issue of interpersonal relationships among board members when they seek to add new personalities to the board.

## Relationship As A Group

Individual relationship among board members naturally melds into a group culture. Effective boards seeds to have meetings marked by open and honest conversations that aim to solicit a range of good ideas from the participants. Members should welcome spirited debate during the discussion, but when a decision is reached, all must be willing to support it. Regular analyses of failings or shortcomings should be undertaken and should not endeavor to assign blame, but rather resemble unemotional autopsies seeking to understand what happened in order to learn from the experience. Members must remember that the board can act only as a body. No single member of the board has the authority to act individually on behalf the board, except as authorized by the full board.

## The Leadership

Effective boards are well led. Usually, one or two leader-members are responsible for creating agendas for and facilitating the discussion in regular board meeting. Some boards regularly rotate leadership roles based on the alignment of topics under discussion and the individual expertise of board members. Good leaders strive not to impose their views, but rather to ensure that all views are heard and discussions move efficiently toward the best resolution of the issues being discussed.

## Relationship With the CEO

The relationship between the CEO and the board is vital to creating effective governance and should be based on mutual trust and respect. This relationship should also aim to maintain a balance between the in dependence of the board and the CEO and the collaboration necessary for them to work toward the best decision for the organization. Typically, the CEO is a great deal more knowledgeable about the operations and affairs of the business than the board, and consequently, he or she must be skilled in providing the board with the information necessary to do its job in a timely and efficient manner.

## Directors' Knowledge of the Business

In order to engage in meaningful discussions and analyses, board members must know or understand the business with reasonable proficiency. One of the key management responsibilities of a board is to decide, with management's input, the businesses in which it will compete. The goal is to select businesses that have attractive characteristics and in which the company can compete effectively. If a company consists of a number of businesses, its corporate structure must also be determined. Often, the multibusiness firm is organized as a holding company operating through decentralized divisions or subsidiaries that report to a central parent organization.

At a high level, knowing the business means understanding the nature of the business at a conceptual level, which encompasses understanding the maturity and structure of the industry and the company's market position within the industry. It also includes understanding the forces that shape the competitive environment, which have been made well known by strategist Michael Porter, including ease of entry, the power of buyers and suppliers, the threat of substitutes, and the rivalry among existing firms.

Directors also must understand the business concept or concepts. In every business, there is (or should be) an underlying logic to the way it approaches the marketplace. If all of the competitors employ the same business concept, they must compete on the effectiveness with which they execute that concept. Real breakthroughs come when a business creates a new concept. Some classic examples of such breakthroughs include Dell's move to sell computers made on demand directly to the consumer; Southwest Airlines' low-cost formula; and Nucor Steel's establishing scrap-melting minim ills as legitimate competitors in the steel industry. All of these strategies created differentiation among the firms in their industries and propelled the innovative companies to rapid growth.

At a fundamental level, knowing the business also requires an understanding of the key customers and their needs, and, more specifically, which of those needs the business is attempting to serve. Understanding the needs of the customers leads to an effective business concept, which in turn requires an understanding of the skills or competencies and resources required to support the chosen strategy.

A competency is a set of organizational capabilities that are needed to function in a given business. They can be further defined as the following:

- *Core competencies:* Those competencies are central to the successful implementation of the selected strategy.
- *Distinctive competencies:* Those competencies that set the business apart from its competitors, generally because it performs them better than others.

In the same vein, the nature of the business and its strategy and growth rate drive the need for resources of all kinds: people and their skills, facilities and technologies, and capital.

For effective performance, the required resources must be obtained in responsible ways, usually well in advance of their need.

### The Legal Obligations of Directors

When individuals serve as directors of businesses, they assume the obli-gation to represent the interests of those owners who cannot represent themselves, undertaking a serious fiduciary responsibility. Effective representation, however, requires more than integrity. It also requires the competence to make sound decisions, Good directors know their limits and turn to more expert advisers when their judgment so dictates. Directors who are "ignorant but honest" fail to fulfill their obligations. Their well-intentioned, incom-petence can be as dangerous as dishonesty.

Even when competent individuals act with the best of intentions in the role of director, business setbacks and failures still might occur. In cases of unsatisfactory results, shareholders can scrutinize the contributing actions of the directors with the advantage of hindsight. They particularly seek answers to question of whether the directors acted-responsibly in fulfilling their obligations. At issue, though, is how "fulfilling their obligations" should be defined

### Who Makes the Rules?

Governments at all levels—federal, state, and local—and various govern-mental agencies write, approve, and interpret the relevant laws and regu-lations for business enterprises. In addition, various stock exchanges and industry associations have established their own regulations and codes of conduct.

The laws pertaining to corporations in the United States have centered on seven main goals:

- To maintain competitive markets via antitrust and fair trade laws
- To regulate noncompetitive markets, such as utilities
- To maintain a balance between capital and labor
- To ensure orderly capital markets
- To protect consumers from unsafe products and fraud
- To ensure equal access to employment, education, housing, and public accommodations
- To protect the environment

These laws and rules frame the context in which corporations must operate. There are also laws that define how corporations are to be gov-erned. The laws that define directors' responsibilities are primarily state laws, as opposed to federal laws, because, with only a few minor exceptions, the states-issue and administer corporate charters through their particular laws and regulations.

### Conclusion

Clearly, a director individually, and a board as a whole, must act in accordance with legal standards spelled out by the state in which the business is incorporated. These laws are often complex. While no layperson can expect to fully understand them, it is essential that all directors have a working knowledge of them and know how and when to seek competent legal advice.

## REFERENCES

1. Lorsch, Jay W., Pawns or Potentate: The Reality of America's Corporate Boards.
2. The information in the section is based on of the Principles of Corporate Governance: Analysis and Recommendations, assembled by the American Law Institute (St Paul, MN: American Law Institute, 1994).
3. Managerial Duties and Business Law (Boston: Harvard Business School Press, 1995).

# Emerging Areas in CSR

A. Jebasheela Mary Margaret

## Introduction

Corporate social responsibility is essentially a concept whereby companies integrate social and environmental concerns in their interaction with their stakeholders on a voluntary basis. This means not only fulfilling legal expectations, but also going beyond compliance and investing in human capital, the environment and relations with stake holders.

## Dependence on Society

In support of the view that corporates have moral and social obligations towards society, some economist, argue that corporates depend on society for a number of facilities, they enjoy such as developed infrastructure, place and tranquility in the work place and attained workforce. They also depend on society for the maintenance of law and order, without which they cannot carry on their productive or distributive activities, and also for reaching to their customers.

If a business body draws so much from society, it has to make its own contribution to the welfare of the latter. It has a debt to pay in the first place. It has to behave as a good citizen in as much as it has to pay its taxes in full and on time, observe the laws of the land & going beyond it, ensure a clean and healthy environment, standards of operational and product safety and help in energy and resource conservation.

## Emerging Areas in CSR

Corporate social responsibility is no longer a trend just among large multinational companies operating in developed countries, more and more emerging market companies are seeking the value of committing to responsible business practices. A strong strategy and reputation as a responsible business can help these companies build trust with local stake holders thereby establishing a local license to operate. Better way of approaching employee concerns, such as progressive labour relations, have also been shown enhance productivity and reduce costs associated with recruitment & turnover. A visible commitment to CSR can help emerging market firms to attract multinational partners, access international source of capital and reach socially.

Corporate social responsibility practice area develops tool and business models and support companies directly in developing strategies and implementing projects in three broad areas.

1. Community development and stakeholder's engagement.
2. CSR strategy and communications.
3. Labour practices and human rights at work.

## LOCAL COMMUNITY DEVELOPMENT AND STAKE HOLDER ENGAGEMENT

The social responsibility team has gathered substantial expertise in Local Community Development and works with IFC (International Finance Corporation) clients to design programs with direct links to business needs and competencies, while also ensuring education and income generation activities for local communities and targets socially excluded groups such as rural populations, indigenous people and women.

The objective is to ensure that the stakeholders impacted by investments are empowered to participate in and benefit from the local community development efforts led by the private sector. Their products and services.

1. Stakeholder mapping and needs assessments.
2. Stakeholder capacity building.
3. Local community development planning.
4. Strategies for livelihood and income generation.

### CSR Strategy and Communication

An integrated CSR strategy combined with effective communications can play in creating reputational business value for a company. Companies that communicate well can also encourage greater uptake of CSR among peers and competitors. The social responsibility practice area thus helps business not only to understand and operate CSR in their core activities, but also to articulate their vision to stakeholders. Their products and services are

1. Assessment of social and environmental opportunities
2. Benchmarking of CSR practices
3. Design of CSR strategies and action plans.
4. CSR awareness rising.

Examples:

### Cairn Energy India Ltd.

IFC assisted cairn energy to enhance its contribution to local development through CSR. This is first supported by analysing business environment in the region and brought experienced CSR specialist to provide advice and expertise to cairn, resulting in building and repairing rainwater harvesting system into villages, enhancing school infrastructure in 9 locations leading to a dramatical increase in student attendence of 40 per cent over the past years.

### Kombi Aluminium Project in Russia

Even after ending project they continue to maintain its focus on stakeholder's engagement program, which proved valuable in resolving conflicts.

### Dana Gas

The social responsibility team has worked with Dana gas, a natural gas resource company in the UAE, top position the company as a regional leader in CSR.

### Labour Practices and Human Rights at Work

The social responsibility team works with the private sector and in partnership with international institutions and global NGOs to provide alternatives to child labour and to remedy discriminations in the workplace. In addition the program is exploring the opportunity to help emerging market companies to understand and work with human rights.

### Conclusion

In an era of intense competition, accentuated by the advent of MNC s it is necessary for them to generate and sustain "goodwill" among their clients and the general public. Active participation in social welfare projects will definitely improve their visibility and place them in a pedestal of public esteem.

## REFERENCES

1. www.csr.finance performance.org.
2. www.csr.org.

# Corporate Social Responsibility

## *A Boon to Emerging Markets*

Ms. P. Juliet
Dr. C. Eugine Franco

### Introduction

In the last twenty years, there has been a change in the nature of the triangular relationship between companies, the state and the society. No longer can firms continue to act as independent entities regardless of the interest of the general public.

The evolution of the relationship between companies and society has been one of slow transformation from a philanthropic coexistence to one where the mutual interest of all the stakeholders is gaining paramount importance. Companies are beginning to realize the fact that in order to gain strategic initiative and to ensure continued existence, business practices may have to be molded from the normal practice of solely focusing on profits to factor in public goodwill and responsible business etiquettes (Reynard and Forstater, 2002). An examination of some of the factors which have led to the development of the concept of corporate social responsibility (CSR) would be ideal starting ground for the conceptual development of suitable corporate business practices for emerging markets.

The business environment has undergone vast changes in the recent years in terms of both the nature of competition and the wave of globalization that has been sweeping across markets. Companies are expanding their boundaries from the country of their origin to the evolving markets in the developing countries which have been sometimes referred to as emerging markets. The current trend of globalization has brought a realisation among the firms that in order to compete effectively in a competitive environment; they need clearly defined business practices with a sound focus on the public interest in the markets (Gray, 2001). The increase in competition among the multinational companies to gain first mover advantage in various developing countries by establishing goodwill relationships with both the state and the civil society is ample testimony to this transformation. Secondly, in most of the emerging markets, the state still holds the key to business success because of the existence of trade and business regulations restricting the freedom of multinational companies to incorporate their previously successful business doctrines which have been tried and tested in the developed nations. The state with its duty of protecting the interests of the general public would naturally be inclined to give preference to companies which take care of the interests of all the stakeholders. Thirdly, emerging markets have been identified as a source of immense talent with the rising levels of education. For example, the expertise of India in churning out software professionals and China in manufacturing has now become internationally renowned. In order to draw from this vast talent pool coming up in developing countries, companies need to gain a foothold in these markets by establishing sound business practices addressing social and cultural concerns of the people. It has been observed that consumers consider switching to another company's products and services, speak out against the company to family/friends, refuse to invest in that company's stock, refuse to work at the company and boycott the company's products and services in case of negative corporate citizenship behaviour (Edenkamp, 2002).

Last but not the least, firms all over the world are beginning to grasp the importance of intangible assets, be it brand name or employee morale. Only firms that have gained the goodwill of the general public and are ideal corporate citizens will be to develop these intangible assets into strategic advantages.

### Defining Corporate Social Responsibility

World Business Council for Sustainable Development defines Corporate Social Responsibility (CSR) as "The continuing commitment by business to behave ethically and contribute to economic development while improving the quality of life of the workforce and their families as well as of the local community and society at large." The European Commission advocates CSR as "Being socially responsible means not only fulfilling legal expectations, but also going beyond compliance and investing more into human capital, the environment and relations with stakeholders."

Thus CSR exhorts firms to diverge from their sole aim of maximising profits and to lay more importance on improving the economic and social standards of the community in their countries of operation. CSR can be thus be simply defined as the additional commitment by businesses to improve the social and economic status of various stakeholders involved while complying with all legal and economic requirements. As Warhust (2001) points out, the three major elements of CSR are product use which focuses on contribution of industrial products which help in well being and quality of life of the society, business practice which focuses on good corporate governance and gives high impetus for the environmental well being and equity which tries for distribution of profits equitably across different societies especially the host community.

## Emerging Markets

The term 'emerging market' was originally coined by IFC to describe a fairly narrow list of middle-to-higher income economies among the developing countries, with stock markets in which foreigners could buy securities. The term's meaning has since been expanded to include more or less all developing countries. World Bank (2002) says that developing countries are those with a Gross National Income (GNI) per capita of $9,265 or less. The World Bank also classifies economies as low-income (GNI $755 or less), middle-income (GNI $756–9,265) and high-income (GNI $9,266 or more). Low-income and middle-income economies are sometimes referred to as developing countries.

The evolution of CSR in these developing economies shows widely varying results. Chambers, Chapple, Moon and Sullivan (2003) evaluate the extent of CSR penetration in seven Asian countries (India, Indonesia, Malaysia, the Philippines, Singapore, South Korea and Thailand). Many researchers have hypothesised that CSR in emerging economies is still in a very nascent stage and suitable mechanisms do not exist to ensure that companies practise CSR with anything other than a charitable outlook. Kemp(2001) states "There are numerous obstacles to achieving corporate responsibility, particularly in many developing countries where the institutions, standards and appeals system, which give life to CSR in North America and Europe, are relatively weak." Chambers, Chapple, Moon and Sullivan (2003) measure the extent of CSR penetration in the seven Asian companies and show that the mean value for the seven countries(even including industrially advanced Japan) is just 41% compared to say a score of 98 per cent for a developed nation like the United Kingdom.

However, there are exceptions to the mean scores. India for example had an average CSR penetration of 72 per cent compared to Indonesia's 24 per cent. The concept of CSR as visualized in the emerging markets and the developed countries have very different understanding.

## Dimensions of CSR and Relevance for Emerging Markets

The Green Paper (2001) by the Commission of the European Communities identifies two main dimensions of CSR, an internal dimension relating to practices internal to the company and an external dimension involving the external stakeholders.

### Internal Dimension

This relates to practices internal to the company which need to be modified to incorporate CSR practices. The various components of the internal dimension of CSR are:

- Human Resources Management
- Work Safety and Health Measures
- Adaptation to change
- Management of Environmental impacts

**(*a*) Human Resources Management:** CSR can be successfully implemented in an organization through precise management of its own work force. The internal dimension of CSR includes elements like providing an environment for lifelong learning for employees, employee empowerment, better information flow, improving the balance between work, family, and leisure, diversified work force, profit sharing and share ownership schemes, concern for employability as well as job security among others. Active follow up and management of employees who are off work due to disabilities or injuries have also been shown to result in cost savings for the companies. Moulding of recruitment policies to include people from ethnic minorities, older workers, women and the long term unemployed would be a significant step forward to incorporating CSR practices in Human Resources Management.

In the context of emerging markets, the availability of cheap labour is an encouraging factor for companies. Dawar and Chattopadhyay (2000) infer from their research that many times, emerging markets are able to provide cheap skilled and unskilled labour at wages which would be substantially cheaper than the normal cost of automation of the job positions. Developed markets have clearly moved towards heavily capital intensive distribution with the introduction of electronic data interchanges, mechanized movement and monitoring of goods, and vending machines that replace salespeople. By contrast labour-intensive distribution remains economical in emerging markets. For example, in emerging markets, Coca-Cola has not invested in vending machines. These are too expensive relative to salespeople. Benjamin, Brandt and Glewwe (2000) report that in China, instead of vending machines, the company has experimented with a pushcart program in which salespeople dispense the company's drinks by the single-serve bottle. Similarly, in India, almost 10% of Coca- Cola sales take place through fountains, where a salesperson dispenses drinks by the paper cup. Daily sales of as little as 100 cups justify the cost of the fountain and the person employed to dispense the drinks.

**(*b*) Work Safety and Health Measures:** Worker safety and labour health have been documented to be having a direct impact on productivity of the labour force. Although legal measures exist in most nations on maintaining standards for ensuring worker safety and providing health benefits, recent trends have made it imperative for companies to adopt a proactive approach to this issue. In emerging markets having significant cost advantages in labour, outsourcing of labour and processes have led to the situation where companies not only need to maintain high safety levels in their own premises but also ensure that their suppliers and other connected parties comply with these principles.

The increased focus on safety standards and employee welfare has led to the development of standards across industries. Mechanisms are being designed especially in emerging markets for measuring, documenting and communicating these qualities thereby saving time, work and costs in the purchasing process.

**(*c*) Adaptation to change:** A recent trend in the global business scenario has been the wide spread use of mergers and acquisitions for business expansion. Also downsizing has been used, often ineffectively, as a cost cutting measure by firms in their relentless push for profits.

According to the Green Paper (2001) by the Commission of the European Communities "Restructuring in a socially responsible manner means to balance and take into consideration the interests and concerns of all those who are affected by the changes and decisions. In practice the process is often as important as the substance to the success of restructuring. In particular this involves seeking the participation and involvement of those affected through open information and consultation.

Furthermore, restructuring needs to be well prepared by identifying major risks, calculating all the costs, direct and indirect, associated with alternative strategies and policies, and evaluating all of the alternatives which would reduce the need for redundancies." However, Bhattacharyya and Rahman (2003) point out that although most emerging economies have labour laws preventing labour retrenchment even in the event of declining sales, in practise lobbying with the bureaucracy and government is an aspect which firms cannot chose to ignore.

**(*d*) Management of Environmental impacts:** The importance of this aspect of CSR cannot be overemphasized. Optimization of resource utilization and reducing environmentally damaging effluents can reduce the environmental impact. This will also enable the firms to affect significant cost savings in energy bills and pollution costs. Many firms in emerging markets have had to face serious repercussions from the state and society for over exploitation of natural resources and disregard for environmental safety measures. Studies by Consultancy and Research for Environmental Management on practices of Dutch multinational companies in India (2004) highlight the importance attached by the companies to maintenance of environmental standards. Many multinational companies are realising to their cost that early compliance with accepted standards will provide strategic advantages in the long run even though cost inefficient in the near future.

### External Dimension

This dimension relates to practices concerning external stakeholders. The significance of this dimension of CSR has come to the forefront with the advent of globalization leading to the development of international standards for business practices.

**(*a*) Local Communities:** The development of positive relations with the local community and thereby the accumulation of social capital is particularly relevant for non-local companies. These relations are being increasingly used by multinational companies to support the integration of their subsidiaries into various markets in which they are present. Deep understanding of the local community and social customs is an asset which can be utilized by the companies to gain strategic advantage. In emerging markets, this is more relevant than ever because of the availability of cheaper labour from the local communities. Companies would find it in their interest to substitute capital substitution with labour and reap the cost benefits. For example, Dawar and Chattopadhyay (2000) point out the instance of Whirlpool. "Whirlpool discovered that it was unable to sell its high priced, fully automatic machines in the emerging markets. It was only after it introduced twin-tub machines that were cheaper and utilized the consumers' labour rather than electronics to complete the entire washing cycle that sales took off. Interestingly, due to the fact that these machines had long disappeared in the developed markets, Whirlpool had to acquire the 'obsolete' technology from Korea."

**(*b*) Business Partners:** Building long term relationships of sound ethical foundation with suppliers, customers (and even competitors in rare occasions) will enable companies to meet customer expectations better while reducing complexity and costs. Companies should realise their CSR practices will be judged taking into account the practices of their partners and suppliers throughout the supply chain. The effect of corporate social responsibility activities will not remain limited to the company itself, but will also touch upon their economic partners.

Companies in emerging markets actually take on additional CSR responsibilities because of the existence of outsourcing opportunities in the form of suppliers and outsourcing agents. Also as part of their social responsibility companies are expected to provide high quality products and services, which meet customer expectations in a manner reflecting the company's concern for the environment and the local conditions. Thus in emerging markets, consumer based business strategies would enable companies to build long lasting relationships with consumers based on trust.

**(*c*) Human Rights:** According to Robbins (2000), "Companies operating in countries where human rights are regularly violated may experience a climate of civil instability and corruption that makes for uneasy relations with government officials, employees, local communities and shareholders."

Amnesty International states:" Companies have a direct responsibility to ensure the protection of human rights in their own operations. They also have a responsibility to use their influence to mitigate the violation of human rights by governments, the forces of law and order or opposition groups in the countries in which they operate." The Caux Round Table Principles state that companies have a responsibility to respect human rights and democratic institutions; and promote them wherever practical.

In the context of emerging markets, operations of companies should not impinge on the land rights of the local community. In particular, the company needs to make sure that people are not forcibly removed from their homes and their livelihoods are not endangered. There is the growing need to develop proper consultative processes with local groups protesting against projects or operations in which they are involved.

Firms also need to build confidence in the local community that people (including union members) participating in peaceful protests against company operations are not intimidated, arrested or in any other way threatened. Also, companies can take steps to ensure forced labour is not used in their own, or their suppliers' operations.

According to Robbins (2000), there are reports of Gulags or prison labour camps in China producing products that are then sold locally or exported. An example of foreign companies benefiting from the ruling regime's abuse of its people is the building of the gas pipeline in Burma. Numerous reports tell of the use of forced labour on a grand scale. Companies need to ensure that human rights principles are withheld in all their operations and related activities in emerging markets.

## Redesigning Marketing Paradigms for Emerging Markets

The last decade has seen a mad rush amongst multinational companies to gain first mover advantages in emerging markets by establishing operations and subsidiaries.

However, most of the firms have found out to their cost that local competition was not as easy to overcome as they had thought with matters made being worse by cutthroat competition amongst the multinationals themselves. Most multinationals are beginning to realise that loss making operations cannot be continued year after year under the pretext of investment for future expectation of profits. It is high time that the local subsidiaries start to deliver profits of their rather than continuing to act as sinks of the firm's global resources.

According to Dawar and Chattopadhyay (2000) "Local operations now realize that the three to five percent of consumers in emerging markets who have global preferences and purchasing power no longer suffice as the only target market. Instead, they must delve deeper into the local consumer base in order to deliver on the promise of tapping into billion-consumer markets". Batra (1999) argues that the usual business strategy of using products that have been historically successful in developed nations will not work in emerging markets. Prahlad and Lieberthal (1998) point out that companies must make the transition in their business strategy of 'thinking globally' to 'thinking locally' as each of the emerging markets represents an intriguing challenge for marketing with its vast diversities existing across nations and even within nations in culture and socio economic conditions. It is in marketing across such diverse cultures and varying conditions that the concept of corporate social responsibility becomes critical to success. In this paper, we will focus on two main paradigms of marketing in which CSR plays an important part.

**(*a*) Customer Segmentation and Consumer behaviour:** There is an urgent need for modifying currently existing customer segmentation techniques. While segmentation based on finer product features may have been successful in the industrially advanced nations, such fine distinctions may not strike a 12cord with consumers in the emerging markets. This is amply demonstrated in the case of consumer products like toilet soaps where market segmentation techniques in the developed nations are based on value provided by products, like fragrance, anti-aging etc. However the mass market in emerging economies with lesser sophisticated consumers may not be compliant to such fine segmentation. Segmentation techniques will need more careful analysis of consumer behaviour with significant input from demographic data. For example, Dawar and Chattopadhyay (2000) point out that "Here, consumers dislike products that evolve too rapidly, making their recent purchases obsolete. Instead, the need is for basic, functional, long lasting products. The Volkswagen Beetle remained the largest selling car in Brazil long after it had been phased out of the affluent markets and despite competitive assaults by other manufacturers with newer models. The largest selling car in China is still the Volkswagen Santana, a model that was phased out of developed markets 15 years ago." Thus clearly, in depth analysis of consumer behaviour is necessary in emerging markets although the level of customer sophistication may be less. Here CSR has an important role to play especially in building up trust in the minds of the consumers. In an emerging market where consumers are looking for functional products which last longer and accelerated obsolescence is not a problem like in developed markets, the consumer perception about the company brand assumes significance. A company which builds the image of producing quality products that last longer though they may not be on the cutting edge of technology will actually be able to gain strategic advantage in emerging economies.

**(*b*) Distribution:** Emerging markets, especially those in Asia have posed significant distribution challenges to multinational companies. Often companies have had to abandon distribution systems tried and tested in developed nations and start developing a customized distribution mechanism specific to the country of operation. Dawar and Chattopadhyay (2000) estimate that that there are 9 million small independently owned grocery shops in China that have limited working capital and, typically, occupy fewer than 300 square feet. Multi layered distribution systems have to be used although this increases the distance between the manufacturers and consumers. Yet in order to achieve volume levels necessary to overcome the thin margins prevalent in emerging markets, this is sometimes absolutely necessary.

CSR is instrumental in relationship building with retailers. Building Relationships in a fragmented retail environment requires an understanding of retailers' interests. Successful manufacturers creatively develop new revenue activities for the retailer. Batra (1999) illustrates the example of United Phosphorous Limited (UPL), an Indian crop protection company, which realized its lost opportunity due to the fact that that in its rural markets small farmers were not applying pesticide at all, or applying it inappropriately due to the lack of application equipment. Most farmers were unable to afford the huge capital cost of the equipment. UPL turned this into their advantage by designing a programme to arrange bank loans for the purchase of application equipment and educated the farmers on additional revenue possibilities from renting the equipment resulting in an added revenue stream for rural retailers and additional sales of pesticides.

## Conclusion

Emerging markets like India have drawn the attention of large MNCs for the potential of market growth. These markets are untapped and give entirely new domain for operations. However many MNCs also take the markets for granted and exploit the laxity in the norms of operations to their advantage. The lack of concern for the local community, the consumers and the environment by these corporations has created large scale public debate and action. It is important in this context to understand that the sustainable business growth is associated with care for the community and markets the corporations operate in. The negative publicity caused by the actions of MNCs has led to suspicion about their operations in the general public in these markets. The case of Coca Cola also proves without doubt that irresponsible corporate behaviour can have repercussion throughout their global markets.

## REFERENCES


1. www.amazon.co.uk
2. www.csrinternational.org/
3. issues.tigweb.org/csr
4. www.csrdigest.com
5. csrinternational.blogspot.com/
6. https://jkmlibrary.pbworks.com/CSR

# The Factors Influencing Corporate Social Responsibility

Rev. Dr. Selvanayakam
S. Muthu Rathinam

## Introduction

Corporate social responsibility and corporate governance are inextricably intertwined. There is today a growing perception among enterprises that sustainable business success and shareholder value cannot be achieved solely through maximising short-term profits, but instead through market oriented yet responsible behaviour. Companies are aware that they can contribute to sustainable development by managing their operations in such a way as to enhance economic growth and increase competitiveness whilst ensuring environmental protection and promoting social responsibility, including consumer interacts.

## Corporate Social Responsibility

Corporate Social Responsibility (CSR) is nothing but what an organisation does to positively influence the society in which it exists. It could take the form of community relationship, volunteer assistance programmes, special scholarships, preservation of cultural heritage and beautification of cities. The philosophy is basically to return to the society what it has taken from it, in the course of its quest for creation of wealth.

According to Browin H.R., social responsibility is defined as "the obligation of businessmen to pursue those policies, to make those decisions or to follow those lines of action which are desirable in terms of objectives and values of society". Business entity is expected to undertake those activities, which are essential for betterment of the society.

Corporate Social Responsibility means open and transparent business practices that are based on ethical values and respect for employees, communities and the environment. It is designed to deliver sustainable value to society at large as well as to shareholders.

### Why Corporate Social Responsibility

There could be several reasons why companies need to be responsible to society. Each of these makes good 'business sense'.

- Internal reasons like employee morale and customer and shareholder satisfaction.
- External reasons like satisfying local communities, publicity and tax benefits.
- Enlightened self-interest wherein a stable social environment and increasing prosperity mean a larger market, and hence more profits in the long term.

### Corporate Social Responsibility—Indian Context

The 1990's have perhaps been the decade of profound change in India's economic paradigm and have significantly affected corporate India. Structural adjustment has meant an increasing role for the corporate sector and freedom from controls-an opportunity of immense proportions. It has also meant competition, both from within and outside, and a breakdown of protections that the sector earlier enjoyed. As with every change, there are winners and losers. But it is undisputed that Corporate India will play, if it is not already doing so, a major role in the lives of all India. This cannot be ignored.

Corporate Social Responsibility (CSR), like many modern ideas, is not new to India. It is part of an ancient tradition, which is currently being practiced by some companies. It has been informed by ideas from the West through business collaboration between companies. Industry associations, who have recognized that it is an essential part of business, have also promoted it.Socially responsible behaviour has two dimensions; one is the stakeholders who have a contractual relationship with the business e.g., employees shareholders, customers and so on. The other is those whose lives are impacted by the behaviour of the business. Of the latter, communities, particularly the most disadvantaged amongst them, are the most crucial.

Effective corporate social responsibility towards any community requires close interaction with current development thinking, which has been constantly evolving. Initially there was welfare and now there is empowerment. Basic needs are gradually becoming basic rights. These ideas seem to gain currency in the view that human development is the ultimate goal and economic growth alone cannot ensure it. Whatever trickles down is not enough.

### CSR Definitions

While the concept of CSR is widely accepted, there is no single, universally accepted definition of CSR. Generally, it refers to business decision-making linked to ethical values, compliance with legal instruments, and respect for people, communities and the environment. Below are some examples of CSR definitions espoused by international organisations.

- Business for Social Responsibility (BSR) defines CSR as "operating a business in a manner that meets or exceeds the ethical, legal, commercial and public expectations that society has of business". Elements of CSR include investment in community outreach, employee relations, creation and maintenance of employment, environmental stewardship and financial performance.
- The European Commission defines CSR in a green paper as a concept in which "companies integrate social and environmental concerns in their business operations and in their interaction with their stakeholders on a voluntary basis".
- The World Business Council on Sustainable Development's (WBCSD) definition of CSR is "the commitment of business to contribute to sustainable economic development, working with employees, their families, the local community and society at large to improve their quality of life".
- The United Nations Conference on Trade and Development (UNCTAD) defines CSR as concerning essentially "how business enterprises relate to, and impact upon, a society's needs and goals". Specifically, CSR touches upon social responsibility standards and performance of multinational corporations, and their roles in developing a stable, prosperous and just global society.

### Factors Influencing CSR

Many factors and influences, including the following, have led to increasing attention being devoted to CSR:

- Globalization—coupled with focus on cross-border trade, multinational enterprises and global supply chains—is increasingly raising CSR concerns related to human resource management practices, environmental protection, and health and safety, among other things.
- Governments and intergovernmental bodies, such as the United Nations, the Organisation for Economic Cooperation and Development and the International Labour Organization have developed compacts, declarations, guidelines, principles and other instruments that outline social norms for acceptable conduct.
- Advances in communications technology, such as the Internet, cellular phones and personal digital assistants, are making it easier to track corporate activities and disseminate information about them. Non-governmental organizations now regularly draw attention through their websites to business practices they view as problematic.

- Consumers and investors are showing increasing interest in supporting responsible business practices and are demanding more information on how companies are addressing risks and opportunities related to social and environmental issues.
- Numerous serious and high-profile breaches of corporate ethics have contributed to elevated public mistrust of corporations and highlighted the need for improved corporate governance, transparency, accountability and ethical standards.
- Citizens in many countries are making it clear that corporations should meet standards of social and environmental care, no matter where they operate.
- There is increasing awareness of the limits of government legislative and regulatory initiatives to effectively capture all the issues that corporate social responsibility addresses.
- Businesses are recognizing that adopting an effective approach to CSR can reduce risk of business disruptions, open up new opportunities, and enhance brand and company reputation.

### Factors Influencing CSR Development

A number of factors and parties have influenced the current concept of CSR and will continue to shape its future development. Parties that are seen as stimulating businesses to adopt CSR practices include consumers, supply chain partners, insurers, banks, investors and shareholders, communities, workers, NGOs, governments, and inter-governmental bodies.

As multinationals, investment interests and NGOs in developed countries have played significant roles in promoting the modern concept of CSR, the impact they have will also be increasingly felt around the world, given growing cross-border trade and investment activities, as well as the use of global supply chains.

1. ***Trade Liberalization and Globalisation:*** Trade liberalisation and deregulation have created more leeway for businesses to pursue their economic objectives. The increased trade in goods and services across borders, including outsourcing, has been accompanied by the rising importance of Multinational Corporations (MNCs) and prevalence of global supply chains. Many MNCs operate and manufacture in countries with lower regulatory standards and sell their products in countries with stricter regulations. As the most important beneficiaries of globalisation and liberalisation of trade regimes, MNCs are increasingly seen as having obligations in the international arena in which they operate. Indeed, a lot of MNCs have adopted codes of conduct concerning their social, economic and environmental activities around the world.

2. ***Increased Expectations of Citizens:*** Citizens in many countries have recognised that corporations should exercise high standards of care not just in their home jurisdictions, but meet standards wherever they operate. They no longer accept corporations which behave well at home, while overlooking or even violating basic norms of consumer, worker, environmental and community protection elsewhere.
3. ***Shrinking Role of Government***: While governments have relied on legislation and regulation to deliver social and environmental objectives in the business sector, shrinking government resources, along with a distrust of regulations, have led to the exploration of voluntary initiatives. Many CSR initiatives have resulted from civil society's frustration with the ability of governments to adequately address the world's growing social and environmental problems.

   Further, there is recognition that the capacity to enforce laws in overseas countries is inadequate given weak or non-functioning governance institutions. Thus, businesses are expected to demonstrate high standards of corporate behaviour consistent with citizen expectations. Businesses should also take on increasing responsibilities where government shows an increasing interest in supporting self-regulation initiatives and may rely more on public-private partnerships to further public policy agendas instead of more intrusive regulatory approaches. In short, there is a perception in some quarters that good CSR practices may decrease the need for new regulations.
4. ***Supply Chain and Labour Codes:*** Outsourcing and subcontracting, including to suppliers outside the home country, have become more commonplace. These activities, however, might make it easier for businesses to avoid responsibilities otherwise required of them. As such, companies need to demonstrate that their partners conduct themselves in a socially responsible manner, so as to take some responsibility over workers throughout the supply chain. Some have adopted codes of conduct to ensure their suppliers observe certain labour codes in light of poor or ineffectual compliance enforced by authorities (including those outside the home country).
5. ***Brand and Risk Management:*** Businesses are more aware these days that a company's value is also contingent on its reputation. Accordingly, implementation of CSR measures developed with stakeholder input can enhance the company's reputation and its brand image. When businesses take the initiative to publicly demonstrate that their operations meet or exceed legal requirements and societal norms, they can better communicate to interested parties that they are systematically reducing commercial risk and other disruptions. In so doing, they ensure other firms' policies or practices do not tarnish their reputation, and potentially open doors to new commercial opportunities.

6. ***Growing Customer and Investor Interests:*** Specifically, companies' ethical conduct has evidently exerted a growing influence over the purchasing decisions of customers, who demand more responsible consumption. Similarly, many investors are making decisions based on ethical criteria, assessing if the invested companies are socially responsible. In addition, there is a greater demand for corporate disclosure from stakeholders regarding CSR activities of businesses. Shareholder activism through pension funds and otherwise has been increasingly common in many developed countries.
7. ***Role of Inter-Governmental Bodies***: Institutions like the United Nations (UN), International Labour Organisation (ILO) and OECD have articulated basic social norms of acceptable corporate conduct at the global level in the form of some modern "soft laws". Targeting corporate behaviour directly, these inter-governmental instruments include the UN Global Compact, the ILO Tripartite Declaration of Principles concerning Multinational Enterprises and Social Policy and the OECD Guidelines for Multinational Enterprises. ILO's Tripartite Declaration is reckoned to be by far the most important inter-governmental CSR instrument. The UN Global Compact, which consists of universal principles covering human rights, labour and environment, is recognised to be a serious act in defining substantive social expectations globally, while providing a flexible structure of corporate-oriented initiatives.
8. ***Role of NGOs:*** NGOs have increasingly participated in CSR advocacy through a range of activities including the development and implementation of standards and certification initiatives.
9. ***Burgeoning CSR industry:*** While many MNCs have staff dedicated to CSR activities, there is a wide range of CSR activities handled by consultants and companies offering CSR services to corporations (including advice on and verification of compliance with management standards and codes of practices). Other companies are involved in CSR-related publications (e.g. on investment in socially responsible companies), sponsoring conferences and initiatives, and promoting and reporting on the interests in CSR activities.
10. ***Advances in Communication Technology:*** Through a growing number of electronic CSR newsletters and CSR websites, the Internet has considerably enhanced the ability to track corporate activities globally and to disseminate information concerning these activities.
11. ***Labour Market Competition:*** There is a perception that employees are looking beyond financial benefits and seeking out employers whose philosophies and operating practices match their own principles. As such, there is a stronger recognition of the potential business benefit

of good CSR practices, such as improved employee morale, increased efficiency and enhanced ability to attract and retain qualified staff. It has also been found that for companies engaged in promoting human resource development as a manifestation of their responsibility towards the employee stakeholder, industrial relations are cordial and collective bargaining is rare.

## Conclusion

CSR has acquired a growing profile internationally over the past decade. Needless to say, CSR advocates point to a host of benefits arising from socially responsible corporate behaviour. The concern of businesses about risk management and brand reputation is also seen as a prime justification or strong component in the business case for CSR practices.

Whether one agrees with the business case for CSR practices, or conversely the idea that business should merely be concerned with maximising profit or return to shareholders (as attested by Nobel-winning economist Milton Friedman), the fact is that CSR has flourished over the past decade. Many factors have contributed to the greater acceptance of CSR among corporations, and the booming industry that it has helped create (see the section on *Factors Influencing CSR Development*). It is also a reality that a growing number of customers, investors and employees around the globe make decisions about what to buy, which companies to invest in and work for based on the socially responsible practices of companies and their overall involvement with the wider community. On the other hand, corporations, especially MNCs with international supply chains, do not hesitate to apply supplier codes to their business partners or suppliers which in, one way or another, mirror certain CSR principles or mimic CSR standards on labour and environment.

## REFERENCES

1. www.essaytown.com
2. www.informaworld.com
3. www.shvoong.com
5. www.palgrave-journals.com
6. www.qfinance.com

# Corporate Social Responsibility

## *A Business Strategy*

Ms. J. Jeya Ani
Dr. Lourdes Poobala Rayen

### Introduction

Many businesses have subscribed to practices that may have had negative effects on their stakeholders. This is now changing as the realization sets in of the true importance of the different stakeholders in any particular business. There are many different manners in which a company can implement corporate social responsibility measures for the benefit of all concerned. The manner in which each different company implements the changes will be dependent on what aspects of the company could be considered as having produced negative effects.

Corporate Social responsibility can often be confused with corporate charity, but it is a very different thing. Corporate charity can involve the donation of money and the provision of opportunities to members of the community and stakeholders. This is very different to the considerations that a company must abide by to ensure that their actions fall with the acceptable corporate social responsibility guidelines that have been established. These can include guidelines that relate to the environmental impact that a particular action can have or they can relate to the impact that an action can have on the local community. The guidelines are intended to ensure that any negative effects that an action could possibly have are eliminated or reduced as far as possible.

### Corporate Social Responsibility

The concept of corporate social responsibility is intended to provide each business with a far greater ability to create sustainable development. This can help to provide ongoing benefits for the business and its stakeholders, regardless of the size of the business. The business can become more competitive once it begins to create and follow guidelines to enforce the concept of corporate social responsibility within the company and its surrounding community. The greater the sustainability of a business's developments, the more successful it can become. The attraction of corporate social responsibility for many businesses is that it can help to increase sustainability without creating negative effects.

The continuing commitment by business to behave ethically and contribute to economic development while improving the quality of life of the workforce and their families as well as of the local community and society at large says World Council for Sustainable Development. The European Commission advocates CSR as "Being socially responsible means not only fulfilling legal expectations, but also going beyond compliance and investing more into human capital, the environment and relations with stakeholders". Thus CSR exhorts firms to diverge from their sole aim of maximising profits and to lay more importance on improving the economic and social standards of the community in their countries of operation.

### Importance of Corporate Social Responsibility

Corporate Responsibility (CR) has emerged as a significant theme in the global business community and is gradually becoming a mainstream activity, according to a new survey by the Economist Intelligence Unit, in cooperation with Oracle Corporation. The growing emphasis on corporate responsibility is affecting the relationship between companies and their various stakeholders, CSR is regarded as a piece of rhetoric intended to placate environmentalists and human rights campaigners. Thus, companies are beginning to regard CSR as a normal facet of business and are thinking about ways to develop internal structures and processes that will emphasize it more heavily. In the not-too-distant future, companies that are not focusing on CR may come to be seen as outliers. As companies focus on non-financial performance, an important yardstick of CSR, the measurement of intangibles, such as customer satisfaction and employee morale, are likely to become less vague and more credible.

The CSR trend is being driven by a variety of factors, such as the erosion of trust in large corporations, the globalization of business, the corporate-governance movement, the rise in importance of socially responsible funds and sheer competitive pressures. This last factor, however, does not necessarily imply that firms emphasising CSR will beat the competition. It may produce such intangible benefits as brand enhancement, stronger employee morale and greater investor confidence. But, on the tangible side, it is harder to prove that CSR leads to higher profits. Indeed, it is easier to quantify the costs of emphasising CSR than the benefits. A full-fledged CR programme at a large multinational can cost tens of millions of dollars, or as

CR practices yield intangible benefits, but it continues to be difficult to quantify the impact, if any, of CR on profits. Although CR dates back several decades, it has taken a long time to gather momentum, because it was perceived in the boardroom as a cost rather than an investment. "The CR movement never really took off until there was a business case for it," says Sunny Verghese, the CEO of Olam. Developing a link between "doing good" and "doing well" is now a major focus of many CR advocates. "All the companies we talk to tell us one thing: show us the business case. Everyone is doing analyses now, trying to pull this together," says Ms

Slater. One term often used is the "triple bottom line," that is, a bottom line for profits, but also for social and environmental benefits, often defined as "economic prosperity, social responsibility and environmental sustainability."

### Poor Practices Can Be Expensive

Of course, a company doesn't have to be dedicated to CR to seek to improve workplace safety, be transparent or build a good brand. But these figures do highlight a negative point: a company that pays no attention to CR is not necessarily going to have lower costs and be more profitable than one that does. In other words, while the bottom-line benefits of CR may be hard to quantify, the reverse is also true: the lack of CR doesn't guarantee higher profits for a company, all other things being equal. "Companies that pollute often have tremendous inefficiencies in manufacturing. For example, coalfired plants with a dirty burn aren't efficient," says Ms Brown. Companies that lack CR may gain some short term advantages over those that have it, she says, but over time it is not clear that they remain competitive. Poor labour relations, high pollution and similar CR problems will erode the performance of a factory, not help it, she says. The same is also true for issues such as corruption. "Bribery is an expensive business model," she says. Whenever companies begin to globalize, they tend to embrace CR faster than those who stay at home, in her view. "You tend to look for sustainable models as soon as you go" abroad, she says, since an outsider entering a new market will be forced to depend on rules to succeed, as it has fewer local connections than entrenched domestic players. This is where some companies can gain an edge by utilizing CR to build a clean image.

### Conclusion

CR is a difficult and elusive topic for companies to deal with. It can often be very costly and yield benefits that are hard to quantify. Perhaps this is one reason why companies have put so much focus on the internal improvements that can be made, such as improving corporate governance and transparency. This could also explain why the most important stakeholders, after customers, are the traditionally important employees and shareholders. There's also the issue of just what standard of CR should companies use and how far companies should go to perform their responsibilities beyond what the laws call for. The issue of what is the "responsibility" of a corporation is far from being settled, and there is an unresolved argument over what CR means. Companies face a plethora of options among the various standards, guidelines, benchmarks and other proposed measures of CR. One point that all can agree on is that CR is not a neutral topic. There is a persistent debate about whether the CR "movement" represents an unjustified intrusion into corporate affairs, and whether companies should invest profits in their own CR projects or return the money to shareholders to let them invest as they see fit. But there is no denying that CR has become an important issue facing the global business community and one that promises to grow in importance in the coming years.

## REFERENCES

1. Article Source: http://EzineArticles.com/455618.
2. Fernando Aguirre, chief executive, Chiquita, "a white paper from the economic intelligence unit" Cincinnati, Ohio.
3. Gavin Anderson, president, Governance Metrics International, A report on economic intelligence unit, New York.
4. www. Graphic.eiu.com.
5. Economic Outlook for 2006-07, Economic Advisory Council to Prime Minister August 2006.
6. EU Green Paper (2001), Promoting a European Framework for Corporate Social Responsibility, Brussels, Commission of the European Communities, Retrieved on August 27, 2004 from www.btplc.com/Societyandenvironment/Reports/GreenpaperonCSR.pdf
7. http://www.csmworld.org

# A Study on Corporate Social Responsibility

K. Pandiyaraj
M. Kanniraj

## Introduction

Corporate social responsibility is necessarily an evolving term that does not have a standard definition or a fully recognized set of specific criteria. With the understanding that businesses play a key role on job and wealth creation in society, CSR is generally understood to be the way a company achieves a balance or integration of economic, environmental, and social imperatives while at the same time addressing shareholder and stakeholder expectations. CSR is generally accepted as applying to firms wherever they operate in the domestic and global economy. The way businesses engage/involve the shareholders, employees, customers, suppliers, governments, non-governmental organizations, international organizations, and other stakeholders is usually a key feature of the concept. While business compliance with laws and regulations on social, environmental and economic objectives set the official level of CSR performance, CSR is often understood as involving the private sector commitments and activities that extend beyond this foundation of compliance with laws.

## Objectives of CSR

To generate awareness and impart skills amongst the corporate, civic bodies and govt. bodies regarding the importance of Corporate Social Responsibility as an effective tool for creating an enabling environment of equitable partnership between civil society and business. To encourage responsible business practices amongst organizations.

## SIGNIFICANCE OF CSR

### 1. Progressive Business Perspective

From a progressive business perspective, CSR usually involves focussing on new opportunities as a way to respond to interrelated economic, societal and environmental demands in the marketplace. Many firms believe that this focus provides a clear competitive advantage and stimulates corporate innovation.

### 2. Sustainable Development

CSR is generally seen as the business contribution to sustainable development which has been defined as "development that meets the needs of the present without compromising the ability of future generations to meet their own needs", and is generally understood as focussing on how to achieve the integration of economic, environmental, and social imperatives. CSR also overlaps and often is synonymous with many features of other related concepts such as corporate sustainability, corporate accountability, corporate responsibility, corporate citizenship, corporate stewardship, etc..

### 3. Firm's Behaviour

CSR commitments and activities typically address aspects of a firm's behaviour (including its policies and practices) with respect to such key elements as; health and safety, environmental protection, human rights, human resource management practices, corporate governance, community development, and consumer protection, labour protection, supplier relations, business ethics, and stakeholder rights.

### 4. Decision-making

Corporations are motivated to involve stakeholders in their decision-making and to address societal challenges because today's stakeholders are increasingly aware of the importance and impact of corporate decisions upon society and the environment. The stakeholders can reward or punish corporations. Corporations can be motivated to change their corporate behaviour in response to the business case which a CSR approach potentially promises. This includes:

1. Stronger financial performance and profitability (e.g. through eco-efficiency),
2. Improved accountability to and assessments from the investment community,
3. Enhanced employee commitment,
4. Decreased vulnerability through stronger relationships with communities, and
5. Improved reputation and branding.

### Three Key Areas of Corporate Social Responsibility

Focusing on three key areas for Corporate Social Responsibility can help create a cohesive map for the present and future:

1. Community Relations,
2. Training and Development, and
3. Cohesive Global Corporate Social Responsibility Platform

### 1. Community Relations

Encouraging Community Relations through your HR team includes implementing reward programs, charitable contributions and encouraging community involvement and practices. Examples of these programs include sending emails and company newsletters to staff members that highlight employees and managers involved in community relations or creating monthly reward programs to recognize efforts by individuals within the company.

### 2. Training And Development

Training and Development programs that explain the connection between the company's core products or services and the society at large, their value to the local community and ways in which employees can get involved in appropriate CSR projects would sustain and direct these initiatives.

### 3. Cohesive Global Corporate Social Responsibility Platform

Global Corporate Social Responsibility policy, centrally managed, is important to acknowledge successes and measurements according to accepted standards. Central to measuring and communicating these results is the use of a Web-based Human Resources Information System (HRIS) that is available globally to employees and managers with any Web browser. In order to encourage and maintain a clear and cohesive global workplace, it is critical for the entire global workforce of a company to be on a single, multi-functioning HR platform, which allows for distributing a sound corporate responsibility plan.

Having a global HR solution that offers companies flexibility, ease of use and the right mix of tools is essential to the success of both employees and employers alike, as they manage and maintain work-life balance and thrive in a changing environment that includes taking on social responsibility. The success of your Corporate Social Responsibility plan is possible with an HRIS that provides the capability to effectively plan, control and manage your goals, achieve efficiency and quality, and improve employee and manager communications.

The flexibility of your HRIS system is critical to tracking and pursuing a sound Corporate Social Responsibility plan and a Web-based system provides an unparalleled level of both scalability and accessibility to implement your Corporate Social Responsibility plan at a global level. This is an increasingly important endeavor, as companies, societies and people coexist productively and in harmony, across the planet we all inhabit.

## Conclusion

India is a fast growing economy and is booming with national and multinational firms. At the same time, the Indian land also faces social challenges like poverty, population growth, corruption, illiteracy just to name a few. Therefore it is all the more imperative for the Indian companies to be sensitized to Corporate Social Responsibility in the right perspective in order to facilitate and create an enabling environment for equitable partnership between the civil society and business.

# Roles of Government in Supporting CSR

Ms. Christina Jeya Devi

## Introduction

One main proposal of this is that the contemporary CSR agenda is founded on the premise that businesses are part of society, their relationship with society is interdependent, and they have the potential to make a positive contribution to societal goals and aspirations. This role of business in promoting positive social progress is well recognized by governments in many developed and developing countries and they have begun to adopt this type of CSR agenda and encourage business in taking initiatives toward positive social development. At the national level, the role of CSR has been put forward as both a mechanism to address welfare deficits, and a means of promoting national competitiveness.86 At the international level, CSR is understood as the mechanism for companies to contribute to sustainable development. For example, CSR is considered to be the strategic solution for socio-environmental challenges in developed economies and was officially adopted by member governments at the European Commission.

## Need for Government Intervention

There are at least four essential reasons why governments should take a CSR agenda seriously, along with implementing the necessary measures to support companies in practicing responsible conduct.

Firstly, citizen groups, civil society organizations, as well as international development agencies have all advocated for inclusive and sustainable development; and governments are expected to play a key role in promoting the economic, social and environmental conditions that favour more inclusive and sustainable development. Governments are under pressure with the challenge of facilitating the transition to a more efficient economy, in conjunction with a fairer and more sustainable society. CSR is widely accepted by many governments around the world as the business sector's contribution to inclusive and sustainable development. Thus, government can utilize a CSR agenda in pursuit of this goal.

Secondly, CSR is considered to play an important role in contributing to the competitiveness of a country. The European Commission stresses the need to link CSR with the competitiveness of companies and national and regional economies, which in turn has been described as fundamental for a nation's sustainability. It also presents a challenge for governments, which need to find ways of designing and implementing policies that encourage CSR practices throughout the business community to promote competitiveness at the national level.

Thirdly, financial crises and fiscal deficit have forced many governments around the world to look for a new approach for developing and funding collective action to deal with social demands that cannot be met by the government alone. The collaborative actions between governments and other sectors (in both the business and civil sectors) are a response to the limitations of government. In addition, business taking an active role in addressing some social causes is seen as a solution to current government financial crises. This allows CSR to present a new governance framework which government can use to create an enabling environment wherein the private sector is encouraged to be more engaged in social mission. CSR therefore becomes a way of promoting good company practices complementing other public efforts for societal progress.

Finally, although CSR is widely viewed as voluntary actions that companies take above and beyond regulatory requirements to improve their ethical, socio-environmental and economic performance, there is growing recognition that governments can and should contribute to shaping enabling conditions in order to see CSR more widely conducted. As Pascal Lamy, Director General of the WTO and former European Commissioner for Trade, has observed, "The societal benefits of corporate responsibility practices will remain limited unless they can be incorporated into broader strategies, and public policies certainly have a role to play in this respect". Government therefore plays an essential role in policy development to promote CSR practice. There are a variety of public policy instruments that governments can use to promote this agenda. The following two sections introduce the roles that governments can play and some broad areas of focus where governments can take action to promote the CSR agenda in their respective countries.

## The Role of Government

No doubt, government actions are essential to creating an enabling environment for private sector development that diminishes risks, lowers costs and barriers of operation, and raises rewards and opportunities for competitive and responsible private enterprises. The challenge for governmental agencies in promoting a CSR agenda is to identify priorities, raise awareness, create incentives and support, and mobilize resources from cross-sectoral cooperation that are meaningful in the national context, as well as building on existing initiatives and capacities. For many developing countries, especially in Asia, there is a significant opportunity for governments to harness current enthusiasm for CSR among enterprises and assist businesses in taking on a bigger role in social development, particularly under the global demands for responsible business practice.

Some key roles which a government can actively choose to engage to support a CSR agenda, include (but are not limited to) the following: regulating, facilitating, brokering, and warranting.

### Regulating

While CSR is normally seen as voluntarily going beyond local requirements, governments can "raise the bar" through stricter regulation. This can come in the form of laws, regulations, penalties, and associated measures to control aspects of business investment or operations. Governments at different levels can regulate the behaviour or practice of business by defining minimum standards for business performance embedded within the legal framework; establishing targets for business to achieve; setting up enforcers and inspectorates to oversee business conduct; promulgating codes or laws to confine undesirable business conduct; or imposing license of operation or mandatory environmental friendly industrial systems. Examples of this include establishing a minimum age for labour forces, emission limit values for particular categories of industrial productions, or requirements for companies to publicize corporate social responsibility reports.

### Facilitating

Through facilitation, governments enable or incentivize companies to engage in CSR to drive social and environmental improvements. In many of the approaches reflected under this role, government plays a catalytic, secondary, or supporting role. For example, government may provide tax incentives and penalties to promote responsible business; ensure business can access information needed; facilitate understanding of minimum legal requirements for issues relating to responsible business practice; include CSR elements in related policy areas (such as industrial policy, trade policy, environmental policy, and labour policy); offer capacity building, business advisory services and technical assistance to business when needed; or, support supply chain initiatives and voluntary certification.

### Brokering

Governments can combine public resources with those of business and other actors to leverage complementary skills and resources to address issues within a CSR agenda. Government can act as a broker in partnering public sector agencies, businesses, civil society organizations and other stakeholder groups in tackling complex social and environmental challenges. Government can do this by initiating dialogue in multi-stakeholder processes; supporting joint government-industry collaboration in capacity building and developing sectoral CSR guidelines; engaging stakeholders in standards-setting processes; promoting public-private partnerships for community development; and mobilizing resources. In this role as broker, government can also stimulate the engagement of key actors in a CSR agenda by, for example, providing funding for research or leading campaigns, information collaboration and dissemination, training, or raising awareness.

### Warranting

Lastly, government can provide political support and public warrant of a CSR concept. In particular, this can be done for specific types of CSR-related initiatives in the marketplace. Warranting can take various forms, including commitment to implement international principles; education or awareness raising programmes; official policy documents; publicity of good CSR practice conducted by other leading companies; specific CSR related award schemes (such as a National Green Business Award); or, endorse specific pro-CSR indicators, guidelines, systems and standards. Government can also lead by example, through things like public procurement or public sector management practices, or direct recognition of the efforts of individual enterprises through CSR award schemes.

### Creating an Enabling Environment

There is substantial evidence that governments around the world have begun to take on a CSR agenda. Some studies emphasize the influence of public policy as a critical factor in establishing a context within which CSR practice can flourish. Public policymakers can thus initiate policies and measures enabling CSR to flourish using several means. Some key means used to introduce an enabling environment for CSR in a country include the following initiatives

### Creating Awareness and Raising Public Support

CSR cannot be imposed against the will of enterprises, but can only be promoted together with them under involvement of their stakeholders. The first step to promote CSR in a country is necessarily to fill the knowledge gaps about the significance and contribution of CSR to business success and sustainability, as well to increase awareness and acceptance among relevant actors. The government can play a crucial role in establishing CSR value and knowledge among the business and the general public through recognition for CSR achievement and spreading CSR information to attain a better understanding of CSR among the public. Initiative can come in the form of publicity, awarding success, campaigning for awareness, networking opportunities, and funding.

### Reforming Regulatory Frameworks to Meet CSR-Related Standards

Government plays an important role in setting standards that reflect a minimum standard of good CSR practice or performance requirements. The government is thus in a position to determine if any legal requirement is needed to ensure compliance with these minimum social and environmental standards. It also can make necessary changes to regulatory frameworks in cases where laws, tax and administrative compliance may hinder the development of responsible business practice. Legislation that supports pro-CSR industrial investment within businesses – for example, pollution charges associated with implementation of the "polluter-pays principle" – can also contribute to pro-CSR production processes. It should be noted that the government role of defining minimum legal requirements on environmental or social issues can be accompanied by access to justice for individuals who are affected by the misconduct of business.

### Providing Support to Increase Capacity and Effectiveness for Business in CSR Initiatives

Other interventions by governmental agencies in some developing countries have included capacity building activities designed to help domestic producers meet CSR standards. Outlines of a broadly complementary initiative in India serve as a good example.106 The Indian Textiles Committee, part of the Ministry of Textiles, has taken up a national campaign to sensitize the textile and clothing industry, particularly in the SME sector, to address emerging challenges resulting from the forthcoming liberalization of the Indian textile and clothing industry. The Committee is working with the Ministry of Commerce, state governments, and local industry and trade associations on the campaign. Approximately 7,500 company representatives will have taken part in 25 workshops. The aim is to disseminate information on various standards and compliance mechanisms including ISO 9000 QMS, ISO 14000 EMS, and Social Accountability (SA8000) standards, as well as offer technical assistance to encourage implementation.

### Conclusion

There is a strong link between CSR and inclusive and sustainable development. CSR provides a strategic and competitive opportunity. It is considered a cross-governmental issue, with a broad agenda related to social, environmental and international issues. Government should therefore seek to develop frameworks within which to assess local or national priorities as they relate to a CSR agenda. Government can help by mapping existing needs, opportunities and constraints in the local or national context in order to define appropriate modes of intervention within an overall national strategy. However, capacity constraints within the government itself should not be overlooked, particularly given the resource implications. Therefore, the CSR strategy of any government should go through a development process wherein locally appropriate modes of intervention are utilized rather than simply copying models from other countries. International cooperation may address the risks of reinventing the wheel and creating different levels of competition distorting requirement. Such cooperation can also mitigate capacity constraints such as by setting up a community of practice.

# Corporate Social Responsibility

## *A Key for Corporate Financial Performance*

Ms. P. Geetha

## Introduction

Still now the question of how corporate social responsibility (CSR) affects financial performance remains open in the academic research. The preponderance of evidence on *CSR* and *financial performance* suggests a positive association; however, a number of methodological problems and mixed results have beleaguered this area of research, limiting the conclusions that can be drawn. While many researchers have relied on various accounting measures of financial performance in empirical *CSR* research, no literature to date has addressed the interaction between CSR business activity with accounting rules guiding earnings measurement CSR diffuses management's attention into projects with uncertain future benefits, allocating resources that could be better invested elsewhere.

## Definition (CSR)

Corporate social responsibility (CSR) has provided considerable challenge to researchers. Difficulty arises, in part, because of the on-going debate surrounding what a corporation's responsibility towards society is. A traditional perspective recognizes that the separation of ownership and control creates a managerial duty to serve the interests of the owners Policies that benefit outside interest groups to the detriment of shareholders violate this duty. Alternative arguments exist for broader responsibilities towards non shareholder stakeholders and towards society's well-being, including arguments based on organizational legitimacy theory, stakeholder theory, and environmental economic theory.

## Relationship Between CSR and CFP

The relationship between CSR and CFP can be explained in two steps:

1. Economic benefits and economic costs of CSR are delineated, based on prior literature.
2. Identified benefits and costs of CSR are discussed in terms of how they would likely be reflected in accounting earnings.

This is accomplished by applying accounting theory to the conclusions drawn in step one. Theories suggesting a positive relationship between CSR and financial performance include:

- stakeholder theory
- organizational legitimacy theory
- political cost theory
- competitive advantage theory
- slack resources theory

## Stake Holders Theory

*Stakeholder theory* argues that a firm's boundary extends beyond the primary stakeholders to include any group that is affected by, or can affect the achievement of the firm's objectives.

Normative stakeholder arguments have emerged declaring firms have a moral obligation to uphold the interests of all corporate stakeholders.

Instrumental stakeholder theory suggests managers "must induce constructive contributions from their stakeholders" to achieve organizational goals efficiently.

A hybrid position between normative and instrumental stakeholder theory maintains CSR is will not result in financial performance gains if it is not based on moral principles or is not genuine.

From an agency perspective, stakeholder relationships act to monitor managerial decision-making and encourage long-term achievement of organizational goals. Using this reasoning, one would have to assume the cost of voluntarily engaging in better environmental and/or social performance is less than the costs that the firm would incur absent any such action. This is similar to what Jensen (2001) calls ***'enlightened value maximization'***. Jensen states, "Enlightened value maximization utilizes much of the structure of stakeholder theory but accepts maximization of the long run value of the firm as the criterion for making the requisite tradeoffs among its stakeholders".

## Organizational Legitimacy Theory

*Organizational legitimacy theory* argues all organizations must be accepted by their environment in order to survive and be successful being socially responsible legitimizes the corporation's role in society. This is closely connected with ***political cost theory**, which* suggests firms engage in CSR to reduce their political or regulatory costs. While some of these benefits are shared by industry peers, firm specific benefits arise for first-moving firms emerge as higher quality and generate the ability to differentiate themselves from industry peers.

### Environmental Economic Theory

*Environmental economic theory* recognizes there are externalities arising from business operations. Corporate attention towards social well-being plays an important role in the efficient allocation of resources to deal with negative externalities, providing a Coasian solution to conflicts between society and corporations.

### Economic Benefits of CSR

Based on prior research, there are three major economic benefits to firms engaging in CSR.

- Firms avoid or mitigate impacts to financial performance arising from negative events and/or externalities.
- Firms create goodwill and/or other intangible assets, favorably impacting financial performance.
- Firms gain efficiencies, reducing costs and improving financial performance.

1. Environmental economic theory, organizational legitimacy, political cost theory, and stakeholder management theory all predict CSR reduces *negative effects to economic earnings when corporate goals and social/environmental goals are not aligned.* With CSR, resources are allocated to social/environmental initiatives to avoid or reduce the economic impact of negative events and/or negative externalities (Heal, 2005). The empirical evidence to support these claim comes primarily from studies involving environmental performance and industrial accidents.
2. The major economic benefit of CSR is *the creation of intangible assets.* As early as 1966, Johnson links corporate giving with competitiveness in the industry including arguments on when differentiation is worthwhile. Such theory grounds some management and marketing literature arguing firms use CSR to attract customers that want to buy products from socially responsible corporations. Marketing statistics support such an argument as does analytical research provide arguments and evidence linking corporate giving, reputational benefits (goodwill), and financial performance.
3. The research on CSR and employees *suggests more productive employees for high CSR firms suggesting reduced economic costs and*

*higher economic earnings.* In sum, the link between CSR and this particular economic benefit is that cost savings result from more efficient processes and employees providing competitive advantage. Socially responsible firms benefit from their ability to provide products and services more efficiently than their less socially responsible industry peers, all else being equal.

### Economic Costs of CSR

The economic costs of CSR, like economic benefits, are not directly observable. The specific CSR initiatives vary by industry based on the potential social and corporate conflicts (potential externalities).

- Socially responsible manufacturers may incur *incrementally higher costs for direct materials, labor, and factory overhead.*
- Many socially responsible manufacturers *buy a certain percentage of raw materials at "fair trade" prices* and/or have adopted formal systems of monitoring of labor in overseas plants.
- More socially responsible service firms may *incur higher labor costs by providing better human resource benefits* for domestic employees relative to firms that are less socially responsible.
- The incremental costs from engaging in CSR will impact economic earnings negatively as they require cash outflows.
- Environmentally responsible firms may have *higher R&D costs* (to search for more efficient, cleaner production processes) and greater investment in PPE (for environmentally friendly equipment), but the incremental costs caused by CSR are not easily traceable.
- Socially and environmentally responsible firms are likely to *spend more time and resources communicating (and auditing) their social and environmental performance* to various stakeholder groups, but again this economic cost is not observable.

A second feature of the economic costs of CSR is that they are more likely to involve significant upfront cash outflows. Consider some of the same examples above. Investing in better monitoring of overseas manufacturing facilities will involve significant upfront cash outflows when getting started.

### Economic Benefits are Reflected in Accounting Earnings

As stated previously, no prior literature has addressed the interaction between CSR business activities with accounting rules guiding earnings measurement. As described above there are three major economic benefits to engaging in CSR.

Firms *avoid or mitigate the economic impact of negative events and/or externalities.* This implies CSR *reduces the probability of compliance* and/or regulatory costs in future periods.

In addition, one would expect firms that are more environmentally responsible to have a lower probability of industrial accidents. This would reduce the probability of expenses related to remediation, litigation, etc. More socially responsible firms potentially reduce expenses associated with accidents and expenses from compliance costs associated with changes in the regulatory requirements. They also avoid the lost sales from reputational damage. Ignoring, for the moment, the costs of being more socially responsible, one would expect higher accounting earnings for such firms, over time, all other things being equal. Levels of accounting earnings would be higher. One might also expect less volatility in accounting earnings for such firms over time, all else being equal. Resources are allocated to resolving operational issues with social and environmental impacts proactively.

The second economic benefit of *generating goodwill and other intangible assets positively* impacts economic earnings.

From a strategic perspective, internally generated competencies and reputational benefits are major categories by which CSR contributes to firm differentiation. Differentiation allows a firm to have a sustainable competitive advantage. A firm that is does not have these same intangible assets may be slower to identify social and environmental threats and slower to respond to social and environmental opportunities, all else being equal. From an accounting standpoint, many of the intangible assets created through CSR (external reputational benefits and internally generated competencies) are not represented on the balance sheet. The value of the firm is equal to the book value of net assets plus goodwill, where goodwill represents the present value of abnormal operating earnings. Goodwill represents future cash inflows from sales. The significance of this particular benefit on accounting earnings will likely vary by industry and possibly over time. The use of cross-sectional samples in this case would understate potential results.

Finally, *efficiency gains impact economic earnings by reducing operating cash outflows.*

CSR gains include more efficient production processes that may reduce the amount of resources required (*raw materials, energy, and labor*) and/or reduce waste. Additionally more socially responsible firms potentially gain from higher quality, more productive employees. Again, temporarily ignoring economic costs, the overall impact to accounting earnings should be reduced operating expenses.

### Economic Cost are Reflected in Accounting Earnings

*Investments in CSR* initiatives that have uncertain future benefits and do not clearly meet the definition of an asset will be expensed. One of the economic benefits described above is the goodwill created from being more socially responsible. The cost associated with this goodwill might include charitable contributions, costs associated with employee volunteer programs, and costs associated with consumer recycling programs. While such costs may be contributing to reputational benefits that positively impact future sales, GAAP requires immediate expensing of such items.

For example, consider a firm that is in the process of *becoming more socially responsible*. There may be large upfront costs associated with consulting fees and costs associated with changes in accounting information systems. While such changes have the potential benefit of helping the firm to be more prepared and able to adapt to changing external demands and crises, the costs may not meet capitalization criteria and are immediately expensed.

Net income is reduced *as these costs are expensed* in the period incurred. Some economic costs of CSR, however, are not immediately expensed. A more socially responsible manufacturer may pay higher costs for raw materials, labor, and factory overhead relative to a less socially responsible industry peer. These costs will be matched with the revenues in the period the goods are sold.

## Conclusion

The current study falls within the research stream of CSR and its relationship with financial performance. By looking specifically at the types of economic benefits and costs associated with CSR, this study provides a comprehensive and inclusive framework for understanding the CSR/financial performance relationship.

This study reviews prior literature and finds three major economic benefits of CSR. First, firms avoid or mitigate impacts to financial performance arising from negative events and/or externalities. Second, firms create goodwill and/or other intangible assets, favorably impacting financial performance. Finally, firms gain efficiencies, reducing operating costs. Specific economic costs of CSR are described in the study include incrementally higher costs for materials, labor, facilities, equipment as well as increased costs to gather and communicate CSR information.

# Corporate Social Responsibility as a Business Strategy

R. Dhanalakshmi
Anand Shankar Raja

## Introduction

CSR is titled to aid an organization's mission as well as a guide to what the company stands for and will uphold to its consumers. Development of business ethics is one of the forms of applied ethics that examines ethical principles and moral or ethical problems that can arise in a business environment. ISO 26000 is the recognized international standard for CSR (currently a Draft International Standard). Public sector organizations (the United Nations for example) adhere to the triple bottom line (TBL). It is widely accepted that CSR adheres to similar principles but with no formal act of legislation. The UN has developed the Principles for Responsible Investment as guidelines for investing entities.

## Corporate Social Responsibility as Business Strategy

There is a visible attention being paid towards social and environmental consequences of business and yet performance in this front is far from satisfactory. Common trait seen across companies is that social concern and business are seen as two independent responsibilities and often at loggerhead. As a consequence, companies lose focus of how social responsibility could have been integrated with the long term business outcomes. Businesses across the world are so obsessed with the immediacy of results that they cannot sight the vast opportunity that discharging of social responsibility holds for the long term sustainability of the organizations. As a result, based on the maturity of strategic thinking in the company.

## CSR as Reactive Strategy

CSR has in general been a reactive strategy for reviving drooping fortunes of the company by gaining the confidence of the communities in which they operate. The case of Shell in Nigeria and that of Nike in Asian countries are just two examples to quote. With such instances on the rise companies have started adopting a "proactive approach" analyzing the cost of not discharging the social responsibility and as a result do the bare minimum to pull on and thus minimizing their spending on this account. CSR is viewed by these companies as a cost and compulsion. This approach only obscures a business from identifying the real potential CSR holds with respect to their core business. Any complacence by such companies may result in the kind of corporate scandals that we are comming across today. Corporate misdeeds are indeed costly, if caught.

The discussions of the "social responsibili-ties of business" are notable for their analytical looseness and lack of rigor. What does it mean to say that "business" has responsibilities? Only people can have responsibilities. A corporation is an artificial person and in this sense may have artificial responsibilities, but "business" as a whole cannot be said to have responsibilities, even in this vague sense. The first step toward clarity in examining the doctrine of the social responsibility of business is to ask precisely what it implies for whom.

Presumably, the individuals who are to be responsible are businessmen, which means in-dividual proprietors or corporate executives. Most of the discussion of social responsibility is directed at corporations, so in what follows I shall mostly neglect the individual proprietors and speak of corporate executives.

In a free-enterprise, private-property sys-tem, a corporate executive is an employee of the owners of the business. He has direct re-sponsibility to his employers. That responsi-bility is to conduct the business in accordance with their desires, which generally will be to make as much money as possible while con-forming to the basic rules of the society, both those embodied in law and those embodied in ethical custom. Of course, in some cases his employers may have a different objective. A group of persons might establish a corporation for an eleemosynary purpose–for exam-ple, a hospital or a school. The manager of such a corporation will not have money profit as his objective but the rendering of certain services.

In either case, the key point is that, in his capacity as a corporate executive, the manager is the agent of the individuals who own the corporation or establish the eleemosynary institution, and his primary responsibility is to them.

Needless to say, this does not mean that it is easy to judge how well he is performing his task. But at least the criterion of performance is straightforward, and the persons among whom a voluntary contractual arrangement exists are clearly defined.

Of course, the corporate executive is also a person in his own right. As a person, he may have many other responsibilities that he rec-ognizes or assumes voluntarily–to his family, his conscience, his feelings of charity, his church, his clubs, his city, his country. He may feel impelled by these responsibilities to de-vote part of his income to causes he regards as worthy, to refuse to work for particular corpo-rations, even to leave his job, for example, to join his country's armed forces. If we wish, we may refer to some of these responsibilities as "social responsibilities." But in these respects he is acting as a principal, not an agent; he is spending his own money or time or energy, not the money of his employers or the time or energy he has contracted to devote to their purposes. If these are "social responsibili-ties," they are the social responsibilities of in-dividuals, not of business.

What does it mean to say that the corpo-rate executive has a "social responsibility" in his capacity as businessman? If this statement is not pure rhetoric, it must mean that he is to act in some way that is not in the interest of his employers. For example, that he is to refrain from increasing the price of the product in order to contribute to the social objective of preventing inflation, even though a price increase would be in the best interests of the corporation. Or that he is to make expendi-tures on reducing pollution beyond the amount that is in the best interests of the cor-poration or that is required by law in order to contribute to the social objective of improving the environment. Or that, at the expense of corporate profits, he is to hire "hardcore" un-employed instead of better qualified available workmen to contribute to the social objective of reducing poverty.

In each of these cases, the corporate exec-utive would be spending someone else's money for a general social interest. Insofar as his actions in accord with his "social responsi-bility" reduce returns to stockholders, he is spending their money. Insofar as his actions raise the price to customers, he is spending the customers' money. Insofar as his actions lower the wages of some employees, he is spending their money. The stockholders or the customers or the employees could separately spend their own money on the particular action if they wished to do so. The executive is exercising a distinct "social responsibility," rather than serving as an agent of the stockholders or the customers or the employees, only if he spends the money in a different way than they would have spent it. Today, enterprises are increasingly aware that their business success does not depend solely on a strategy of maximising short-term profits, but on protecting the environment and on promoting their social responsibility, including the interests of consumers.

There was wide consensus on the importance of CSR in the activities of enterprises, since they must be aware of the following points:

- globalisation has made the organisation of enterprises more complex since the increasing extension of business activities abroad has led to new responsibilities at global level, particularly in relation to developing countries;

- the image, reputation and consequently the success of enterprises depends on their commitment to consumers;
- to allow them to better calculate the success and the risk factors inherent in a company, the financial institutions ask for the disclosure of information going beyond traditional financial reporting;
- it is clearly in the interest of enterprises to contribute to knowledge-development and innovation if they wish to enjoy the advantages of a skilled workforce;
- developing practices which take account of environmental and social considerations helps to modernise business activities and thereby increases their long-term competitiveness.

**Obstacles**

There are many obstacles to developing CSR, the main ones being the following:

- Insufficient knowledge of the relationship between CSR and business performance;
- Insufficient knowledge of the CSR concept on the part of consumers and investors;
- Lack of a consensus concerning the general CSR concept arising from differences between Member States;
- Insufficient emphasis on CSR in university education;
- Lack of resources for actions to promote CSR in small and medium-sized enterprises (SMEs);
- Lack of instruments to communicate and administer CSR activities;
- Lack of a coherent strategy by public authorities.

**Principles for Community Action**

Given the deficits observed in relation to CSR, the Commission proposes to build its strategy on a number of principles:

- the voluntary nature of CSR;
- the credibility and transparency of CSR activities;
- focus on Community action which adds true value;
- a balanced approach to CSR in the economic, social and environmental spheres and in relation to consumers' interests;
- attention to the specific needs of SMEs;
- compatibility with existing international agreements and instruments (for example labour standards of the International Labour Organisation (ILO), guidelines of the Organisation for Economic Cooperation and Development (OECD), etc.).

## Concrete Actions

More specifically, the Commission plans to focus on the following actions:

**Spreading information on the benefits of CSR for business and states:** Despite the broad consensus regarding the importance of CSR for enterprises, at present they find it difficult to measure exactly what the practical impact of such action will be. The Commission therefore proposes to launch studies showing the positive impact of CSR actions on business competitiveness, to support activities to increase awareness of CSR, and to analyse and disseminate information on socially responsible practice.

**Increasing the exchange of good practice between businesses and between member states:** The enterprises themselves have emphasised the importance of exchanging their respective experience and good practice in the field of CSR. They must therefore improve existing forums through better networking and coordination. The same is valid for the Member States which have developed CSR policies which differ because they reflect national traditions.

## Developing CSR Management Skills

CSR principles must be integrated into general education and into business administration training. Moreover, the structural funds, and in particular the European Social Fund, must be used to promote CSR in management training and training for other employees;

## Encouraging SMEs To Adopt CSR Strategies

Since the CSR concept was developed mainly for large enterprises, it is especially important to put an end to the indifference of SMEs. The main problems of SMEs in this respect are insufficient awareness and limited resources. It is therefore necessary to study SME-specific aspects of CSR strategy, foster the exchange and dissemination of good practice, introduce SME associations and business support organisations to the concept of CSR, facilitate cooperation between large companies and SMEs and raise awareness among SMEs with regard to the impact of their activities on developing countries;

## Conclusion

This doesn't mean that you can't run a profitable business. In fact, CSR can help you improve your business performance. By looking ahead, you're ready to cope with new laws and restrictions. You avoid costs such as wasted energy or paying unnecessary waste fees. Perhaps most importantly, you can keep winning business from increasingly demanding customers. Every business firm (private, public, small, big) every of these organisations are tempted to scale the profits which is their primary motto and then service which is their secondary motto. Thus in order to scale the pinnacles of success corporate social responsibility must be linked with business; many new strategies must be identified, implemented to find the desired result. On a sample of 3,434 companies that declared their financials for three years,

# Corporate Social Responsibility As Business Strategy

**Mrs. P. Priya, Venkatesha Balaji Manian**

## Introduction

The Globalization of the businesses, the issues and the challenges before the business community has never been as turbulent and unpredictable as they are today. Intensive competition, emerging new multilateral trading order and the need for sustainable development have generated extensive debate on the process and style of Corporate Governance. Corporate governance (CG) is one of the most talked about topics in business, indeed in society, today. Most academics, business professionals, and lay observers would agree that CG is defined as the general set of customs, regulations, habits, and laws that determine to what end a firm should be run. An important theme of corporate governance is to ensure the accountability of certain individuals in an organization through mechanisms that try to reduce or eliminate the principal-agent problem. A related but separate thread of discussions focuses on the impact of a corporate governance system in economic efficiency, with a strong emphasis shareholders' welfare. There are yet other aspects to the corporate governance subject, such as the stakeholder view and the corporate governance models around the world.

## Corporate Social Responsibility Means

- An obligation, beyond that required by the law and economics, for a firm to pursue long term goals that are good for society.
- The continuing commitment by business to behave ethically and contribute to economic development while improving the quality of life of the workforce and their families as well as that of the local community and society at large about how a company manages its business process to produce an overall positive impact on society.

- Conducting business in an ethical way and in the interests of the wider community.
- Responding positively to emerging societal priorities and expectations.
- A willingness to act ahead of regulatory confrontation.
- Balancing shareholder interests against the interests of the wider community.
- Being a good citizen in the community.

## Dimensions of Corporate Responsibility

- *Economic* - responsibility to earn profit for owner.
- *Legal* - responsibility to comply with the law (society's codification of right and wrong).
- *Ethical* - not acting just for profit but doing what is right, just and fair.
- *Voluntary and philanthropic* - promoting human welfare and goodwill being a good corporate citizen contributing to the community and the quality of life.

## Corporate Social Responsibility As Business Strategy

There is a visible attention being paid towards social and environmental consequences of business and yet performance in this front is far from satisfactory. Common trait seen across companies is that social concern and business are seen as two independent responsibilities and often at loggerhead. As a consequence, companies lose focus of how social responsibility could have been integrated with the long term business outcomes. Businesses across the world are so obsessed with the immediacy of results that they cannot sight the vast opportunity that discharging of social responsibility holds for the long term sustainability of the organizations.

As a result, based on the maturity of strategic thinking in the company, CSR is being implemented in one or more of the following ways as shown here:

## CSR as Reactive Strategy

CSR has in general been a reactive strategy for reviving drooping fortunes of the company by gaining the confidence of the communities in which they operate. The case of Shell in Nigeria and that of Nike in Asian countries are just two examples to quote. With such instances on the rise companies have started adopting a "proactive approach" analyzing the cost of not discharging the social responsibility and as a result do the bare minimum to pull on and thus minimizing their spending on this account. CSR is viewed by these companies as a cost and compulsion. This approach only obscures a business from identifying the real potential CSR holds with respect to their core business. Any complacence by such companies may result in the kind of corporate scandals that we are coming across today. Corporate misdeeds are indeed costly, if caught.

### CSR as Image Building Exercise

Efforts of companies to recover from the effects of not discharging social responsibility can broadly be classified as damage control exercise as far as their image is concerned. Here the businesses have their back against the wall. However, CSR today is seen by companies as an opportunity for building corporate image. Keen on drawing attention of media and general public, companies announce their plans for various kinds of philanthropic activities. There is nothing wrong with this kind of approach, except for the fact that such initiatives are not emphasized in the maze of important and urgent business calls. If a company can develop a systematic and deliberate approach for maintaining the focus on social welfare activities, this will not only enhance its image in the immediate future but consistency on this front will help the company in building a positive reputaion of societal concern. Such image will definitely help the company in its future business forays in the region.

On the other hand, the image building campaign includes CSR reporting where a series of disjointed anecdotes of companies' contribution to society are highlighted, which are in no way related to implementation of the business strategy of the company. This underlines the fact that potential of CSR as a tool for image building is more easily comprehended by corporate offices rather than as a means of creating a sustainable business.

### CSR for Improved Operating Efficiency

There are other set of companies that take care of environment because not only does it help in operating within the environmental norms set by statutory authorities but also reducing their costs by improving operating efficiency. Operating barely within the norms set by statutory authorities is being in the compliance mode. As companies deliberately plan and move beyond the compliance mode, find the case for integration of CSR and business goals, where improved productivity or operational efficiency in current time frame also results in better environmental conditions that fosters better living conditions for future generations. This in fact is a business necessity today for improved profitability for industry and cleverly used by companies for projecting a business case for CSR and showcasing the integration of CSR and business outcomes.

### CSR as Source of Competitive Advantage

Business must have clear understanding of the communities that they impact and must give a serious thought to the question—How the strategy helps these communities grow qualitatively along with the business in the short and long term? The answer to this question may not be obviously forthcoming but an open debate among the executives and strategic managers may open up options, that may help improve the quality of life indicators for the communities around in a way that enhances business opportunity for tomorrow if not the current profitability.

The challenge for industry today is to identify social issues that drive its competitiveness both now and in the future. For this to happen managers must first believe that social concern or CSR as it is popularly known is a source of business opportunity and competitive advantage. This integration then would pave way for all round sustainability and growth. Sooner than most of the experts suspect, the issues relating to climate change and social responsibility in the area of operations will be decisive factors for survival of businesses. CSR has the potential to change the way business is conducted the world over.

### Reports of CSR Business Strategy

In tough economic times, corporate social responsibility often takes a back seat to corporate survival. But, as The New York Times reported last week, that is definitely not the case at the global pharmaceutical giant GlaxoSmithKline.CEO Andrew Witty has made access to life-saving drugs in the poorest corners of the globe his company's mission. In the process, he is changing the face of an industry once widely criticized for charging prohibitively high prices while millions in the developing world died of diseases that now barely raise an eyebrow in more affluent nations.

In a speech at the Harvard Medical School last year, Witty promised that Glaxo would discount drugs it sells in poor countries by more than 75 percent. In a move that likely shocked many in an industry known for its R&D secrecy, Glaxo also announced that it would publish on the Web a list of 13,500 chemicals that attack malaria, making the list it available to anyone doing research related to the disease. And if the malaria vaccine that Glaxo has been developing for more than 23 years passes clinical trials, Mr. Witty has promised that it will be sold in poor countries at a markup of only five percent.

This commitment to social responsibility and transparency is a breath of fresh air in an era of unprecedented—and in many cases, well justified—anger aimed at Corporate America. But the satisfaction that comes from helping the less fortunate and the obvious reputational benefits of doing so are not the only reasons that Witty's strategy is a winning one.

### Corporate Social Responsibility Practices In India

Corporate governance is used to monitor whether outcomes are in accordance with plans and to motivate the organization to be more fully informed in order to maintain or alter organizational activity. Corporate governance is the mechanism by which individuals are motivated to align their actual behaviors with the overall participants.

Also, with the recent spate of corporate scandals and the subsequent interest in corporate governance, a plethora of corporate governance norms and standards have sprouted around the globe. In the last few years the thinking on the topic in India has gradually crystallized into the development of norms for listed companies. The problem for private companies, that forms a vast majority of Indian corporate entities, remains largely un-addressed. The agency problem is likely to be less marked there, as ownership and control are generally not separated. Minority shareholder exploitation, however, can very well be an important issue in many cases.

Development of norms and guidelines are important step in a serious effort to improve corporate governance. The bigger challenge in India, however, lies in the proper implementation of those rules at the ground level. More and more it appears that outside agencies like analysts and stock markets (particularly foreign markets for companies making GDR issues) have the most influence on the actions of managers in the leading companies of the country. But their influence is restricted to the few top (albeit largest) companies. More needs to be done to ensure adequate corporate governance in the average Indian company.

Even the most prudent norms can be hoodwinked in a system plagued with widespread corruption. Nevertheless, with industry organizations and chambers of commerce themselves pushing for an improved corporate governance system, the future of corporate governance in India promises to be distinctly better than the past.

"*Corporate Social Responsibility Practices in India* sets a realistic agenda of grassroots development through alliances and partnerships with sustainable development approaches. At the heart of solution lies intrinsic coming together of all stakeholders in shaping up a distinct route for an equitable and just social order...." The above lines epitomize the soul of the National Survey on corporate social responsibility.

## Corporate Social Responsibility Practices In India

***Times Foundation,*** the corporate social responsibility wing of the Bennett, Coleman & CO. Ltd., in partnership with ***TNS India*** and ***IRRAD*** undertook a national survey to understand the underlying dynamics of CSR and the current situation in India.

CSR is not new to India, companies like TATA and BIRLA have been imbibing the case for social good in their operations for decades long before CSR become a popular cause. Inspite of having such life size successful examples, CSR in India is in a very nascent stage. It is still one of the least understood initiatives in the Indian development sector. It is followed by a handful of public companies as dictated by the very basis of their existence, and by a few private companies, with international shareholding as this is the practice followed by them in their respective foreign country. Thus the situation is far from perfect as the emphasis is not on social good but rather on a policy that needs to be implemented.

A lack of understanding, inadequately trained personnel, non availability of authentic data and specific information on the kinds of CSR activities, coverage, policy etc. further adds to the reach and effectiveness of CSR programmes. But the situation is changing. And CSR is coming out of the purview of 'doing social good' and is fast becoming a 'business necessity'.

The 'business case' for CSR is gaining ground and corporate houses are realising that 'what is good for workers—their community, health, and environment is also good for the business".

As we are aware, corporate governance, as a subject of significance for both public policy and markets, is of recent origin. It is useful to recognise that it is a dynamic concept, in terms of scope, thrust and relevance. The issue is approached very differently today compared to original view. The point to be noted is that corporate governance should be viewed as an ongoing process subject to rapid changes based on experiences, developments and policy-setting.

## Conclusion

Corporate Governance is basically no more than getting appropriate controls over what management does for some public bodies such as share holders and to insure some supervision over the management structure itself. It includes a fair, efficient and transparent administration to meet certain well-defined objectives. It is a system of structuring, operating and controlling a company with a view to achieve a long-term strategic goals to satisfy share holder, creditors, employees, customers and suppliers with the legal and regulatory requirements, apart from meeting environmental and local community needs.

Corporate Governance leads to the building of legal, commercial and institutional framework. It also demarcates the boundaries within which these functions are performed. Failure in corporate governance is a real threat to the future of every corporation. Corporate governance as a business ethics issue is a hundred times more powerful than the internet or globalisation and can destroy business in a week. To make matters worse, standards of governance are changing rapidly in response to random events which capture public imagination. In business ethics, what was good is becoming bad and what was considered bad is now good. Standards for corporate governance that have worked for decades are looking old fashioned or immoral while other practices that raised questions are becoming totally acceptable.

# Corporate Social Responsibility

## *An Overview*

**Dr. N. Magesvaran**
**S. Karthik**

## Introduction

CSR is generally understood to be the way a company achieves a balance or integration of economic, environmental, and social imperatives while at the same time addressing shareholder and stakeholder expectations. CSR is generally accepted as applying to firms wherever they operate in the domestic and global economy. The way businesses engage/involve the shareholders, employees, customers, suppliers, governments, non-governmental organizations, international organizations, and other stakeholders is usually a key feature of the concept. CSR is often understood as involving the private sector commitments and activities that extend beyond this foundation of compliance with laws.

## Role of Human Resource In Promoting Corporate Social Responsibility

The world is a smaller place thanks to the Internet, global trading and new communication and technology advances. More U.S. companies are expanding overseas, and now manage a global workforce that has unique benefits, rules/laws, and different languages and currencies. With this global expansion comes a "responsibility."

When companies are global, an important challenge in garnering success is to respect other cultures and workforce environments and start forming a global profile or social consciousness. Recognize these differences with a sound Corporate Social Responsibility (CSR) plan that can simultaneously increase shareholder value, boost employee engagement and increase employer brand recognition. Human Resource Departments play a critical role in ensuring tnat the company adopts Corporate Social Responsibility programs. Furthermore, HR can manage the CSR plan implementation and monitor its adoption proactively, while documenting (and celebrating) its success throughout the company. Human Resources technology can help with a Corporate Social Responsibility program, including reducing the company's carbon footprint to benefit the planet. Start with these areas:

1. Implement and encourage green practices.
2. Foster a culture of social responsibility.
3. Celebrate successes.

**1. Implement and Encourage Green Practices for Corporate Social Responsibility:** Implement green practices to assist in environmental waste reduction, while promoting and encouraging stewardship growth, better corporate ethics and long-lasting practices that promote both personal and corporate accountability. The value inherent in embracing green aspects of corporate responsibility is clearly understood, given the direct impact that rising energy and utility costs has on employees' pocketbooks. Conservation has become an accepted means of making our planet healthier. Reducing each employee's carbon footprint is a great way of getting energy conservation and recycling waste initiatives off the ground. Here are suggestions to start:

1. Recycle paper, cans and bottles in the office; recognize departmental efforts.
2. Collect food and donations for victims of floods, hurricanes and other natural disasters around the globe.
3. Encourage reduced energy consumption; subsidize transit passes, make it easy for employees to car pool, encourage staggered staffing to allow after rush hour transit, and permit telecommuting to the degree possible.
4. Encourage shutting off lights, computers and printers after work hours and on weekends for further energy reductions.
5. Work with IT to switch to laptops over desktop computers. (Laptops consume up to 90% less power.)
6. Increase the use of teleconferencing, rather than on-site meetings and trips.
7. Promote brown-bagging in the office to help employees reduce fat and calories to live healthier lives and reduce packaging waste, too.

**2. Foster a Culture of Corporate Social Responsibility:** Creating a culture of change and responsibility starts with HR. Getting the younger employees, who are already environmentally conscious; excited about fresh Corporate Social Responsibility initiatives is a great way to begin. A committed set of employees who infuse enthusiasm for such programs would enable friendly competition and recognition programs.

Over the past few years, major news organizations have reported on large, trusted companies that have failed employees, shareholders and the public (i.e. Enron, Lehman, WaMu). These failures created a culture of mistrust in the corporate world. All too often, employees and employers at all levels, who competed for advancement and recognition in harsh workplaces, were forced to accept corporate misconduct and waste as "business as usual."

Employer brands are being eroded and the once sacred trust that employees had with stable pensions, defined benefits and lifelong jobs, are being replaced with pay for performance and adjustment to new learning goals. In this environment, Corporate Social Responsibility can go a long way in rehabilitating the employer brand with potential new hires and society at large. It can help defeat the image that corporate objectives are rooted in single minded profit at the expense of society and the environment. Social and community connections that are encouraged by employers give employees permission to involve their companies in meaningful ways with the community. Employers can connect with their employees and the community through:

1. Company matches to employee charitable contributions;
2. Community programs and volunteer days;
3. Corporate sponsorship of community events; and
4. Encouraging employees to participate in walkathons, food banks, and so forth.

**3. Celebrate Corporate Social Responsibility Successes:** Celebrating success is important to sustain the momentum of any CSR program. Involving company leaders and praising the success of these initiatives, gives the program real meaning. In the rapidly expanding global workplace, the celebration of these successes not only drives the implementation of Corporate Social Responsibility initiatives, but also allows sound corporate HR practices to enable them.

Additionally the publicity about these successes creates a mutual understanding of the cultures within each region that the company serves. The local population knows that, in addition to providing jobs, the company takes an active interest in, and participates in, local issues.

## Corporate Social Responsibility / Human Resource

Indian companies are now expected to discharge their stakeholder responsibilities and societal obligations, along with their shareholder-wealth maximisation goal. Nearly all leading corporates in India are involved in corporate social responsibility (CSR) programmes in areas like education, health, livelihood creation, skill development, and empowerment of the weaker sections of the society. Notable efforts have come from the Tata group, Infosys, Bharti Enterprises, Coca Cola India, Pepsico and ITC Welcome group, among others. In fact, four Indians, including Sunil Mittal, Chairman and Managing Director of the Bharti Group, NRI businessman Anil Agarwal, Shiv Nadar, HCL Technologies Chairman and NGO activist Rohini Nilekani were featured in the Forbes list of '48 Heroes of Philanthropy' recently.

Corporate India has spread its CSR activities across 20 states and Union territories, with Maharashtra gaining the most from them. About 36 per cent of the CSR activities are concentrated in the state, followed by about 12 per cent in Gujarat, 10 per cent in Delhi and 9 per cent in Tamil Nadu.

Assocham's 'Eco Pulse Study' on CSR for 2009-10, released in June 2009, says some 300 corporate houses, on an aggregate, have identified 26 different themes for their CSR initiatives. Of these 26 schemes, community welfare tops the list, followed by education, the environment, health as well as rural development. Of the 300 corporate houses, 74 are from the chemical sector, contributing 12 per cent to the overall CSR initiatives. As many as 62 companies in the FMCG and consumer durable sector are placed at second position with a CSR initiative contribution of 10.15 per cent.

Further, according to a survey carried out in June 2008 by TNS India (a research organisation) and the Times Foundation, over 90 per cent of all major Indian organisations surveyed were involved in CSR initiatives. The leading areas that corporations were involved in were livelihood promotion, education, health, environment, and women's empowerment.

In another study undertaken by automotive research company, TNS Automotive, India has been ranked second in global corporate social responsibility. The study was based on a public goodwill index and India received 119 points in the index against a global average of 100. Thailand was at the top slot with 124 points. Now there are plans to also introduce CSR in the small and medium enterprises (SME) sector to increase its reach in remote areas.

### Csr Initiatives and Green Measures

India Inc has joined hands to fine-tune all its activities falling under CSR. For this, it has set up a global platform to showcase all the work done by Indian firms. Confederation of Indian Industry (CII) and the TVS Group have collaborated to form the CII-TVS Centre of Excellence for Responsive Corporate Citizenship. It will provide consultancy services and technical assistance on social development and CSR.

- Reliance Industries and two Tata Group firms—Tata Motors and Tata Steel—are the country's most admired companies for their corporate social responsibility initiatives, according to a Nielsen survey.
- The Indian paints industry is making its products more environmentally friendly by opting for water-based paints and making it carcinogen-free.

- The heating, ventilation, air-conditioning and refrigeration (HVAC) industry is working to get rid of its 'global warmer' stigma through greater use of gases with zero ozone depletion potential (zero ODP).

Sustainable Technologies and Environmental Projects Ltd (STEPS) is planning to start a project to change plastic, organic and electronic waste into petroleum without the usual harmful residue

## Conclusion

Corporate Social Responsibility is one such niche area of Corporate Behaviour and Governance that needs to get aggressively addressed and implemented tactfully in the organizations. At the same time CSR is one such effective tool that synergizes the efforts of Corporate and the social sector agencies towards sustainable growth and development of societal objectives at large.

# Corporate Social Responsibility

## *As a Key to Deliver Sustainable Value to the Society*

J. Divya Merry Malar

### Introduction

Corporate Social Responsibility (CSR) is the responsibility recognized by the companies for acting in socially responsible manner. There is no single universally accepted definition of CSR, but it means business decision making linked to ethical values, legal compliance and respect for people, community and environment. Corporate houses should see CSR as a responsibility not imposed by outside forces, but guided by conscience and the best practice of giving back in society, people, communities and environment, what they took back from them. If an organization has to function effectively and efficiently in the long run it has to be accountable to the society at large.

### CSR - No more Charity

CSR is no more equated to philanthropy and corporate charity that involves cash donations to members of the community. With business focusing on maximization of profit, sustainability was not a popular concern among companies until recently. Now in the era of globalization, multi-national companies the concept of CSR takes the idea of sustainability and combines its three pillars economy, ecology and society with concrete corporate action. During the past decade consumers and communities have become sensitive to business practices of companies and are supportive of companies that are concerned with the general welfare of the society.

### Need for CSR

The concept of CSR is becoming a vital strategy for companies to survive in a tough competitive market environment. In a condition where market shift and consumer preferences are more unpredictable and complex adopting CSR strategy would be a powerful tool for survival. There is a growing perception among enterprises that sustainable business success and shareholders' value cannot be achieved solely through maximizing short term profits, but instead through market oriented yet responsible behavior. With increase media attention, pressure from non-government organizations and rapid global information sharing there is a surging demand from civil society consumers, government and others for corporate to conduct sustainable business process.

When a company does not adhere to the ethical values and engage in harmful business practices, it damages its corporate image. Reputations that take decades to build up can be received in hours through incidents such as corruption, scandals or environmental accidents as it happened in the case of Sathyam Computers and Union Carbide. In this context, it is apt to recollect the words of Mr. Narayana Moorthy the mentor and ex-chairman of Infosys who in an interview to a T V channel said "every company should have a value base and it should pay a cost for its value.

### CSR Delivers Sustainable Value to the Society

A business is not just a money making entity. It has a very responsible role to play in the welfare of the society and companies operating on good values will give in value and deliver value.

A company needs to implement CSR measures for the benefit of all kinds of people associated to it. It is responsible to its stake holders, consumers, suppliers, employees, government, business partners and can deliver sustainable value to the society in the following ways:

(*a*) Share holders - maximization of profit leads to higher dividend. This increases share value and retains, attracts new investors.

(*b*) Employees - fair pay, equal opportunities, work force from local area, training and education work force.

(*c*) Consumers - product safety, avoidance of price fixing, innovative products, quality of service would enhance their and corporate image in the eyes of consumers.

(*d*) Suppliers - fair trading, setting standards for supplies and source of supplies would indicate the company's commitment toward ethical behavior.

(*e*) Community - addressing social challenges like poverty, population growth, illiteracy, corruption and efforts to reduce the sufferings around us would result in sustainable development of the society

(*f*) Environment – combating global warming, pollution control, conservation of energy and other scarce resources, using environmental friendly ingredients and components recycling and non-wasteful packaging, would help to sustain environment for future generations.

## Sustainable Value and Sustainability of the Business

CSR generates superior long term performance that result in sustainable and inclusive growth of a business. A company creates sustainable value by being responsible to the society and share holders. When a company uses local labour and material, the economic impact in areas where it operates is sustainable and long-term.

Values build bases of CSR. They create trust and a clear positioning in the market. This strength gives a company high profile and creates competitive advantage. Environmental initiatives to reduce waste, re-use materials, re-cycle and conserve water and electricityresults in decreased operating cost, reduce advertising cost and gives free publicity. Sustainable development is the development that meets the needs of present generation without compromising the ability of future generation to meet their needs.

Social development and operational activities should be designed in such a manner, these activities deliver sustainable value to the society at large, as well as share holders. It is necessary to create shared value not just 'share holders value' for the business of the future to remain strong. CSR delivers sustained business growth and profitability while creating benefits to the society, planet and delivering good values for all.

## Role of Indian Corporate in Delivering Sustainable Value to the Society

India has become one of the fast growing economies of the world. It is going at the rate of 9 per cent As an emerging market all are looking at India from an international perspective. Though India has a strong economic growth, the socio-economic problems like poverty, literacy, lack of health care are still ubiquitous and the government has limited resources to tackle the challenges. This scenario has opened up several areas for big corporate to contribute towards social developments. It is high time they maintain harmony between business vision and vision for society.

Most of the leading corporate in India have realized the importance of CSR and involved in CSR programmes in areas of education, health, livelihood creation, skill development and empowerment of weaker section of the society. Notable efforts have come from Tata group, Bharathi enterprises, ITC welcome group, Infosys, Wipro, HCL and Indian oil corporation.

Mr. Azim Premji founder of Wipro, had recently contributed Rs. 8,846 crores to a Trust established by him to provide education to the disadvantage sections of our society. According to Nelson Survey release in May 2009 Reliance and Tata motors are the most admired companies of CSR. Mr. Pranai Roy of NDTV 24 × 7, English News channel organized a programme in collaboration with Toyota in 2009 to provide solar lamps to remote Indian villages which has no electricity. They collected money to adopt 55 villages. On 12$^{th}$ December 2010, they again organized " Save the Tigers" programme in collaboration with Aircel and generated more than Rs. 5 crores.

According to a study by Financial Paper Economic Times, donations by listed companies grew by 8 per cent during the fiscal year 2009. This study showed that 760 companies donated 170 million dollars in 2009. The 2010 list of Forbes, Asia's 48 Heroes of Philanthropy contains four Indians. India has been named among the top 10 Asian countries paying and increasing importance towards Corporate Responsibility disclosure norms. India was ranked 4$^{th}$ in the list according to social enterprise CSR Asia's Asian Sustainability Ranking release in October 2009.

### Role of Government in the Practice of CSR

The Central Government is working on a frame work for quantifying the CSR in initiatives of companies. As per the guidelines of the government, companies with the net profit less than 22.5 million US dollars need to allocate 3 to 5 per cent of profit for CSR, net profit between 22.5 – 112.5 million US dollars to allocate 2 to 3 per cent of profit and companies with net profit more than 112.5 million US dollars to allocate 2 to 5 per cent on net profit for CSR. The government made mandatory for all public sector companies to spend 2 per cent of net profit on CSR.

### Conclusion

The concept of CSR is seen as being important for the continued well being of the vast majority of companies and essential for the community that surrounds them. The continuous technological evolution and new market demand in a more globalised environment, CSR gives a helping hand to add value to the business of companies. The attraction of CSR for many businesses is that it can help to deliver sustainable value to the society and thus increasing sustainability of the business without negative effects. CSR plays a crucial role in building a just, equitable, humane and sustainable society.

## REFERENCES

1. Philip Kotler and Nancy Lee, CSR – Doing the most good for your company and your cause
2. www.rimweb.in
3. en.wikipedia.org

# Corporate Social Responsibility in India

M. Charlet Rose Mary Vijaya
Dr. Lourdes Poobala Rayen

## Introduction

Corporate Social Responsibility (CSR) is viewed as a comprehensive set of policies, practices and programs that are integrated into business operations, supply chains, and decision-making processes throughout the organization—wherever the organization does business—and includes responsibility for current and past actions as well as future impacts. CSR involves addressing the legal, ethical, commercial and other expectations society has for business, and making decisions that fairly balance the claims of all key stakeholders. Effective CSR aims at "achieving commercial success in ways that honor ethical values and respect people, communities and the natural environment." Simply put it means "what you do, how you do it and when and what you say."

## Need for CSR

While the interests of shareholders and the actions of managers of any business enterprise have to be governed by the laws of economics, requiring an adequate financial return on investments made, in reality the operations of an enterprise need to be driven by a much larger set of objectives that are today being defined under the term CSR. The broad rationale for a new set of ethics for corporate decision making, which clearly constructs and upholds a organization's social responsibility, arises from the fact that a business enterprise derives several benefits from society, which must, therefore, require the enterprise to provide returns to society as well. A business cannot succeed in a society which fails. This, therefore, clearly establishes the stake of a business organization in the good health and well being of a society of which it is a part. More importantly, in this age of widespread communication and growing emphasis on transparency, customers of any product or service are unlikely to feel satisfied in buying from an organization that is seen to violate the expectations of what is deemed to be ethically and socially responsible behaviour. It is becoming increasingly evident that organizations that pay genuine attention to the principles of socially responsible behaviour are also finding favour with the public and are the preferred choice for their goods and services.

### CSR in India

Mahatma Gandhi, the charismatic visionary leader who brought the cause of India's independence from British colonial rule, was a person who in several respects was ahead of his time. His view of the ownership of capital was one of trusteeship, motivated by the belief that essentially society was providing capitalists with an opportunity to manage resources that should really be seen as a form of trusteeship on behalf of society in general. Today, the world is coming round full circle in emphasizing this concept through an articulation of the principle of social responsibility of business and industry.

A much less publicized but deeper aspect of the importance of CSR in India comes to light when one considers CSR as a concept that covers a range of issues under the fabric of sustainable development. This is a crucial terminology for developing nations in the world today. Protection of the environment and a country's natural resources are a key element of this concept. Additionally, there is this equally important need to ensure that society does not suffer from disparities of income and provision of basic services like health care, education and literacy.

### Current Status of CSR in India

CSR is fast gaining momentum as an important aspect of business practice in India. An appreciative quantum of roundtables and networks pertaining to CSR are being established and doing good work. There are several bodies now emerging on the Indian scene that focus on issues of CSR. For instance, the Corporate Roundtable on Development of Strategies for the Environment and Sustainable Development - Business Council for Sustainable Development (CORE-BCSD) of India is a grouping of Indian corporates trying collectively and individually to build in sustainable development concepts into their operations (see Box A). Initiated by The Energy and Resources Institute (TERI), CoREBCSD India includes some of the most innovative, some of the largest and also the most forward looking organizations in the country. Subject experts from these corporates identify and conceptualize projects. A team of industry members and TERI researchers then works to develop appropriate solutions/strategies for use by the industry. Currently the Roundtable includes some of the leading Indian corporates, such as:

- The Associated Cement Companies Limited
- Bharat Heavy Electricals Limited

- Bharat Petroleum Corporation Limited
- Century Textiles & Industries Limited
- Gas Authority of India Limited
- Gujarat Ambuja Cements Limited
- Hindustan Lever Limited
- Infrastructure Leasing & Financial Services Limited
- ITC Limited - Paper Brands & Speciality Papers Division

## The Rewards of CSR

CSR is a business strategy that works. In a world where brand value and reputation are increasingly seen as an organization's most valuable assets, CSR can build the loyalty and trust that ensure a bright sustainable future. In our complex, global society, corporations are becoming increasingly visible. These businesses are not judged on their results but on their behavior too. Thus CSR should be an integral part of every aspect of business life. The following are some of the benefits of CSR.

- Improved financial performance
- Better risk and crisis management
- Reduced operating costs
- Increased worker commitment
- Good relations with government and communities
- Enhanced brand value and reputation
- Long-term sustainability for your organization and society
- Long-term return on investments
- Increased productivity
- A license to operate

## Conclusion

CSR today, is seen as something more far-reaching, engaging at a much wider level with business' operations and relations with communities. It embraces the 'triple bottom line' and requires attention to be paid not only to economic performance, but to environmental and social impacts as well. It is essentially about business' contribution to sustainable development and how best to maximize that contribution. Sustainable development is a very vague term and simply setting that as a goal does not take a business very far. "Putting CSR into operation, bringing it to the heart of corporate culture without losing sight of core business objectives, while also avoiding the traps of paternalism and philanthropy, is a complex task, requiring clear-sighted analysis and detailed implementation.CSR has become increasingly important to companies/businesses over the last few years, with more and more companies responding to stakeholders' calls for increased accountability by incorporating and integrating CSR into their organization/business policies. In time, the public is likely to become increasingly discriminating, less willing to take general claims on trust, and more keen to see specific action. In this case, if companies are to maintain their standing and stake out leadership in the future, CSR cannot be an additional extra - it must run into the core of every business' ethics, and its treatment of employees and customers. Thus, CSR is becoming a fast-developing and increasingly competitive field. The case for demonstrating corporate responsibility is getting stronger as expectations among key opinion formers, customers and the public are increasing. Being a good corporate citizen is increasingly crucial for commercial success and the key lies in matching public expectations and priorities, and in communicating involvement and achievements widely and effectively.

## REFERENCES


1. Corporate Social Responsibility – Perceptions of Indian Business. Available at: www.csmworld.org/public/pdf/social_respons.pdf
2. Franz von Däniken (Secretary of State of the Department of Foreign Affairs, Switzerland) What Should and Can Governments Do to Encourage CSR. Business and Global Corporate Citizenship: Best Practice for the Future (May 2001). Available at:http://www.eda.admin.ch/sub_ecfin/g/home/docus/ethic.Par.0003.UpFile.pdf/sp_010504_wiltonp ark_e.pdf
3. Why Corporate Social Responsibility? The European Business Campaign. Available at: http://www.csrcampaign.org/why/default.aspx.
4. Corporate Social Responsibility – Prof. Kevin Kolben (Rutgers Business School, USA)Availableat:http://www.indianngos.com/corporate/interviews/kevinkolben/fullinterview.htm
5. The business case for CSR. The Gateway to Corporate Social Responsibility Website (UK). Available at: http://www.societyandbusiness.gov.uk/business casecsr.shtml.
6. Responsibility Orange UK Report 2002. Available at: http://www.orange.co.uk/about/community/documents/fullreport_2002.doc
7. The business case for corporate social responsibility – Available at: http://www.weforum.org/site/homepublic.nsf/Content/The+business+ case+for+ corporate+social+responsibility

# Corporate Social Responsibility

## *Creating Shared Value*

Dr. B. Revathy
K.S. Arockiasamy

Corporate social opportunity is a concept whereby organizations consider the interests of society by taking responsibility for the impact of their activities on customers, suppliers, employees, shareholders, communities and other stakeholders, as well as the environment. CSR approach basically leads a business to operate in a manner that meets or exceeds the ethical, legal, commercial and public expectations that society has of business. Elements of CSR include investment in community outreach, employee relations, creation and maintenance of employment, environmental stewardship and financial performance. Many people believe it is no longer enough for a company to say that their only concern is to make profits for their shareholders, when they are undertaking operations that can fundamentally affect (both negatively or positively) the lives of communities in countries throughout the world.

Thus, Corporate Social Responsibility is a concept whereby organizations consider the interests of society by taking responsibility for the impact of their activities on customers, suppliers, employees, shareholders, communities and other stakeholders, as well as the environment. This obligation extends beyond the statutory obligation to comply with legislation and sees organization voluntarily taking further steps to improve the quality of life of employees and their families as well as the local community and society at large.

Till 1990s CSR was understood purely in terms of *"philanthropy"* or charity. In the new environment, companies have realized that without a healthy community the new business ventures cannot prosper. Most companies initiated action in the early 90's and now have a formal policy in place. CSR taken up by various genres of companies primarily focuses on poverty alleviation, environmental protection & sustained development.

Considered as pioneers in the field of CSR, the Tata group has played an active role in nation building & social economic development. Since the early 1990's, the Tata group has placed equal importance on maximizing financial return as on fulfilling its social & environmental responsibilities popularly known as the *triple bottom line.* Most of the Indian companies are now expected to discharge their stakeholders' responsibilities and social obligations along with shareholder wealth maximization goal. Most of the leading corporates in India are involved in corporate social responsibility programs in the areas like education, health, livelihood creation, skill development and empowerment of the weaker sections of the society. Notable efforts have come from the Tata group, Infosys, Bharti Enterprise, Coca-Cola India, PepsiCo, ITC, Welcome group, among others. In fact, four Indians, including Sunil Mittal-chairman and Managing Director of the Bharti Group, Anil Agarwal-Chairman of mining outfit Vedanta Resources, Shiv Nadar, Chairman-HCL Technologies and NGO activist Rohini Nilekani were featured in the Forbes list of *"48 Heroes of Philanthropy"*- recently.

Globalization, deregulation, privatization and a redrawing of the lines between state and market have changed the basis on which business houses are expected to contribute to the public good. Meanwhile, the relationship between companies and civil society has moved on from paternalistic philanthropy to re-examination of the roles, rights and responsibilities of business in society.

These dynamics combined with the macro changes like globalization and the associated growth in competition, increased size and influence of companies, war for talent i.e. companies competing for expertise and increased importance of intangible assets etc. have led to the emergence of a new approach to Corporate Social Responsibility with companies recognizing that improving their own impact and addressing wider social and environmental problems will be crucial in securing their long-term success. Increasingly, high profile companies are implementing CSR processes such as public commitment to standards, community investment, continuous improvement, stakeholder engagement and corporate reporting on social and environmental performance.

The basic drivers of CSR consist of:

| | |
|---|---|
| Values | A value shift has taken place within businesses v/here they not only feel responsibility for profit earning but also for social and environmental good. |
| Strategy | Being more socially and environmentally responsible is important for the strategic development of a company. |
| Pressure Groups | Pressure groups like consumers, media, the state and other public bodies are pressing companies to become more socially responsible. |

A number of factors and parties influence the current concept of CSR and will continue to shape its future development. Parties that are seen as stimulating businesses to adopt CSR practices include consumers, supply chain partners, insurers, banks, investors and shareholders, communities, workers, NGOs, governments, and inter-governmental bodies etc. In present scenario, various factors like trade liberalization and globalization, increased expectations of citizens, brand and risk management, growing customer and investors interest, burgeoning CSR industry, advances in communication technology & labour market competition etc also influence CSR development. While discussing various factors managerial ethics is an aspect that requires special attention. Manager's ethical standards in the enterprise determine the type of response it will make as it reacts to the tension between the forces for change and stability. *Proactive responses* are likely to be more ethical since they will go beyond minimum legal requirements. They are more consistent with the high social expectations. *Reactive responses* on the contrary either conform only with the minimum legal requirements. So, more proactive choices means long term social responsiveness enhancement & more reactive choices means sufficient for the moment and decrease in the long-term social responsiveness. Hence, ethics affect an enterprise's action through the decisions that its managers make.

India was ranked fourth in the list, according to social enterprise CSR Asia's Asian Sustainability Ranking (ASR). Assocham's 'Eco Pulse Study' on CSR for 2009-10, released in June 2009, says some 300 corporate houses, on an aggregate, have identified 26 different themes for their CSR initiatives. Of these 26 schemes, community welfare tops the list, followed by education, the environment, health as well as rural development. Further, according to a survey carried out in June 2008 by TNS India (a research organization) and the Times Foundation, over 90% of all major Indian organizations surveyed were involved in CSR initiatives. The leading areas that corporations were involved in were livelihood promotion, education, health, environment and women's empowerment.

### Creating Shared Value

"A coherent corporate social responsibility strategy based on integrity, sound values and a long-term approach, offers clear business benefits to companies and a positive contribution to the well-being of society". (World Business Council for Sustainable *Development*) Creating Shared Value means thinking long term while at the same time delivering strong *Annual* results. Successful creation *of long term shareholder value* is dependent also on the creation of value for society. Creating shared Value for Society & investor means going beyond customer benefits. It means examine multiple points where business houses touch society & making very long term investment that benefit both public shareholders. It is not philanthropy or an add-on activity but a fundamental part of business strategy. For a business to be successful in the long run, it has to create value, not only for its shareholders but also for society. Practicing CSR gives companies the double advantage of a healthier business and an improved image. We can examine some Business Cases in this respect like Nestle: simultaneous benefits for Nestle and society: One of the fundamental Nestle Corporate Business Principles is that 'we will not sacrifice long-term development for short-term gain. Nestle's long-term objective is to create sustainable value for its shareholders. To do this, they need to create value for the societies where they operate. Nestle's approach is based on :

- A long-term view;
- Understanding of countries and cultures;
- Responsibility and accountability

| Nestle's Actions | Value For Nestle | Value of Society |
|---|---|---|
| Expertise and support or farmers | Securing suppliers of high-quality raw materials. | Improved yield and increased incomes. |
| Providing ongoing R&D and expertise to suppliers | Improving community relationships and product quality. | Reducing exploitation of natural resources. |
| Building brands through responsible marketing | Entering new and emerging markets. | Widening access to nutritional products. |
| Increasing volume and value of sales | Achieving competitive shareholder returns. | Generating local Investment and economic growth. |
| Creating Shared Value | | |
| = Organisational value + Social value | | |

The above table shows how Nestle's actions in various ways generate value for business and societies where they are present.

In the same way, The ITC groups e-choupal project gives access to IT kiosks to four million farmers across nine states in India. These kiosks provide information about the weather, crop prices and fertilizers. This has increased farmers income by 30-40 per cent. As a business, this gives them access to reliable source of farm produce. ITC's Social and Farm Forestry project also provides a comprehensive package of support to tribal areas. It includes loans, planting of saplings, which are later used 'by ITC for wood pulp. The project has generated 28 million days of employment. ITC has also earned carbon credits from nearly 75,000 acres of green cover, According to the spokesperson; ITC is probably India's largest company to have a positive carbon and water balance. Its projects cover the twin goals of creating social development and shareholder value. It serves ITC's Triple Bottom Line-Economic performance, Social performance, Environmental performance.

Beverages Company Coca-Cola India has been awarded the 'Golden Peacock Global Award for Corporate Social Responsibility -2008'. The Indian arm of the world's largest soft drinks company Coca-Cola India is all set to come up with an India specific arm for its corporate social responsibility (CSR) activities this year, starting with a corpus of $10 million. The Company's general CSR activities linked to developing the areas around its plant sites will continue as it is. It has 45 plants across the country and involves itself with community education, health & sanitation projects. About Rs. 4-5 crore is being spent on these activities. Apart from this, Coca-Cola is also pumping back the entire three million cubic meter of water that it currently consumes for its operations back into the water cycle through rain water harvesting (RWH) structure. Company's water recycling, harvesting, and recharging projects saved more than 100 million liters of water in 2006. That's 35 per cent of water usages over six year. So there is the direct benefits of using less water, power and land etc. This is a direct way of measuring benefits.

| Value for Business | Value for Society |
|---|---|
| Direct benefits of using less water, power and land etc. Hence, less cost & as a result increased profit so high shareholder value. | Environmental Benefits like saving of valuable water resources by water recycling, harvesting, and recharging projects |
| = Creating Shared Value | |

Light on some more business cases:

| Company | Value for Business House | Value for Society |
|---|---|---|
| NTPC (Power gene a ration) | Recycling by-products of power generation reduces costs of buying raw material Community programmes improve local relations | Environmental management and community development |
| IndianOil Corporation | A set of core values for themselves– Care, Innovation, Passion and Trust. They take pride in being able to claim all our countrymen as their customers. | About one-fourth of the community development funds are spent on the welfare of Scheduled Caste and Scheduled Tribe beneficiaries. |
| | = Creating Shared Value | |

After going through the above-mentioned business cases one can say that CSR may produce such intangible benefits as good image of the organization, brand enhancement, stronger employee morale and greater investor's confidence. Through voluntary commitment to CSR, companies hope to send a positive signal about their behavior to their various stakeholders, and by doing so make an investment in their future and help to increase profitability. In the broadest sense, stakeholders can be considered to be anyone affected by the activities of an enterprise, or whose activities affect the enterprise. Generally, stakeholders include for example, employees, shareholders, investors, consumers, regulators and non-government organisations (NGOs). These stakeholders have taken an increasingly important role in promoting the concept of CSR and its sustainability. When companies take a strategic approach to CSR it would have a positive effect on mainstream business performance. The research, however, also shows how business benefits go beyond (he long-term intangible measures of success, to include direct financial measures. Some of them are :

**Building Reputation**

In general, public prefer companies that are seen to be positively contributing to the environment and society. A good reputation is one of the most valuable intangible assets a company can have, and maintaining it as a key motivation for companies to engage in responsible business. By being responsible, companies can enhance brand value by managing and influencing the expectations of their customers and companies can build trust through actions that increase customer satisfaction and add to shareholder value.

**Employee Satisfaction & Retention**

There is a "war for talent" - businesses are dependent on their employees to deliver and create value. Responsible business practice is increasingly a contributing factor in attracting and retaining a talented and diverse workforce, and in being an employer of choice. Builds employee morale and loyalty and creates a more motivated, engaged and inspired workforce that can improve long-term productivity. It may be mentioned here that companies in which the level of employee satisfaction is low are likely to be the least effective in CSR initiatives. It is not possibles to generate goodwill in the external environment without taking care of the needs and aspirations of the employees; charity really does begin at home.

| Value for Business Houses | Value for Society |
|---|---|
| By maximizing the performance of people by motivation and skills to perform to their full potential and achieve superior business results and future sustainable growth. | It offers employment opportunities worldwide, provides tlie potential for a better standard of Irving and sell-development. |
| = Creating Shared Value | |

**Financial Performance**

Responsible busir ess opens opportunities to reduce present and future costs to the business by improving competitiveness, market positioning and profitability. It helps to understand how company should use natural resources and energy and the operational benefits of managing these more effectively & integrating environmental specifications into new assets, which can reduce recycle costs and improve efficiency.

## Global Competitiveness

Business operates in a global economy and as such stakeholder views are shaped by what they see happening in the world around them. Businesses have the opportunity to address a unique set of global challenges using responsible business strategies. Companies benefit by:

- Opening doors to new markets, new opportunities and new relationships.
- Setting the scene for long-term profitability and operational security.
- Increasing the competitiveness and better understanding the needs of the communities in which they operate.

**Increased Revenue Base**

CSR can boost factors that drive revenue in important ways. CSR initiatives and cause-related marketing could build reputation and goodwill among suppliers and customers. Employees who, identified with the social mission, are likely to be motivated, committed and more prepared to make sacrifices as a team member.

Environmental footprints:

| Value for Business Houses | Value for Society |
|---|---|
| Building high-quality, high-performing lactones with good and continuously Improving environmental performance, supported by strong local businesses, enable to achieve sustainable profitable growth. | Major investments in rural areas help workers acquire new skills and higher income, develop local suppliers and entrepreneurs, and raise environmental standards. |
| = Creating Shared Value | |

A simple Approach to introducing CSR in a structured way:

1. **Assess :** Assessment of the actions and actions should be relevant for business as well as society.
2. **Commit :** Commitment to a statement being a responsible business means to the company and clear ethical values from the top down.
3. **Tell :** Set ethical and business cases, communicate them and promote them at every opportunity.
4. **Integrate :** Responsible business behaviour across different functions and activities within the business.
5. **Organize :** The project management, the details, relevant business resources and set targets.

6. **Nurture :** Involve clients and supply chain. Once the programmes are established, companies can have greater impact and raise their profile by widening their resources.

## Conclusion

The business of business is to create sustainable value.

Primary objective of the business is to create maximum wealth for their shareholders and various stakeholders & CSR is one of the most reliable and consistent way to do so. Stakeholders and customers are increasingly concerned about the environmental and social impacts of the products they buy. It follows that businesses can maximize their long term returns by minimizing their negative impacts. As a constructive partner in the communities in which it operates, it has been taking concrete action to realise its social responsibility objectives, thereby building value for its shareholders and customers. The Corporation should respect human rights, values its employees, and invests in innovative technologies and solutions for sustainable energy flow and economic growth.

Besides focusing primarily on the welfare of economically and socially deprived sections of society, it also aims at developing techno-economically viable and environment-friendly products and services for the benefit of millions of its consumers, while at the same time ensuring the highest standards of safety and environment protection in its operations.

## REFERENCES

### I. Books and Reports:

1. Andriof, J. *et al.*, (eds) Unfolding Stakeholder Thinking. Volume 1 : Theory, Responsibility and Engagement. Greenleaf, 2002.
2. Andriof, J. *et al.*, (eds) Unfolding Stakeholder Thinking. Volume 2 : Relationships, Communication, Reporting and Performance. Greenleaf, 2003.
3. Crowther, D. and Capaldi, N. (eds) The Ashgate Research Companion to Corporate Social Responsibility. Ashgate, 2008.
4. Bakan, J. The Corporation : The Pathological Pursuit of Profit and Power. Free Press, 2004.
5. Charkham, J. Keeping Better Company : Corporate Governance Ten Years on. Oxford University Press, 2005.
6. Crane, A. *et al.*, (eds) The Oxford Handbook of Corporate Social Responsibility. Oxford University Press, 2008.
7. Corporate Social Responsibility in India - An Empirical Research By Bernadette Dsilva.
8. CSR could Prove to be a Valuable Asset in an Age of M&As, as it Helps Firms Spread their Brand Name - Maitreyee Handique.
9. Corporate Social Responsibility is no Longer Just an Addition, it is a key Differentiator." Prasad Chandra, CMD, BASF South Asia.

10. Frederick, W. Corporation be Good! The Story of Corporate Social Responsibility. Dog Ear Publishing, 2006.
11. Kotler, P. and Lee, N.(eds) Corporate Social Responsibility : Doing the Most Good for your Company and your Cause. Wiley, 2005.
12. Nicholls, A. Fair Trade : Market-driven Ethical Consumption. Sage, 2005.
13. Olsen, L. Making Corporate Responsibility Work : Lessons from Real Business. Ashridge Centre for Business and Society, 2004.
14. Olsen, L. and Gitsham, M. Catalogue of CSR Activities : A Broad Overview. Ashridge Centre for Business and Society, 2005.
15. Phillips, R. Stakeholder Theory and Organizational Ethics. Berrett-Koehler, 2003.
16. Schwartz, P. When Good Companies do bad things. Wiley, 1999.
17. Sethi, S. Setting Global Standards : Guidelines for Creating Codes of Conduct in Multinational Corporations. Wiley, 2003.
18. Steger, U. The Business of Sustainability. Palgrave Macmillan, 2004.
19. Tully, S. (ed) Research Handbook on Corporate Social Responsibility. Edward Elgar, 2005.
20. Van Tulder, R. International Business-society Management : Linking Corporate Responsibility and Globalization. Routledge, 2006. London.
21. Visser, W. *et al.*, (eds) The A to Z of Corporate Social Responsibility. Wiley, 2007.
22. Vogel, D. The Market for Virtue : The Potential and Limits of Corporate Social Responsibility. Brookings Institute Press, 2005.
23. Werther, W. and Chandler, D. (eds) Strategic Corporate Social Responsibility. Sage, 2006.
24. Zadek, S. *et al.*, Responsible Competitiveness : Corporate Responsibility Clusters in Action. AccountAbility, 2005.

**II. Databases and Journals:**

1. E., Williams, C. A. and Ganapathi, J. 2007 Putting the s back in Corporate Social Responsibility: A Multilevel Theory of Social Change in Organizations. Academy of Management Review, 32 (3), 836-863.
2. Basu, K. and Palazzo, G. 2008 Corporate Social Responsibility: A Process Model of Sensemaking. Academy of Management Review, 33 (1), 122-136. Accounting, Organizations and Society.
3. Futures – Example: Warhurst, J. 2005 Future Roles of Business in Society. Futures 37 (2-3) 151-168.
4. Harvard Business Review.
5. International Affairs – Example Article: Blowfield, M. and Frynas, J. 2005 Setting New Agendas : Critical Perspectives on Corporate Social Responsibility in the Developing World. International Affairs 81 499-513.
6. Journal of Management Studies – Occasionally has Special Issues on Corporate Social Responsibility, for Instance 43 (1) January 2006. Example Article: McWilliams, A., Siegel, D. and Wright, P. 2006 Corporate Social Responsibility: Strategic Implications. Journal of Management Studies, 43 (1) 1-18.
7. New York Times Magazine – Which ran Milton Freidman's Famous Article The Social Responsibility of Business is to Increase its Profits, September 13 1970. Strategic Management Journal.

**III. Online magazines:**

1. Business Ethics Magazine http://www.business-ethics.com/
2. Corporate Social Responsibility Newswire http://www.csrwire.com/
3. Ethical Corporation http://www.ethicalcorporation.com/

**Websites:**

1. http://www.iocl.com/Aboutus/corporatesocialresponsibility.aspx
2. http://timesfoundation.indiatimes.com/articleshow/4662536.cms
3. http://ebooks.cambridge.org/ebook.
4. http://en.wikipedia.org/wiki/Corporate_social_responsibility
5. http://www.greenleaf-publishing.com
6. http://www.bl.uk/reshelp/findhelpsubject/socsci/topbib/csr/csr.pdf
7. www.itcportal.com
8. www.coca-colaindia.com

# Corporate Social Responsibility Facilitates Customer Relationship

Dr. C. Eugine Franco

In modern business, especially in a country like India where mixed economy is prevailing, any business is bound to have a lot of responsibilities towards the different sectors of the society. The obligation which the business houses have towards the different parts of the society is known as social responsibility of a business. The corporate social responsibilities (CSRs) are: responsibility towards the employees, customers, government, suppliers, owners and other investors and the society as a whole.

CSR is connected with treating the stakeholders of the firm ethically or in a socially responsible manner. Stakeholders exist both within a firm and outside. The aim of the social responsibility is to create higher and higher standards of living, while preserving the profitability of the corporation for its stakeholders, both within and outside the corporation.

The Indian business scenario presents a varied type of CSR focus. There are companies who definitely allocate time and financial resources towards CSR activities year after year, whereas, there are others who totally ignore this aspect. The customer is the focal point of business. In fact, the whole organization exists because of its customers. Needless to say, it is imperative that the company must fulfill its responsibilities towards the customer. The basis for the continuity of relationship between the company and the customer over a period of time is value maximization.

Maximizing customer value means cultivating long-term customer relationships. Companies are now moving away from wasteful mass marketing to precision marketing designed to build strong customer relationships. Today's economy is supported by information businesses. Information has the advantages of being easy differentiate, customize, personalize and dispatch over networks at incredible speed.

Customer Relationship Management (CRM) is the process of carefully managing detailed information about individual customers and all customer "touch points" to maximize customer loyalty. A customer touch point is any occasion on which a customer encounters the brand and product- from actual experience to personal or mass communications to casual observation. For a hotel, the touch points include reservations, check-in and check-out, frequent-stay programs, room service, business services, exercise facilities, laundry service, restaurants and bars.

A responsible entrepreneur's first and foremost concern is not making profit but building better customer relationship. In the modern corporate world which is characterized by highly dynamic, complex and competitive, winning customers' confidence towards a business house has greater significance and too difficult. Of the several promotional strategies like advertising, personal selling, sales promotion, packaging, public relations and publicity, the last two elements are more significant. The primary business of any business enterprise is customer retention. An enterprise could retain and enhance its customer base only by satisfying the expectations of its customers as to all the four Ps of goods marketing namely Product, Price, Place and Promotion. A corporate's social responsibility heavily relies upon marketing a right product, at a fair price, through proper distribution channels and by due promotional strategies. Further , in the case of services marketing along with the above said four Ps the additional three Ps such as pleasing People, appropriate Process and proper Physical evidences are of great use in satisfying the expectations of the customers.

A satisfied customer speaks well of the corporate's product and trade practices. Conversely, an unsatisfied customer speaks ill of the enterprise. Thus, word of mouth promotion i.e. publicity plays a vital role in Customer Relationship Management (CRM). An enterprise that operates under the 'societal marketing concept' does market only those goods and services which ensure provision of customer satisfaction and promotion of social well-being. Such enterprise has Corporate Social Responsibility (CSR) as an integral part of its total marketing system. Further, such enterprise applies the concept of CSR in all its aspects and endeavours. Accordingly, CSR and CRM are complementary and supplementary to each other. An enterprise that duly discharges its social responsibility eventually manages customer relationship effectively.

It is reported that TATA Steel earmarks 12-14 per cent of their profit after tax for welfare activities; for the spread of computer education alone, INTEL Corporation Spends about $100 million every year; and Gujarat Ambuja Cements Ltd. has restored 3979 wells which benefited 3940 farmers.

All these CSR initiatives and activities indeed lead to increased reputation in the public about these corporations. Further, these CSR initiatives and activities develop deep relationship between the corporations and their stakeholders such as customers, employees and investors. The CSR initiatives that have been taken by the Microsoft Bill Gates and by the philanthropist Warren Buffet are the evidences of CSR facilitates CRM. Recently, the founder chair person of Wipro Technologies Mr. Azim Premji has announced that 1300 schools are going to be set up across the nation for the development of the country. This CSR initiative builds better image about Wipro Technologies in the minds of both the present and potential customers. Thus, it is evident that CSR facilitates CRM.

## REFERENCES

1. Business Environment, 2nd edition, Namita Gopal, Tata McGraw Hill Education Private Ltd., New Delhi.
2. Marketing Management, Philip Kotler, 13th edition, Pearson Education, New Delhi.

# Corporate Social Responsibility

## *A Sustainable Business Approach*

**Dr. M. Julias Ceasar**

Organizations have developed a variety of strategies for dealing with the intersection of societal needs, the natural environment, and corresponding business imperatives. At one end of the continuum are organizations that do not acknowledge any responsibility to society and the environment. And on the other end of the continuum are those organizations that view their operations as having a significant impact as well as reliance on society at the economic, social, and ecological levels. Thus a variety of strategies, alliances and partner-ships, and approaches are being used around the globe to respond to issues of CSR. The aspiration of many corporations to contribute to a better world is great, but translating that aspiration into reality remains a challenge for organizations at the global level.

Corporate responsibility or sustainability is therefore a prominent fea-ture of the business and society literature, addressing topics of business ethics, corporate social performance, global corporate citizenship, and stakeholder management. Redefined management practice can be an important source of new ideas about shifting toward an integrated rather than fractured knowledge. It means that the role and meaning of socially responsible leader-ship needs to be updated with a clear understanding of what is required, both in leadership itself and in the field of leadership development.

### Approaches to Implementing CSR

The first theme focuses on why CSR gets started in or-ganizations and how it is or can be well implemented. As to why CSR gets started, some argues that CSR can be seen as either an integral part of the business strategy and corporate identity, it can be used as a defensive policy, with the latter being used more often by companies targeted by ac-tivists. The rationale for CSR can be based on a moral argument, a rational argument or an economic argument is representative of a group of studies that create testable propositions related to the conditions under which organizations will move toward CSR. Experts see corporations' level of social responsibility as being influenced by factors such as financial conditions of the firm, health of the economy, and well-enforced state regulations.

Why companies take on CSR is discussed in terms of the specific initiatives under which CSR may fall. Ways of describing these rationales vary, from the more sceptical view of cause-related marketing to a more generous attribution of genuine socially responsible business practices. To ascertain how CSR is implemented in organizations, an analysis of a developmental framework is carried to show change in awareness, strategy, and action over time, and posits stages of CSR from elementary to transforming take more of a how-to approach, offering a principle-based framework for mastering what is called as a "new rules of the game." Examples of principles include harness-ing innovation for the public good, putting people at the centre, and spreading economic opportunity.

(*a*) **Drivers of On-going Commitment:** On-going commitment can derive from either economic self-interest (i.e., a solid business case) or from ethical grounding (i.e., the moral impor-tance of sustainable development). Oftentimes, of course, both of these apply. Value addition is considered to be significant and positive aspect of building the business case for CSR, much effort has focused on CSR in an attempt to demonstrate that positive CSR can be linked to improved financial perfor-mance. There is a growing sense that looking after the people and the commu-nity as well as the environment are all relevant to long-term business survival. Though the business case for CSR appears strong, it also reflects the fact that there are doubts as well as cynicism.

A good example of the contrast between CSR as business case and CSR as ethical issue. In its cross-cultural analysis of communication of CSR activities in U.S. and European corporations, there is a demonstration that U.S. companies justify CSR using economics or bottom-line terms and arguments in their communi-cations, whereas European Union companies rely more heavily on language or the theories of citizenship, corporate accountability, or moral commitment. Results also indicate that European companies do not value sustainability to the exclusion of financial elements, but instead project sustainability commit-ment in addition to financial commitment. U.S. companies focus more heavily on financial justifications, whereas European Union companies incorporate both financial and sustainability elements in justifying their CSR. European companies have a leading role in the CSR movement as a sustainable development opportunity. One source of on-going CSR commitment is focused on the need for corporations to take an active role in poverty reduction efforts. This often concludes with a call for a more explicit acknowledgement of poverty in the corporate citizenship field and for corporate leadership, it in such a way as to accelerate its reduction, and take an active role in poverty reduction efforts. Companies must push to seek something other than the lowest short-term cost for the highest short-term gain. Misconceptions and inaccurate assumptions exist about business opportunities and profitability available at the bottom of the economic pyramid. By serving the poor, business can gain new sources of rapid revenue growth and greater efficiencies with cost reduction initiatives for the multinational corporations, which also translates to increased purchasing power for the local consumers, as well as access to innovation.

**(*b*) Corporate Identity and Ethics:** The key attributes that define a company's essential character and the contemporary turn to values reflect an evolution in what has sometimes been called the personality of the corporation—or the corporation's identity (Paine, 2003). Corporate identity reflects what a company really is, rather than what a company might advocate. Many companies have established a corporate identity using branding, which has become a focal point of their success and competitive advantage. These stances helped differentiate the firm's offerings and made responsibility figure prominently in its corporate identity in the minds of consumers.

According to Archie Carroll (1991), a firm's pyramid of CSR starts with economic responsibilities and continues with legal, ethical, and discretionary responsibilities respectively. However, what was ethical or even discretionary in Carroll's model is becoming increasingly necessary today because of the changing environment within which businesses operate and because the ethical responsibilities are more likely to stand on par with economic and legal responsibilities as foundational for business success. CSR can be a way of matching corporate operations with societal values at a time when these parameters are changing rapidly. As such, ethical behaviour is a prerequisite for strategic CSR. A company's ethical behaviour is the mirror image of its culture, a shared set of values and guiding principles deeply ingrained throughout the organization, and the ethical behaviour and culture become part of the definition of corporate identity.

**(*c*) CSR and Accountability:** Accountability is one of the processes whereby a leader, company, or organization seeks to ensure integrity. In a global stakeholder society, accountability is among the key challenges of organizations. Responsible leaders are concerned with reconciling and aligning the demands, needs, interests, and values of employees, customers, suppliers, communities, shareholders, nongovernmental organizations (NGOs), the environment, and society at large. A company's track record in terms of CSR accounting will be effective when appropriate CSR measures are included in its internal as well as its supplychain activities. Furthermore, it must reflect a growing need for dissemination of good practice in CSR accountability and a need for more pressure to be exerted on NGOs to prove themselves as ethical, transparent, and accountable as those they seek to influence.

A relevant point raised in some study has to do with the effectiveness of strategies undertaken by communities to demand corporate accountability. It further argues that the success of community-based strategies for corporate accountability is conditional upon the right combination of state, civil, societal, and corporate factors. Accountability is more than making false promises. In the oil, gas, and mining sectors, despite the promise of CSR and the spending of over US $500 million in 2001 alone on a long list of community development programs and other CSR initiatives, the effectiveness of the initiatives has been increasingly questioned. There is mounting evidence of a gap between the stated intentions of business leaders and their actual behaviour and impact in the real world of financial funding.

CSR requires accountability by all leaders, individuals, organizations, stakeholders, customers, and community members, and yet accountability is complex. The factors which influence the effectiveness of corporate accountability are multiple and tightly interconnected. This interconnectedness and its relationship to accountability are represented by experts, which uses the idea of considering a business as an interconnected web of relationships, with the consequences of every action the company takes having an impact on both the world and the company's long-term business.

**(*d*) Partnering with Stakeholders:** CSR is strictly embedded with a multitude of business actors. With the call for sustainability and the new role of business in society, and with increased expectations and new rules and tactics, leadership is bound to come into contact—and conflict—with key stakeholders in the arena of responsible business, global versus regional and local needs, and different national cultures. Although companies strive to engage in CSR together with their stakeholders, they are simultaneously struggling to understand the true relationship behind this and first of all, who their stakeholders are. In both the business and academic literature, the shareholders are now renamed as one of many key stakeholders, and they are seen as competing for influence with employees, customers, consumers, suppliers, competitors, trade unions, the environment, the local communities, and the society at large, to name a few and the most recurrent ones. Two basic relationship models may help to explain how leaders can best interact with multiple and diverse stakeholders. The insideout approach suggests that leaders can manage their CSR activities and achieve favourable reputations with their stakeholders by building CSR activities across the country.

Corporate Social Responsibility and Sustainable Business boundaries and in a framework where the decision-making point resides inside the organization and where communication with stakeholders is a means to deliver information already developed and perhaps even implemented. CSR reporting for stakeholders can be one such practice and has sometimes been used as a tool in the marketing communicator's toolbox. This can backfire, feeding scepticism toward CSR and its terminology from trade unions as well as from the activist opposition. An alternative approach is based on substantial attention and engagement with the stakeholders to reach CSR goals. Communication is not just a device for alignment; the decision-making process is negotiated and concepts or key actions developed. The stakeholders in this model are actors, together with the company, in achieving sustainable development. This differentiation is similar to that seen in others that focus on the difference between stakeholder identity the extent to which the corporations and their stakeholders' interests are linked and stakeholder management the incorporation of stakeholders' interests into operational decision making. Despite the debate, real stakeholder engagement ultimately leads to a combination of organizational and social learning, which is a basis for long-term change based on trust, but which is not always clearly quantifiable or predictable in the short term.

Whatever the approach to stakeholders, well-intentioned efforts sometimes produce disappointing results, or conflicting stakeholder demands cause problems. Nevertheless, leadership efforts to deal rationally with stakeholders, with uncertainty, and with constraints lead to greater potential for sustainability in terms of culture, structure, and output. Corporations need to engage with stakeholders to develop valuable CSR-related actions. Stakeholders face challenges and threats that are more likely to partner with corporations on CSR-related issues and corporations and stakeholders are more likely to succeed when a longterm vision is embraced. The corporate leadership should have a holistic approach to engage with stakeholders and that the vital link between business and stakeholder management is leadership.

**(*e*) Leadership Capabilities and Competencies:** The pivotal role of leadership is initiating and developing CSR programs and initiatives within and across organizations. Leaders in the world of business are the first true planetary citizens, they have worldwide capability and responsibility and their decisions affect economies as well as societies. The role of the leader in guiding business toward sustainable social responsibility is complex and vast, and it has been alleged that it requires a unique array of leadership skills and competencies. A change in management thinking has been from process to people. Leadership styles and leadership capabilities and competencies most prevalent among leaders whose organizations have successfully experienced changes in organizational strategy and focus, transitioned towards and achieve more socially responsible behaviours.

Responsible leaders are defined as people of the highest integrity and deep understanding of difficult concepts such as sustainable development, committed to building enduring organizations in association with others, leaders who have a deep sense of purpose and are true to their core values. Leaders of socially responsible organizations have been associated with the charismatic leadership style; the connection between top managers and firm outcomes depends to a large extent on the managers' charismatic leadership under conditions of perceived environmental uncertainty. Charismatic leadership style communicates an innovative vision, energizes others to innovate, and accelerates innovation processes and CSR; interactive leadership characteristically empowers employees to innovate and to become innovation leaders themselves. The transformational leader is able to communicate so enthusiastically that the result is pulling people to commit to the vision of the leader on sustainability. Some effective organizational models for CSR, however, support a simultaneous transformational and visionary leadership style, together with a need for transparency. Moreover, CEOs' intellectual stimulation is found to be significantly associated with the propensity of the firm to engage in strategic CSR or those CSR activities that are most likely to be related to the firm's corporate and business-level strategies.

Leadership competencies consistent with "responsible" leaders include courage, business acumen, passion, having a life ("you can't think out of the box if you are always in the box"), compassion, sense of humour, and vision for legacy (instead of vision for activity). A leader should be remembered as a person who is designed a society that is educated, environmentally friendly, safe, and economically sustainable. Other leadership attributes are related to sustainable social success and leaders' values such as integrity, teamwork, respect, and professionalism are part of global responsible leadership. The success is attributed to leaders' relentless focus on clients, continuous communication of values and beliefs, a large amount of engaging with others, accountability, and reliability (van de Loo, 2006), as well as a long-term perspective.

The challenge for today's leaders is to perform effectively in an environment of uncertainty and ambiguity while reconciling the diversity of interests, needs, and demands of multiple stakeholders. When the question is how the CSR concept can be locked into corporate DNA, the conclusion would be that the issue is less about sustainability with a big *S* and more about leadership with a big *L*.

*(f)* **Organizational Challenges and Limitations:** Companies face challenges and limitations as they implement CSR. These usually relate either to political issues or to organizational-level concerns and are often embedded in culture. The complexity of operating in a global society places new demands on organizations and their leadership.

As the roles and responsibilities of government are being redefined and the boundaries between business and government become less clear, the business leaders are facing a daunting array of challenges. In the new age of

CSR, the needs of the stakeholders, consumers, employees, national as well as international regulators, watchdogs, NGOs, and activist groups have to be satisfied (Hatcher, 2002). It identifies the opportunities and limitations of CSR. The CSR rhetoric including the blurred boundaries of CSR, the under development of the civic society, the economic reality, the ethical standards, and the attempts at self-regulation of business considers the biggest challenge in the field of CSR implementation to be the development of leaders for a sustainable global society, asking what kind of leader is needed for building a sustainable global society and how best can develop individuals with these leadership capabilities. The task and challenge will be to develop leaders for a sustainable global society by encouraging imagination and the accomplishment of a positive change.

Leadership is the art of building and sustaining relationships with all relevant stakeholders, and it requires socialized, not personalized, leaders. Here, the challenge is to develop leaders who can relate in different ways, who are able to align different values into a common vision, who can listen to and care for others and ultimately serve them. Meeting these challenges requires the joint efforts of a global society and responsible leadership committed to diversity, ethics, and values.

## Conclusion

There is a growing awareness that business needs to manage its relationship with the wider society. Corporate leaders are responsible for their corporations' impact on society and the natural environment beyond legal compliance and the liability of individuals. To the novice, this annotated bibliography offers a short but nevertheless deep introduction to the field. More experienced leaders can gain new perspectives on how to grow in their approach to sustainability and how to develop innovative business models in accordance with the triple bottom line (TBL) namely the society, environment and business.

CSR is becoming a leading principle of top management and of entrepreneurs. The number of observations in research in this field clearly delineated models, leadership competencies, accountability, and structure of partnerships as well as organizational challenges and limitations and ethics. Organizations can reexamine their pattern of behaviours in the TBL framework and begin their journey toward a sustainable approach that is integrated into their business strategy.

# Corporate Social Responsibility

## *Issues and Challenges in India*

F.X. Robert Bellarmine

### Introduction

In a societal structure, we have many stakeholders, one amongst them are companies or Corporate Houses. These Corporate houses are meaningfully contributing from their kitty which impact their internal stakeholders and also openhandedly support societal initiatives. In India companies like TATA and Birla are practicing the Corporate Social Responsibility (CSR) for decades, long before CSR become a popular basis. There are many instances where corporate have played a dominant role in addressing issues of education, health, environment and livelihoods through their corporate social responsibility interventions across the country. As per United Nations and the European Commission, Corporate Social Responsibility (CSR) leads to triple bottom-line: profits, protection of environment and fight for social justice. It is expected that Civil society, activist groups, Government and corporate sectors should work together to create appropriate means and avenues for the marginalized and bring them to the mainstream. The success of CSR lies in practicing it as a core part of a company's development strategy. It is important for the corporate sector to identify, promote and implement successful policies and practices that achieve triple bottom-line results.[1]

At one end of the spectrum, CSR can be viewed simply as a collection of good citizenship activities being engaged by various organizations. At the other end, it can be a way of doing business that has significant impact on society. For this latter vision to be enacted in India, it will be necessary to build CSR into a movement. That is to say, public and private organizations will need to come together to set standards, share best practices, jointly promote CSR, and pool resources where useful. An alliance of interested stakeholders will be able to take collective action to establish CSR as an integral part of doing business—this is not a passing fad. There are more than 1,000,000 registered companies in India out of which less than 1 per cent companies are traded on the Indian Stock Exchange. A new Trend has started in Corporate is the establishment of special committees within the board of directors to oversee CSR activities. Groups of corporate are being encouraged to come together to promote CSR. In 2006, Europe created the European Alliance for CSR. It currently consists of 70 multinational corporate houses and 25 national partner organizations and has become a unique resource for building capability in CSR.[2]

### Definition of CSR

The well accepted definition of CSR is not a common term; MNC's prefers sustainable development or sustainable business while several Indian companies talk about responsible business or Triple P (People, Planet, and Profit). It is important to note that Indian companies and stakeholders give a broader definition of CSR then MNC and stakeholders. According to the Indian Corporate: "Sustainable development implies optimizing financial position while not depleting social and environmental aspects and CSR implies supporting issues related to children, women and environment".

These corporate refer in its definition of CSR to community development. In the context of Western community, development is often seen as charity. In the Indian context it is seen as a large responsibility of a corporate, not only by stakeholders but also by the local Indian management. The background of this is that stakeholders see the large western companies as capitalist islands in a developing country. This position gives them a certain responsibility towards the community. Most of the MNC's leave room to their Indian daughter company to develop initiatives in this field; sometimes they have a special fund. All kinds of initiatives are developed by the interviewed Indian companies, many times bottom up initiated by the employees.

Nearly all leading corporate in India are involved in corporate social responsibility (CSR) programs in areas like education, health, livelihood creation, skill development, and empowerment of weaker sections of the society.

### Issues and Challenges

Many companies think that corporate social responsibility is a peripheral issue for their business and customer satisfaction more important for them. They imagine that customer satisfaction is now only about price and service, but they fail to point out on important changes that are taking place worldwide that could blow the business out of the water. The change is named as social responsibility which is an opportunity for the business.

Some of the drivers pushing business towards CSR include:

*The Shrinking Role of Government:* In the past, governments have relied on legislation and regulation to deliver social and environmental objectives in the business sector. Shrinking government resources, coupled with a distrust of regulations, has led to the exploration of voluntary and non-regulatory initiatives instead.

*Demands for Greater Disclosure:* There is a growing demand for corporate disclosure from stakeholders, including customers, suppliers, employees, communities, investors, and activist organizations.

*Increased Customer Interest:* There is evidence that the ethical conduct of companies exerts a growing influence on the purchasing decisions of customers. In a recent survey by Environics International, more than one in five consumers reported having either rewarded or punished companies based on their perceived social performance.

*Growing Investor Pressure:* Investors are changing the way they assess companies' performance, and are making decisions based on criteria that include ethical concerns. The Social Investment Forum reports that in the US in 1999, there was more than $2 trillion worth of assets invested in portfolios that used screens linked to the environment and social responsibility. A separate survey by Environics International revealed that more than a quarter of share-owning Americans took into account ethical considerations when buying and selling stocks.

*Competitive Labour Markets:* Employees are increasingly looking beyond paychecks and benefits, and seeking out employers whose philosophies and operating practices match their own principles. In order to hire and retain skilled employees, companies are being forced to improve working conditions.

*Supplier Relations:* As stakeholders are becoming increasingly interested in business affairs, many companies are taking steps to ensure that their partners conduct themselves in a socially responsible manner. Some are introducing codes of conduct for their suppliers, to ensure that other companies' policies or practices do not tarnish their reputation.

## Challenges

*Lack of Community Participation in CSR Activities:* There is a lack of interest of the local community in participating and contributing to CSR activities of companies. This is largely attributable to the fact that there exists little or no knowledge about CSR within the local communities as no serious efforts have been made to spread awareness about CSR and instil confidence in the local communities about such initiatives. The situation is further aggravated by a lack of communication between the company and the community at the grassroots.

*Need to Build Local Capacities:* There is a need for capacity building of the local non-governmental organizations as there is serious dearth of trained and efficient organizations that can effectively contribute to the ongoing CSR activities initiated by companies. This seriously compromises scaling up of CSR initiatives and subsequently limits the scope of such activities.

***Issues of Transparency:*** Lack of transparency is one of the key issues brought forth by the survey. There is an expression by the companies that there exists lack of transparency on the part of the local implementing agencies as they do not make adequate efforts to disclose information on their programs, audit issues, impact assessment and utilization of funds. This reported lack of transparency negatively impacts the process of trust building between companies and local communities, which is a key to the success of any CSR initiative at the local level.

***Non-availability of Well Organized Non-governmental Organizations:*** It is also reported that there is non-availability of well organized nongovernmental organizations in remote and rural areas that can assess and identify real needs of the community and work along with companies to ensure successful implementation of CSR activities. This also builds the case for investing in local communities by way of building their capacities to undertake development projects at local levels.

***Visibility Factor:*** The role of media in highlighting good cases of successful CSR initiatives is welcomed as it spreads good stories and sensitizes the local population about various ongoing CSR initiatives of companies. This apparent influence of gaining visibility and branding exercise often leads many nongovernmental organizations to involve themselves in event-based programs; in the process, they often miss out on meaningful grassroots interventions.

***Narrow Perception towards CSR Initiatives:*** Non-governmental organizations and Government agencies usually possess a narrow outlook towards the CSR initiatives of companies, often defining CSR initiatives more donor-driven than local in approach. As a result, they find it hard to decide whether they should participate in such activities at all in medium and long run.

***Non-availability of Clear CSR Guidelines:*** There are no clear cut statutory guidelines or policy directives to give a definitive direction to CSR initiatives of companies. It is found that the scale of CSR initiatives of companies should depend upon their business size and profile. In other words, the bigger the company, the bigger is its CSR program.

***Lack of Consensus on Implementing CSR Issues:*** There is a lack of consensus amongst local agencies regarding CSR projects. This lack of consensus often results in duplication of activities by corporate houses in areas of their intervention. This results in a competitive spirit between local implementing agencies rather than building collaborative approaches on issues. This factor limits company's abilities to undertake impact assessment of their initiatives from time to time.

## Recommendations

In order to crystal gaze the future of CSR in India and take time bound steps to mainstream it, the recommendations of the survey are firm indications of the existing state of affairs in the CSR domain; they correspondingly call for necessary and appropriate steps to be initiated to put CSR on firmer ground. Keeping in view the broad results of the survey, the following recommendations are listed for serious consideration by all concerned stakeholders for their effective operationalization to deepen CSR in the company's core business and to build collaborative relationships and effective networks with all involved.

There is a need for creation of awareness about CSR amongst the general public to make CSR initiatives more effective. This awareness generation can be taken up by various stakeholders including the media to highlight the good work done by corporate houses in this area. This will bring about effective changes in the approach and attitude of the public towards CSR initiatives undertaken by corporate houses. This effort will also motivate other corporate houses to join the league and play an effective role in addressing issues such as access to education, health care and livelihood opportunities for a large number of people in India through their innovative CSR practices. Thus, the social justice agenda of the day would be fulfilled more meaningfully.

Appropriate steps be undertaken to address the issue of building effective bridges amongst all important stakeholders for the successful implementation of CSR initiatives. As a result, a long term and sustainable perspective on CSR activities should be built into the existing and future strategies of all stakeholders involved in CSR initiatives.

Only medium and large corporate houses are involved in CSR activities, that too in selected geographical areas. This issue builds a case for more companies to be brought under the CSR domain. To address the issue of reaching out to wider geographical areas, the involvement of small and medium enterprises (SMEs) in the CSR domain will be essential. It is recommended that a campaign should be launched to both spread awareness on CSR issues amongst the general public as well as to involve SMEs to participate more actively in CSR initiatives. This will help CSR reach out to other locations and cover a large number of communities and help companies play a valuable role in addressing various social and development issues. This approach will help CSR get ingrained into the DNA of core business activities of companies.

Corporate houses and non-governmental organizations should actively consider pooling their resources and building synergies to implement best CSR practices to scale up projects and innovate new ones to reach out to more beneficiaries. This will increase the impact of their initiatives on the lives of the common people. After all, both corporate houses and non-governmental organizations stand to serve the people through their respective projects and initiatives. It is recommended that the projectisation, scaling up and sustainability of CSR projects need to be safeguarded at all costs for their efficiency and efficacy.

Many CSR initiatives and programs are taken up in urban areas and localities. As a result, the impact of such projects does not reach the needy and the poor in the rural areas. This does not mean that there are no poor and needy in urban India; they too equally suffer from want of basic facilities and services. While focusing on urban areas, it is recommended that companies should also actively consider their interventions in rural areas on education, health, girl child and child labor as this will directly benefit rural people. After all, more than 70 per cent people still reside in rural India.

Government should consider rewarding and recognizing corporate houses and their partner non-governmental organizations implementing projects that effectively cover the poor and the underprivileged. Incentives to be offered to the private sector to strengthen their good work must include a formal partnership with local administration, easy grant of 12A, 80G and Foreign Contribution Regulation Act (FCRA) license and other fiscal incentives including matching project grants and tax breaks for social and development projects. This will be instrumental in encouraging enhanced voluntary participation of greater number of corporate houses in CSR activities.

CSR as a subject or discipline should be made compulsory at business schools and in colleges and universities to sensitize students about social and development issues and the role of CSR in helping corporate houses strike a judicious balance between their business and societal concerns. Such an approach will encourage and motivate young minds, prepare them face future development challenges and help them work towards finding more innovative solutions to the concerns of the needy and the poor. It is recommended that involvement of professionals from the corporate sector, on Governmental organizations and business schools would be key in ensuring youth participation in civic issues.

## Conclusion

The concept of corporate social responsibility is now firmly rooted on the global business agenda. But in order to move from theory to concrete action, many obstacles need to be overcome. A key challenge facing business is the need for more reliable indicators of progress in the field of CSR, along with the dissemination of CSR strategies. Transparency and dialogue can help to make a business appear more trustworthy, and push up the standards of other organizations at the same time.

**Acknowledgement**

*This research paper is based on the book "Corporate Social Responsibility Practices in India, Times Foundation , the corporate social responsibility wing of the Bennett, Coleman & CO. Ltd.* in partnership with *TNS India* and *IRRAD* undertook a national survey to understand the underlying dynamics of CSR and the current situation in India.

**Glossary**

*ACCSR - Australian Canadian Corporate Social Responsibility*

*ASR - Asian Sustainability Ranking*

*CSR - Corporate Social Responsibility*

*CREM - Consultancy and Research for Environmental Management*

*FCRA - Foreign Contribution Regulation Act*

*ILO - International Labor Organization*

*MNC - Multinational Companies*

*NGOs - Non-governmental organizations*

*PSU - Public sector undertakings*

*SAP - System Application & Products*

*SRI - Socially Responsible Investment*

*TNC - Transnational Companies*

*UN - United Nation*

## REFERENCES

1. Dr. Suri Sehgal, Chairman & Founder Institute of Rural Research & Development (IRRAD) Gurgaon.
2. Professor Leo Burke, Associate Dean and Director, Executive Education, Notre Dame University,USA.
3. CREM-Report, nr. 03.650.
4. Indian Brand Equity Foundation, www.ibef.org.
5. ACCSR's State of CSR in Australia Annual Review 2010/11.
6. http://www.chillibreeze.com/articles_various/CSR-in-India.asp.
7. International Conference on Technology and Business Management March 28-30, 2011.

# Corporate Social Responsibility a Tool for Business Sustainability

J. Mexon P. Rayan

## Introduction

The role of business man by and large has been understood in terms of a commercial business paradigm of thinking that focuses purely on economic parameters of success. As corporate have been regarded as institutions that cater to the market demand by providing products and services and have the onus for creating wealth and jobs, their market position has traditionally been a function of financial performance and profitability. However, over the past few years, as a consequence of rising globalisation and pressing ecological issues, the perception of the role of corporate in the broader societal context within which it operates, has been altered. Stakeholders (employees, community, suppliers and shareholders) today are redefining the role of corporate taking into account the corporate' broader responsibility towards society and environment, beyond economic performance, and are evaluating whether they are conducting their role in an ethical and socially responsible manner.

As a result of this shift (from purely economic to 'economic with an added social dimension'), many forums, institutions and corporate are endorsing the term Corporate Social Responsibility (CSR). They use the term to define organisation's commitment to the society and the environment within which it operates. The World Business Council on Sustainable Development's (WBCSD) report was titled Corporate Social Responsibility: Making Good Business Sense and the OECD Guidelines for Multinational Enterprises which includes a discussion on how CSR is emerging as a global business standard. Further, there is a global effort towards reinforcing CSR programmes and initiatives through local and international schemes that try to identify best-in-class performers.

In today's competitive global market, companies aspire to be more socially responsible as well as sustainable and comparatively less worried about maximizing profits, sustainability being seen itself as an achievement. An increasing number of companies are requiring teams that can virtually, performing without the regional boundaries. The issues related to the software project management in multi-cultural and multi-location teams are not always visible to many but they definitely exist. Factors enhancing the need for CSR identified by Boston College (2005) are:

- Globalization and the associated growth in Competition
- Increased size and influence of companies
- Retrenchment/repositioning of government and its Roles
- War for talent; companies competing for expertise
- Growth of global civil society activism
- Increased importance of intangible assets.

### What is Corporate Social Responsibility?

The term "corporate social responsibility" came into common use in the late 1960s and early 1970s after many multinational corporations formed the term stakeholders, meaning those on whom an organization's activities have an impact. It was used to describe corporate owners beyond shareholders as a result of an influential book by R. Edward Freeman Strategic management: a stakeholder approach in 1984. Proponents argue that corporations make more long term profits by operating with a perspective, while critics argue that CSR distracts from the economic role of businesses. Others argue CSR is merely window-dressing, or an attempt to preempt the role of governments as a watchdog over powerful multinational corporations.

According to Philip Kotler and Nancy Lee (2005) define CSR as "a commitment to improve community well being through business practices and contributions of corporate resources" whereas Mallen Baker refers to CSR as "a way companies manage the business processes to produce an overall positive impact on society". According to World Business Council for Sustainable Development "Corporate Social Responsibility is the continuing commitment by business to behave ethically and contribute to economic development while improving the quality of life of the workforce and their families as well as of the local community and society at large".

The term is often used interchangeably for other terms such as Corporate Citizenship and is also linked to the concept of Triple Bottom Line Reporting (TBL), which is used as a framework for measuring an organization's performance against economic, social and environmental parameters. The rationale for CSR has been articulated in a number of ways. In essence it is about building sustainable businesses, which need healthy economies, markets and communities.

The key drivers for CSR are:

- **Enlightened self-interest** - creating a synergy of ethics, a cohesive society and a sustainable global economy where markets, labour and communities are able to function well together.
- **Social investment** - contributing to physical infrastructure and social capital is increasingly seen as a necessary part of doing business.
- **Transparency and trust** - business has low ratings of trust in public perception. There is increasing expectation that companies will be more open, more accountable and be prepared to report publicly on their performance in social and environmental arenas.
- **Increased public expectations of business** - globally companies are expected to do more than merely provide jobs and contribute to the economy through taxes and employment."

### Corporate Sustainability and CSR

Corporate sustainability is a business approach that creates long-term consumer and employee value by not only creating a "green" strategy aimed towards the natural environment, but taking into consideration every dimension of how a business operates in the social, cultural, and economic environment. Also formulating strategies to build a company that fosters longevity through transparency and proper employee development.

Corporate sustainability is an evolution on more traditional phrases describing ethical corporate practice. Phrases such as corporate social responsibility (CSR) or corporate citizenship continue to be used but are increasingly superseded by the broader term, corporate sustainability. Unlike the other phrases that focus on "added-on" policies, corporate sustainability describes business practices built around social and environmental considerations.

Sustainability refers to an organization's activities, typically considered voluntary, that dem-onstrate the inclusion of social and environmental concerns in business opera-tions and in interactions with stakeholders (van Marrewijk & Verre, 2003). It is no longer acceptable for a corporation to experience economic prosperity in isolation from those agents impacted by its actions. A firm must now focus its attention on both increasing its bottom line and being a good corporate citizen. Keeping abreast of global trends and remaining committed to financial obligations to deliver both private and public benefits have forced organizations to reshape their frameworks, rules, and business models. To understand and enhance current efforts, the most socially responsible organi-zations continue to revise their short- and long-term agendas, to stay ahead of rapidly changing challenges.

In addition, a stark and complex shift has occurred in how organizations must understand themselves in relation to a wide variety of both local and global stakeholders. The quality of relationships that a company has with its employees and other key stakeholders—such as customers, investors, suppliers, public and governmental officials, activists, and communities—is crucial to its success, as is its ability to respond to competitive conditions and corporate social responsibility (CSR). These major transformations require national and global companies to approach their business in terms of sustainable development, and both individual and organizational leadership plays a major role in this change.

Organizations have developed a variety of strategies for dealing with this intersection of societal needs, the natural environment and corresponding business imperatives. Organizations can also be considered on a developmental continuum with respect to how deeply and how well they are integrating social responsibility approaches into both strategy and daily operations worldwide. At one end of the continuum are organizations that do not acknowledge any responsibility to society and the environment. And on the other end of the continuum are those organizations that view their operations as having a significant impact as well as reliance on society at the economic, social and ecological levels, thus resulting in a sense of responsibility beyond the traditional boundaries of the organization. Most organizations can be placed somewhere in between.

Corporate responsibility or sustainability is therefore a prominent feature of the business and society literature, addressing topics of business ethics, corporate social performance, global corporate citizenship, and stakeholder management. Management education can be an important source of new ideas about shifting toward an integrated rather than fractured knowledge economy, but this means also that the role and meaning of socially responsible leadership needs to be updated. Much further research is needed to create a clearer understanding of what is required, both in leadership itself and in the field of leadership development.

## Role and Impact of CSR on Corporate Sustainability

CSR and corporate sustainability movements are building an impressive momentum with the support from governments and the investment community through Socially Responsible Investing (SRI) and associated corporate sustainability indexes. There is no doubt that businesses are doing far more than ever before to tackle the sustainability challenge by recognising their social responsibilities, reducing their environmental impacts, guarding against ethical compromises, creating governance transparency and becoming more accountable to their stakeholders. However, despite the progress achieved, CSR and corporate sustainability as business practiced approaches are at the infancy stage with relatively few real adopters and questionable impact.

On the positive side, success stories from responsible companies, for example the leading companies in SRI indexes, confirm that outstanding financial performance is not incompatible with good sustainability performance. The motivations of companies to address corporate responsibly and sustainability varies widely from instrumental approaches using responsible practices as a means of maximising profits to intrinsic approaches committing the company to upholding its values and principles irrespective of the impact on financial performance. The key business drivers are:

(*a*) Strong brand and reputation;

(*b*) Employer of choice;

(*c*) Market position;

(*d*) Trust of the financial markets and increased shareholder value;

(*e*) New 'green' products/services and new markets.

It is becoming clear that leading companies of the future will have missions and strategies to constantly increase shareholder value but as an integral part of those strategies will also and act upon the potential for:

- Addressing the interests of a broad range of stakeholders.
- Building societal value.
- Contributing to coalitions aimed at increasing the capacity for sustainable development.

As the business case for Corporate Responsibility and Sustainability is becoming clearer it is also becoming evident that it could take some time before Corporate Responsibility and Sustainability becomes part of mainstream business practice. It is widely recognised that implementation of Corporate Responsibility and Sustainability requires time to reach maturity and the speed of achieving mainstreaming is dependant on leadership, training and organisational capabilities to integrate CSR and sustainability policies in the overall business strategy and in core operational processes. Socially and environmentally responsible behaviour is multisided and is related to all functions, decisions and processes in a company. The width and complexity of the Corporate Responsibility and Sustainability scope makes mainstreaming a change management challenge necessitating carefully planning and possibly long term commitment to developing appropriate capabilities.

### Key Challenges in Corporate Responsibility and Sustainability Management

- Managing in an integrated manner the full lifecycle of CRS strategy formulation, implementation, evaluation and evolution incorporating stakeholder participation;
- Aligning responsibility strategy to corporate strategy focusing on:

Rationalizing and harmonizing the economic, compliance, ethical, and sustainability dimensions of corporate responsibility and sustainability in the context of stakeholder requirements;

Managing non-financial risk, particularly to brand, reputation, local license to operate and to performance instability as an integral part of corporate sustainability management.

Integrating eco-design and other sustainability requirements into product and service offerings:

- Managing the sustainability performance optimization process to continually increase stakeholder satisfaction;
- Developing strategic responsibility and sustainability capabilities

Corporate Responsibility and Sustainability as a company's verifiable commitment to operating in an economically, socially and environmentally sustainable manner that is transparent and increasingly satisfying to its stakeholders. Stakeholders include investors, customers, employees, business partners, local communities, the environment and society. The emphasis is on transparent and verifiable stakeholder driven business operation delivering optimized sustainability performance and associated competitive advantage.

Sustainable business operation means addressing the needs of present stakeholders while seeking to protect, support and enhance the human and natural resources that will be needed by future stakeholders.

## Conclusion

Corporate Social Responsibility has an undeniable effect on both society and businesses, but this practice depends on the companies availability to get involved which is at the discretion of the managers and shareholders. For a real satisfactory implementation of the Corporate Social Responsibility as well as the more specific challenges of corporate sustainability continue to be an elusive goal at the corporate management level. In this corporate world every concerns wants to sustain a long period in the market. Only with the help of adapting Corporate Social Responsible policies in their concern they attain this target, otherwise it is difficult in the modern business world. In today's competitive global market, companies aspire to be more socially responsible as well as sustainable and comparatively less worried about maximizing profits, sustainability being seen itself as an achievement. So, business concerns realized that in order to sustain a long period in their field they should adopt certain social responsibilities.

## REFERENCES

1. D Wood, 'Corporate Social Performance Revisited' (1991) 16(4) The Academy of Management Review.
2. ASOCIO policy paper on Corporate Social Responsibility, June 2004.
3. Theory of Corporate Social Responsibility: Its evolutionary path and the road ahead, by Boli and Hartsuikar, 2001.
4. Boston College Centre for Corporate CommunityRelations (2000), "Making the Business Case:Determining the Value of Corporate CommunityInvolvement".
5. Brundtland Commission, (1987), "Our CommonFuture".
6. www.managementmarketing.ro/pdf/articole/194.pdf
7. www.bus.wisc.edu/business-sustainability/resources/organizations
8. www.ccl.org/leadership/pdf

# The Role of Government in Developing Corporate Social Responsibility

A. Oliver

## Introduction

Corporate Social Responsibility (CSR) is a concept whereby Companies integrate social and environmental concerns in their business operations and in their interaction with their stakeholders on a voluntary basis. At the same meaning, 'a corporation's ultimate success can be measured not just by the traditional financial bottom line, but also by its social/ethical and environmental performance'. Corporation means do business and make a profit, they also assert that the only responsibility corporation has CSR in the interest of businesses, in particular when stakeholders such as employees, consumers, civil society organizations and governments demand and value the perspective efforts. The government plays an important role in shaping and promoting CSR in recent years, The government sees Corporate Restructuring as the business contribution to sustainable development goals and play an important role in setting standards in areas such as environmental protection, health & safety and employment rights. The government provides policy and institutional framework that stimulates companies to raise their performance beyond minimum legal standards.

***I. Reasons Why Governments Promote CSR:*** Governments care about promoting and fostering CSR to take full advantage of their strengths and abilities to compensate for the insufficient market and establish a good institutional foundation and external environment for CSR.

*(a) CSR enhance the regional and national competitiveness:* CSR can enhance the regional and national competitiveness. Zadek introduces the concept 'Corporate Responsibility Clusters' and divides it into challenge clusters, market-making clusters, partnership clusters and statutory clusters. He

proposes that Corporate Responsibility Clusters offer a pivotal mechanism for scaling up corporate responsibility practices through their effective integration into national and regional competitiveness strategies. Zadek concludes that generations of corporate responsibility, that are legal compliance, 1st Generation Non-strategic Corporate Responsibility, 2nd Generation Strategic Corporate Responsibility, and 3rd Generation Competitive Responsibility. CSR that connect to the national competitiveness belong to 3rd Generation Competitive Responsibility.

*(b) CSR contribute to achieving the sustainable development:* Sustainable development is a pattern of resource use that aims to meet human needs while preserving the environment so that these needs can be met not only in the present, but also for future generations. The term was used by the Brundtland Commission which coined what has become the most often-quoted definition of sustainable development as development that 'meets the needs of the present without compromising the ability of future generations to meet their own needs'. The field of sustainable development can be conceptually broken into three constituent parts: environmental sustainability, economic sustainability and sociopolitical sustainability. Some researchers view environmental and social challenges as opportunities for development action. This is particularly true in the concept of sustainable enterprise that frames these global needs as opportunities for private enterprise to provide innovative and entrepreneurial solutions. Company is the main body of modern economic and social development, and it need contact with the external environment in the production and management process. Social responsibility can promote company to adopt initiatively energy-saving and environmental protection technology, reduce consciously consumption of natural resources and pollution, and protect actively the ecological environment. Global Compact appeal the social responsibility that a company abide include the demand of sustainable development. Businesses should support a precautionary approach to environmental challenges, undertake initiatives to promote greater environmental responsibility and encourage the development and diffusion of environment friendly technologies.

*(c) CSR contribute to the realization of new social governance:* CSR is not simply a feature of the new global corporation but is also increasingly a feature of new societal governance. New governance and CSR in fact became two complementary concepts, both implying and prompting that the steering of societies is no longer a sole matter of governments, but rather one of all three societal domains working together through new governance arrangements. The government view CSR as the complement of the social policies and the innovation of the social governance. Through the use of social policies, government can enhance the equity and justice of the society and realize the social harmony. In other words, new governance and CSR both highlight 'the public role of private enterprises'.

***II. CSR and Sustainable Development:*** Globally, there is a transition from a planned economy to a market economy, there are still different opinions on awareness and understanding of CSR. Under the circumstance of sustainable development, CSR faces the following challenges:

(a) *Corporate development caused deterioration of ecological environment:* Corporate develop rapidly to enhance high economic returns, at the same time energy consumption is too high, the waste of resources and other issues is still serious. It began to outbreak frequently the water crisis and has sounded the alarm of environmental pollution.

(b) *Enterprise credit system needs to be developed:* The dishonesty of companies in the economic field is mainly due to defaulted loans, breach of contract, false advertising, fake and shoddy products, and quality fraud. Relevant survey of the departments of state shows that enterprises in arrears account for 80 per cent of the total number of enterprises, breach of contract account for 71 per cent, the tort account for 47 per cent, false information account for 31 per cent, fake and shoddy products account for 28 per cent and quality fraud account for 13 per cent.

***III. Public Policies to Foster CSR:*** The public sector roles in supporting CSR could be divided into four broad categories: mandating, facilitating, partnering, and endorsing. Mandating includes laws, regulations, penalties, and associated public sector institutions that relate to the control of some aspect of business investment or operations. Facilitating: Setting clear overall policy frameworks and positions to guide business investment in CSR, development of nonbinding guidance and labels or codes for application in the marketplace, laws and regulations that facilitate and provide incentives for business investment in CSR by mandating transparency or disclosure on various issues, tax incentives, investment in awareness raising and research, and facilitating processes of stakeholder dialogue. Partnering: Combining public resources with those of business and other actors to leverage complementary skills and resources to tackle issues within the CSR agenda, whether as participants, conveners, or catalysts. Endorsing: Showing public political support for particular kinds of CSR practice in the marketplace or for individual companies; endorsing specific award schemes or nongovernmental metrics, indicators, guidelines, and standards; and leading by example, such as through public procurement practices. Considering the real situation government should give priority to the following policies.

(a) *Raise CSR Awareness:* Government should raise CSR awareness among companies, consumers, investors and civil society organizations. When companies are aware of CSR that are the obligations they should do, they will be willing to do it from the heart. Only when the consumers and investors realize that CSR relate to the sustainable development of national economy and the benefit themselves, they will give the incentive and pressure to the companies through the manners of choosing investor objective, service and goods.

*(b) Promote Companies Bring into Effect the Reporting System:* More and more companies produce and publish reports to the society about their social, environmental and economic impact. The nations and governments support the social and environmental reports system all over the world, though encourage the plus companies to try, at the same time make the guidelines for the companies to follow, establish the basic rules for social and environmental balances.

*(c) Encourage Companies to Take Management Standard:* Management standard is a tool to evaluate companies about the performance of economy, society and environment. Although the management standard doesn't involving all the aspect of CSR, it still provides the basic standard to evaluate the performance of companies. Management standard experience is from quality management system to environmental management system then to responsibility management system. Nowadays the management standard has been accepted by most companies all over the world. The companies take part in the certification of the management standard actively. They still worry about the problem about costs. The government should consider providing the necessary financial support and encouraging companies to take these management standards.

*(d) Provide the Financial Aid for Companies:* The government should provide pension and investment funds in order to award the social and environmental performance for the companies. This measure will encourage listed companies to implement CSR strategies. Government should put the ethical and social standard in government purchases. There are many successful cases related the public purchases to CSR. Local governments play an important role in providing technical support and financial aid for the dissemination of CSR as an investment.

## Conclusion

The government is the main force to encourage the companies to fulfill CSR. It should realize that CSR is essential for the sustainable development of society and economy. Through the public policies of CSR, the government can promote and foster CSR. Furthermore, government should cooperate with non-governmental organizations to promote CSR and it is also necessary to establish the department in the government to take the public policies to promote CSR.

# Corporate Social Responsibility in Co-operative Institutions

R. Ravindran

## Introduction

The main objective of co-operation is to serve the society. If a person has co-operation between his mind and body, he will lead a healthy life. In the same way if there is co-operation among people, society will have peace and property. Co-operation saves society by rendering financial support, good quality products and services.

Corporate social responsibility means responsibility of organisation towards the welfare of society. A business organisation has to fulfill the society's needs beyond its profit need. Co-operative institution satisfy the consumers by providing best quality products and services at a very reasonable price. But there is an area where co-operative institutions have to give more importance, that is corporate social responsibility. From this article the writer will explain that in a detailed manner.

***I. C.SR in Human Resources Management:*** Many Co-operative Institution like Central District Co-operative Banks, Super Markets, Primary Co-operative Societies and other co-operative organisations do not have enough human resources. These problems create injustice to employees of co-operative institution. Minimum number of employees have to finish the work of maximum numbers of employees. That means employees have heavy work load, but they are getting very low salaries than their actual work. Proper working environment has not been provided to the employees of co-operation. They do not have staff room, enough tools and of enough welfare schemes.

Following are the pit falls in CSC in Human Resource Management in most of co-operatives.

1. Man Power Planning
2. Wage and Salary Administration
3. Training
4. Welfare Schemes

*1. Man Power Planning:* Co-operatives have poor man power planning. They never do the serious human resource planning. Many of the co-operatives (60%) posts are filled. Tirunelveli District Central Co-operative bank, total strength of Head Office is 130. But present staff strength is 58, it affect the performance of bank. They do not have staff of marketing, administration and technical section. They existing workers of bank have heavy work. One person does the work of three persons.

Take Nellai Super Market, they do not have enough staff to carry out their regular operative functions as well as marketing functions, Tirunelveli Central Co-operative Bank's 26 branches have very minimum number of workers. Every branch has only two persons it affects the efficiency of the bank.

*2. Wage and Salary Administration:* In all the co-operatives banks the employees are getting very low salary. Their salary level is lower than Govt. and Private sector workers.

Because of this workers have very low morale. They are getting low salary but doing heavy work. This is injustice.

In the salary package of co-operative workers, numbers of allowances and perks are very minimum.

Tirunelveli District Central Co-operative Bank's employee getting low salary than other district Central Co-operative Bank, the reason is bank has accountable heavy loss due to cancellation of debt to farmers in the year 2006. Tirunelveli District is one of the major districts which is dependent on agriculture sector.

*3. Training:* Even though co-operatives have enough training centre in around Tamil Nadu, they are not able to give training programs to their employees due to shortage of human resource. If the existing people are on training, its affect the regular work co-operatives.

*4. Welfare Schemes:* Up to present days, there is pension schemes to the workers of co-operatives. During the service, they are getting low salary, and so the scope of savings are very minimum. This leads the workers unhappy life after their retirement.

Now Government has proposal to implement the pension schemes. But it will take some time to implement it.

There are the major or pitfalls in CSR in Human Resource Management.

***II. CSR in Financial Management:*** Financial Management means managing inflow and outflow fund. Most of the co-operatives, do not have proper financial management because there is no separate person to manage the financial activities. This lead to poor financial planning and poor execution of financial plans. Almost all the co-operatives have problem of shortage of fund. Due to this they could not do their operation in full capacity. This leads to incurance of losses, therefore working people get low salary.

No Co-operative provides any fund for social responsibility activities because of this they do not carry out any social responsibility tasks. The major reason is poor financial management.

The following are pitfalls of financial management.

1. Financing Decision
2. Investment Decision
3. Dividend Decision

*1. Financing Decision:* Co-operatives are very poor in their financing activity. They are not able to arise enough fund for their operation. Find can be arised from Government, issue of shares and debentures, borrowing from APEX institution like NABARD, RBI, Borrowing loans from financial institutions.

Central as well as State Governments do not allocate enough fund to the co-operative, since profitability co-operatives are very low, they couldn't collect money from issue of shares and debentures. Even APEX institutions are not providing enough funds to the co-operatives, this leads to shortage of fund.

*2. Investment Decision:* Co-operatives are not having good investment policy. Many of co-operatives do not have own building and good infrastructure facility. Because of this, efficiency of operation of business of co-operatives are low.

*3. Dividend Decision:* Many co-operative are incurring losses on every year. So they never pay the dividend for last ten years. This leads to lesser marketability of shares of co-operatives.

***III. CSR in Marketing Management:*** Marketing process of satisfying consumers needs. Co-operative institution lacking in the following areas.

*1. Poor Infrastructure:* There is enough building to accomplish their operations. And also they are not attractive.

*2. Poor Advertisement:* Many co-operatives do not advertise sufficiently for this leads to great injustice, that is good quality products reasonable price is available but it is not known by majority of people. In Tirunelveli, Nellai Supermarket provides best quality products at reasonable price. But 90 per cent of people residing in Tirunelveli do not know about Nellai Super Market. This is because of poor advertisement.

*3. Poor Promotional Activities:* Co-operatives are not giving importance to because. There is no separate personnel to look after such activities.

*4. Poor Customer Relation Management:* Most of co-operatives fail to have effective customer relation management. They do not conduct customers' meeting. There is no actives like getting feedback of customers, sendings greetings to the customers on special occasions.

The co-operatives have to give more consideration in marketing area. Because they are very poor in following marketing areas.

1. Product Management
2. Pricing
3. Promotion
4. Distribution

*1. Product Management:* Due to Shortage of fund, co-operatives having lesser varieties of products in their sale centre. Many products are not available. This leads to low sales and low profit.

In Nellai Super Market, Due to shortage of fund. They do not have enough varieties of products. So consumers get lesser satisfaction.

*2. Pricing:* Even the price of products of co-operatives are less than other organisation. They fail to provide price offer on important periods like Deepavali and Pongal.

*3. Distribution:* Co-operatives do not have enough vehicles for the distribution. So that they are spending more cost on distribution it reduces their profitability.

*4. Promotion:* Co-operatives do not spend the enough amount on 1. Advertisement, 2. Sales Promotion. 3. Personnel Selling, 4. Public Relations.

This leads to lesser awareness among the people.

***IV. CSR in Development of Societies:*** Co-operatives only providing best quality products and services at reasonable price. They are not providing schemes/programs for development of societies like construction signal lights, providing awareness programs against any evil habits, free coaching of technical education and so on.

Co-operatives are lacking there functions of social responsibility.

Co-operatives are not spending fund on development process of societies. They fail to provide signal lights, technical coaching class to weaker sections, awareness programs on environmental protections, against evil habits, sex education, women empowerment, social harmony and son.

***V. Remedial Measures:*** Following are remedial measures of co-operatives in CSR.

1. Appoint enough human resource.
2. For the reasonable salary.
3. Provide need able allowance and perks.
4. Introduce pension schemes with out any delay.

5. Provide training program at regular interval.
6. Government, APEX institution must provide enough fund to the co-operatives.
7. Co-operatives must interest their fund in need able fixed and current assets.
8. Dividend must be paid on annually.
9. Varieties of products, infrastructure of sales centre must be improved.
10. Provided price offer on special occasional.
11. Provide enough fund for promotional activities.
12. Purchase needable transport modes.
13. Spend fund on social welfare development programs.
14. Provide separate department to the social responsibility activities.
15. Carry out social audit on every year to verify effectiveness of social responsibility of co-operatives.

**Conclusion**

Co-operatives must under take the social responsibility so that their service motto will be fullfiled. Co-operatives have to think of social responsibility in a serious manner at of the present situation. If they fail to accommodate social responsibility in their operation, co-operative concept will be moved out of business environment.

# HR's Role in Promoting Corporate Social Responsibility

S. Lawrence Leve

## Introduction

Corporate social responsibility (CSR) is an expression used to describe what some see as a company's obligation to be sensitive to the needs of all of the stakeholders in its business operations.

A company's stakeholders are all those who are influenced by, or can influence, a company's decisions and actions. These can include (but are not limited to): employees, customers, suppliers, community organizations, subsidiaries and affiliates, joint venture partners, local neighborhoods, investors, and shareholders (or a sole owner). One of the most frequently asked questions for all those individuals and organizations dealing with CSR issues is the obvious - just what does "Corporate Social Responsibility" mean anyway? Is it a stalking horse for an anti-corporate agenda? Something which, like original sin, you can never escape? Or what?

Different organizations have framed different definitions - although there is considerable common ground between them. I believe CSR is about how companies manage the business processes to produce an overall positive impact on society. Companies need to answer to two aspects of their operations. 1. The quality of their management - both in terms of people and processes (the inner circle). 2. The nature of, and quantity of their impact on society in the various areas.

Outside stakeholders are taking an increasing interest in the activity of the company. Most look to the outer circle - what the company has actually done, good or bad, in terms of its products and services, in terms of its impact on the environment and on local communities, or in how it treats and develops its workforce. Out of the various stakeholders, it is financial analysts who are predominantly focused - as well as past financial performance - on quality of management as an indicator of likely future performance.

### Definitions

The World Business Council for Sustainable Development in its publication "Making Good Business Sense" by Lord Holme and Richard Watts, used the following definition. "Corporate Social Responsibility is the continuing commitment by business to behave ethically and contribute to economic development while improving the quality of life of the workforce and their families as well as of the local community and society at large"

The same report gave some evidence of the different perceptions of what this should mean from a number of different societies across the world. Definitions as different as "CSR is about capacity building for sustainable livelihoods. It respects cultural differences and finds the business opportunities in building the skills of employees, the community and the government" from Ghana, through to "CSR is about business giving back to society" from the Phillipines.

Traditionally in the United States, CSR has been defined much more in terms of a philanthropic model. Companies make profits, unhindered except by fulfilling their duty to pay taxes. Then they donate a certain share of the profits to charitable causes. It is seen as tainting the act for the company to receive any benefit from the giving. The European model is much more focused on operating the core business in a socially responsible way, complemented by investment in communities for solid business case reasons. Personally, I believe this model is more sustainable because:

> Social responsibility becomes an integral part of the wealth creation process - which if managed properly should enhance the competitiveness of business and maximize the value of wealth creation to society. When times get hard, there is the incentive to practice CSR more and better - if it is a philanthropic exercise which is peripheral to the main business, it will always be the first thing to go when push comes to shove. But as with any process based on the collective activities of communities of human beings (as companies are) there is no "one size fits all". In different countries, there will be different priorities, and values that will shape how business act.

### HR's Role in Corporate Social Responsibility

Companies increasingly need to co-ordinate their CSR activities and demonstrate their commitment to CSR. Effective CSR depends on being seen as important throughout an organization. Delivery, not rhetoric, is the key to stakeholders developing trust in an organization.

HR has a key role in making CSR work. CSR without HR runs the risk of being dismissed as PR or shallow 'window-dressing'. And CSR is an opportunity for HR to demonstrate a strategic focus and act as a business partner. CSR needs to be embedded in an organization's culture to make a change to actions and attitudes and the support of the top team is critical to success. HR already works at communicating and implementing ideas, policies, cultural and behavioural change across organizations. Its role in influencing attitudes and links with line managers and the top team mean it is ideally placed to do the same with CSR.

HR is also responsible for the key systems and processes underpinning effective delivery. Through HR, CSR can be given credibility and aligned with how business run. CSR could be integrated into processes such as the employer brand, recruitment, appraisal, retention, motivation, reward, internal communications, diversity, coaching and training.

The way a company treats its employees contributes directly to it being seen as willing to accept its wider responsibilities. Building credibility and trusting their employer are being increasingly seen as important by employees when they choose who they want to work for.

The world is a smaller place thanks to the Internet, global trading and new communication and technology advances. More U.S. companies are expanding overseas, and now manage a global workforce that has unique benefits, rules/laws, and different languages and currencies. With this global expansion comes a "responsibility."

When companies are global, an important challenge in garnering success is to respect other cultures and workforce environments and start forming a global profile or social consciousness. Recognize these differences with a sound Corporate Social Responsibility (CSR) plan that can simultaneously increase shareholder value, boost employee engagement and increase employer brand recognition.

Start with these areas:

- Implement and encourage green practices.
- Foster a culture of social responsibility.
- Celebrate successes.
- Share and communicate the value of corporate social responsibility to employees and the community.

### Problems in Human Resources Involvement with CSR

The trust built through successful CSR is hard to regain if lost. HR needs to ensure that their organization's CSR can stand up to the inevitable scrutiny by stakeholders, and that training and communication mean it's embedded throughout the culture of an organization. HR needs to be an active business partner working with other functions, for example finance, PR/marketing etc. It will need to look beyond the boundaries of usual practice and arguably work on its own PR. CSR is a strategic opportunity which is market-led and is restrained by bureaucracy. It needs dynamism, creativity, imagination and even opportunism.

### CSR Strategy

Clarify your core values and principles.

Make sure you know who your key internal and external stakeholders are and which issues affect your relationship with them. et the top team on board, and know how to sell the benefits of CSR to different stakeholders. Understand how the CSR strategy is aligned to your business strategy and HR practices. Get endorsement for the CSR strategy from inside and outside your organisation. Communicate, consistently. Training is vital, as CSR will only have an impact if employees are engaged: attitudes or behaviour won't change otherwise. Effectively measure and evaluate CSR, otherwise the time, effort and money invested are based on assumptions, not results.

Direct results (such as saving fuel resulting in lower carbon emissions) and indirect results (increased employee satisfaction) of CSR strategies can be shown to contribute to business performance. One way outcomes can be measured is through a balanced scorecard approach, which allows for the different types of factors that contribute to a business's bottom line including internal people, processes and customers.

### Conclusion

One thing that is for sure - the pressure on business to play a role in social issues will continue to grow. Over the last ten years, those institutions which have grown in power and influence have been those which can operate effectively within a global sphere of operations. These are effectively the corporate and the NGOs. Those institutions which are predominantly tied and manage events. These include national governments, police, judiciary and others.

There is a growing interest, therefore, in businesses taking a lead in addressing those issues in which they have an interest where national government have failed to come up with a solution. The focus Unilever has on supporting a sustainable fisheries approach is one example. Using the power of their supply chain, such companies are placed to have a real influence. National governments negotiating with each other have come up with no solutions at all, and ever-depleting fish stocks. That is not to say businesses will necessarily provide the answers - but awareness is growing that they are occasionally better placed to do so than any other actors taking an interest. CSR has a wide range of potential meaning and the first module of this site addresses the issue of definition as well the nature of the challenges calling for public and private sector action on CSR.

## REFERENCES

1. B.Wenther Williams, Chandler David-Strategic Corporate Social Responsibility: Stakeholders In A Global Environment.
2. Blake, D.H. ,The Management of Corporate Social Policy.
3. Chatterjee N.N, Social Responsibility of Business: Some Indian Myths & Realities Decision Vol. 8, Sep. 1976.
4. Chris C Ganotis, Managerial Attitudes Towards Corporate Social Responsibility, Paper Presented at University of California at Berkley (Nov 9-11, 1972).
5. web:http://lmadurasinghe.googlepages.com

# Corporate Social Responsibility in Advertisements

## *An Overview*

R. Mareeswaran
B. Muthu Prabhu

### Introduction

Today the market is full of numerous products to cater all our needs. When there are products to satisfy all our needs, advertisement acts as a medium which can assist in promoting all the available market products. With the booming market economy, competition becomes imperative and the role of advertising becomes more important.

In recent times, it has seen that major companies have started advertising with a social message. The new generation is much more aware and can not be targeted easily. So companies have changed their methodology of presenting their new product to the market. it is just another marketing funda or its really a new revolution in the Indian Marketing Industry.

### Advertising as A Media

Media today is the fastest means of communication and advertising reaches out to countless people in one go. The new products can be launched through T.V, Radio or the Newspapers. Advertising plays a major role in establishing any brand to attract more and more customers. Advertising promises more choice, better value, new and improved products. It helps us to analyze different kinds of products at one site.

### Realities of Advertisements

Advertising should be honest, decent and truthful and should provide relevant information. Misguiding people by exaggerated advertising would only present a wrong picture in front of the masses. Some ethical codes and values should be abided by while advertising for a certain brand. Taking advantage of the lack of knowledge or inexperience of the customers should not be encouraged. Advertising has the power to make people believe, they should possess something which they never dreamt of. Trust is an essential element for building up any relationship; this applies to the consumers and advertisers as well. The advertiser should always provide a clear picture and honest information to the customer.

Words and images have a magical power which should not be misused. The rivalry and competition among certain products is clearly reflected in the advertisements which of course affect the public values.

### Corporate Social Responsibility by Advertisements

- Idea's "What an idea Sirji",
- Aircel's "Save our Tigers" campaign,
- Tata Tea's "Jaago Re",
- Nokia's "Green Phone".

Every major giant is targeting the new generation consumers. New generation means here the "People of Youngistaan" which believes in changing the world.

### Building Green World

The following messages are insisted in the recent advertisements:

- Green Phones - The next Generation eco friendly Phones
- 100 Ways to Save the Environment
- How Earth's Temperature is Changing - Past 150 Years History
- Dark Complexion, falling hair, any problem or anything under the sun.

### 'Advertising and Social Responsibility'

The Findings of a study by the *Indian Institute of Mass Communication (IIMC), 'Delhi,* in 1982 reveals that:

Of the total number of advertisements sampled, only about 3.3 per cent were factual and informative about the product without any emotional or psychological appeal. The most popular appeal was ego satisfaction in over 50 per cent of the advertisements of consumer goods.

Certain stereotypes are associated with certain types and particular brands of consumer goods. This appeal was pointedly in non-durable consumer goods, such as clothes, leather goods, cosmetics and toiletries and other personal care articles.

This is very much evident in advertisements aimed at the young, the teenagers-foods, soft drinks, coffee, biscuits, chocolates, etc. Cigarette advertisements use a wide variety of appeals from the strong outdoor stereotype to the happy relaxed mood.

### Health

Health is another area of emotional and psychological appeal. This approach has been found particularly suitable for baby foods, health foods and drugs and pharmaceuticals advertisements. This is also a powerful appeal in baby care products, such as toilet soap and massage oils. Toothbrushes and toothpastes also use the same appeal.

### Celebrities

In advertising of all such products, the emphasis often is on maternal love and care. On the other hand, a whole range of products are stereotyped as status symbols and are associated with public personalities like sportspersons, film stars, and stereotypes of people in high places, at economically and socially higher levels.

### Emotional Messages

Advertising basically appeals to the elemental human emotions. But this is not enough, although it provides a very strong appeal. The emotional appeal needs to be linked with information about the benefits to be derived from the product or service backed by convincing arguments. This becomes difficult when there is very little difference between the different brands of products on the market. In such a situation there seems to be no other alternative but to try to win consumer support by flattering his or her ego or resorting to a whole range of basic psychological and emotional appeals including the most primordial, i.e. sex appeal.

### Findings of the IIMC Study Result

The IIMC study reveals that only 1.4 per cent of the total advertisements used relevant information about the product to persuade a purchase. Among these were baby foods, certain books such as dictionaries, certain health foods and personal care articles. The largest percentages of advertisements were found to be low on information but very high on motivation through psychological and emotional appeals. A little over two out of five advertisements fall on this category. What are important however, are that such categorizations as informative and emotive are not always mutually exclusive.

In most cases the approach is a combination of both these elements. It is usually a question of which way the message is tilted-i11fonnative to persuade or appeals to the emotions to motivate. Sometimes it is difficult to draw the line, for instance, a baby care consumer goods.

### Social Responsibility

Such messages could also hit home with consumers who are aware, now more than ever, of their responsibility as voters. "There is an indication that we are taking ourselves more seriously and involving ourselves in the process". "Many brands are riding the social cause wave. But only few are on a political platform—it needs to find a fit with the category. The movement is towards self-governance.

The Responsibilities of most of the brand advertisement insists the following messages to the society:

- Save tree
- Awareness about health
- Awareness about sanity problems
- Awareness about child birth
- Awareness about population control
- Energy saving
- Avoidance of deforestration
- Green House Effect
- Escape from accidents, etc.

## Conclusion

In recent years, most of the companies' advertisements focused about the societal values. This is possible due to certain positive aspects for the company welfare. It may increase the goodwill and turnover of the product. The advertisements which insists the awareness about the society shows the social responsibility of the corporation. We hope that, it will give the responsible youth to the society.

# Corporate Social Responsibility among Private and Government Hospitals

R. Jai Ganesh

## Introduction

Corporate Social Responsibility is a form of corporate self-regulation integrated into a business model. CSR policy functions as a built-in, self-regulating mechanism whereby business monitors and ensures its active compliance with the spirit of the law, ethical standards, and international norms.

## Objectives of CSR

The Objectives of CSR is to:

- Embrace responsibility for the company's actions
- Encourage a positive impact through its activities on the environment, consumers, employees, communities, stakeholders and all other members of the public sphere.
- CSR-focused businesses would proactively promote the public interest by encouraging community growth and development,
- It voluntarily eliminating practices that harm the public sphere, regardless of legality.
- CSR is the deliberate inclusion of public interest into corporate decision-making, and the honouring of a triple bottom line: people, planet, profit.

## Corporate Social Responsibility in Private Hospitals

Being responsible means finding the right balance between what patients want and what governments can afford, and that staff are willing to provide the care needed. Doing this affects the entire hospital value chain. Doing this well, ensures the long term success that shareholders demand.

**Stakeholders**

- Customers (patients and families) served by hospitals;
- Employees working in hospitals;
- Governments who have a vital interest in public health;
- Electorates that can vote them out of office if they are dissatisfied with the health service they receive;
- Shareholders are also primary stakeholders and Society.

CSR and the Hospital Value Chain

| R&D | Purchasing | Production | Outpatient Care | Marketing & Sales | Management Policies |
|---|---|---|---|---|---|
| Natural Capital<br>> Biopiracy<br>> Patenting traditional remedies | > Environmental damage<br>> Waste<br>> Pollution<br>> GHGs | > Pollution/Spills<br>> Emissions/GHGs<br>> Use of water<br>> Use of energy<br>> Bandage/parts disposal | | | > 3 'R's<br>- Reduce<br>- Reuse<br>- Recycle |
| Social Capital<br>> Compution<br>> Intellectual property<br>> Abuse of indigenous people's knowledge | > Corruption<br>> Social inequity<br>> Abuse of indigenous people<br>> Intellectual property | > Corruption<br>> Social inequity | > Corruption<br>> Social inequity<br>> Ethical marketing<br>> Generics v. brands | > Corruption<br>> Social inequity<br>> Ethical marketing<br>> Generics v. brands | > No comption<br>> Obey the law<br>> Avoid politics<br>> Support education |
| Human Capital<br>> Discrimination<br>> Human Rights<br>> Union Rights<br>> Health & Safety<br>> Working hours | > Discrimination<br>> Human Rights<br>> Unicon Rights<br>> Health & Safety<br>> Working hours | > Discrimination<br>> Human Rights<br>> Unicon Rights<br>> Health & Safety<br>> Working hours | > Discrimination<br>> Unicon Rights<br>> Health & Safety<br>> Working hours | > Discrimination<br>> Unicon Rights<br>> Health & Safety<br>> Working hours | > Diversity & Inclusion<br>> Meritocracy<br>> Respect Union Rights<br>> Good Health & Safety<br>> Good working hours<br>> Pay for performance |

**Fig. 50.1**

**CSR Equals Capital Stock Renewal**

Another way of looking at CSR is to regard it as a form of Capital Stock Renewal reflecting the need to preserve natural capital (by minimizing the hospital's environmental footprint), to improve social capital (by supporting the institutional framework of laws and acceptable business practices) and to invest in human capital (by empowering and training staff). If we look at CSR in this way, we can see how it affects the hospital value chain in figure 1:

As can be seen, there are a number of issues hospitals must address if they are to behave responsibly across the value chain.

### The Business Case for CSR

The socially responsible behaviour across the hospital's value chain ensures that the role of private hospitals as legitimate healthcare providers will be accepted by both government and electorates alike. It will:

- Preserve access to patients and their demand for services provided because patients will not feel 'scalped';
- Guarantee the supply of willing and motivated staff;
- Keep governments 'on side' as they will not have political repercussions to fear;
- As a result, provide access to quality partners and investors from around the world.

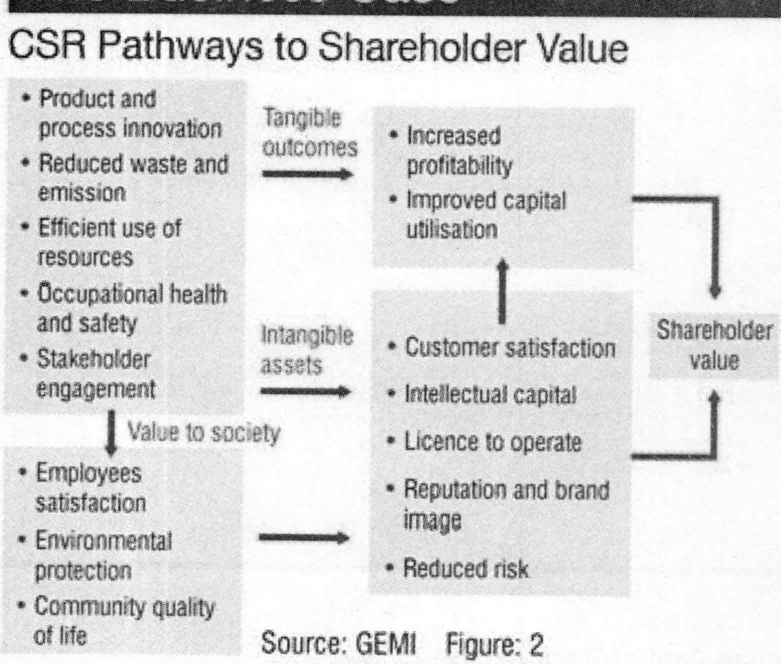


**Fig. 50.2**

### Corporate Social Responsibility in Government Hospitals

As a responsible corporate entity committed to discharge its social obligations, the government has contribute generously towards the development of the areas located nearer to the hospitals and other areas of operation.

- Medical & Health Care
- Drinking water
- Education
- Environment
- Development of village infrastructure

### Medical Facilities in Districts

- It providies medical, educational and other facilities to the villages situated around its location.
- To improve the medical infrastructure, it starts its operation in the area of Cardio-Thoracic Surgery Centre, Neo-Natal Special Care Unit, 64-Slice CT Scan Centre, Central Oxygen supply system and other facilities.
- Medical Camps are being regularly organized in the villages where free check-up and medicines are provided.
- Education & Mid-Day Meal.
- Supply of Potable Water.

### Medical & Health

- Health services are managed by Qualified Doctors and paramedical staff.
- Regular annual Monitoring of Occupational Health.
- Health facilities extended to employees dependents.
- Contribution to Panchayats for schools.
- Organising regular Blood donation camp.
- Oranising awareness programme regarding accidents, eye donation and other parts donation.

### Conclusion

In the modern era, both government and private hospitals are voluntarily take responsibility in the development of society. This type of change is evolved due to the heavy competition in the medical field. All the hospitals are ready to give their helping hands to the needy people. Also it performs the awareness camp to the people regarding donating eyes and others parts of a body, provide medicines, eye camp, regular check up for senior citizens, providing awareness about the impact of diseases, and its preventive measures.

# Corporate Social Responsibility a Key for Corporate Financial Performance

A. Nishani
N. Sudha

## Introduction

The field of corporate social responsibility has grown exponentially in the last decade. More than half of the Fortune 1000 companies issue corporate social responsibility (CSR) reports. A larger number of companies than at any time previous are engaged in a serious effort to define and integrate CSR into all aspects of their businesses. An increasing number of shareholders, analysts, regulators, activists, labor unions, employees, community organizations, and news media are asking companies to be accountable for an ever-changing set of CSR issues. There is increasing demand for transparency and growing expectations that corporations measure, report, and continuously improve their social, environmental, and economic performance.

The definition of corporate social responsibility is not abstruse. According to *Business for Social Responsibility* (BSR), corporate social responsibility is defined as "achieving commercial success in ways that honor ethical values and respect people, communities, and the natural environment." McWilliams and Siegel (2001:117) describ e CSR as "actions that appear to further some social good, beyond the interest of the firm and that which is required by law." A point worth noticing is that CSR is more than just following the law (McWilliams & Siegel, 2001). Alternatively, according to Frooman (1997:227), the definition of what would exemplify CSR is the following: "An action by a firm, which the firm chooses to take, that substantially affects an identifiable social stakeholder's welfare."

A socially responsible corporation should take a step forward and adopt policies and business practices that go beyond the minimum legal requirements and contribute to the welfare of its key stakeholders. CSR is viewed, then, as a comprehensive set of policies, practices and programs that are integrated into business operations, supply chains and decision-making processes throughout the company and usually include issues related to business ethics, community investment, environmental concerns, governance, human rights, the marketplace as well as the workplace.

Each company differs in how it implements corporate social responsibility, if at all. The differences depend on such factors as the specific company's size, the particular industry involved, the firm's business culture, stakeholder demands, and how historically progressive the company is in engaging CSR. Some companies focus on a single area, which is regarded as the most important for them or where they have the highest impact or vulnerability—human rights, for example, or the environment—while others aim to integrate CSR in all aspects of their operations. For successful implementation, it is crucial that the CSR principles are part of the corporations values and strategic planning, and that both management and employees are committed to them. Furthermore, it is important that the CSR strategy is aligned with the company's specific corporate objectives and core competencies.

### Business Case for CSR

Corporate social responsibility is about the integration of social, environmental and economic considerations into the decision-making structures and processes of business. It is about using innovation to find creative and value-added solutions to societal and environmental challenges. It is about engaging shareholders and other stakeholders and collaborating with them to more effectively manage potential risks and build credibility and trust in society. It is about not only complying with the law in a due diligent way but also about taking account of society's needs and finding more effective ways to satisfy existing and anticipated demands in order to build more sustainable businesses. Ultimately, it is about delivering improved shareholder and debt holder value, providing enhanced goods and services for customers, building trust and credibility in the society in which the business operates, and becoming more sustainable over the longer term.

While there are different ways to frame the benefits because they are interrelated, they generally include the following:

- stronger financial performance and profitability through operational efficiency gains.
- improved relations with the investment community and better access to capital.
- enhanced employee relations that yield better results respecting recruitment, motivation, retention, learning and innovation, and productivity.

- stronger relationships with communities and enhanced licence to operate.
- improved reputation and branding.

### Stronger Financial Performance and Profitability

Businesses can use CSR and corporate sustainability to produce direct benefits for the bottom line. For example, operational efficiencies can be achieved through reducing energy and materials as input factors for production. Wastes can also be reduced and materials can be recycled. These sorts of actions from eco-efficiency can produce concurrent environmental and economic benefits for the company and thereby contribute to stronger financial performance and more positive profitability. Operational efficiencies can be achieved in other facets of CSR such as streamlining the way that information is provided to the investment community as well as to other stakeholders that demand increased transparency. Managing potential risks and liabilities more effectively through CSR tools and perspectives can also reduce costs. Using corporate responsibility and sustainability approaches within business decision-making can result not only in reduced costs but can also lead to recognizing new market opportunities such as when new manufacturing processes are developed that can be expanded to other plants, regions or markets. There are various studies that have examined the relationship between CSR and corporate financial performance and most of the evidence suggests that the links are positive.

### Enhanced Employee Relations, Productivity and Innovation

A key potential benefit from CSR initiatives involves establishing the conditions that can contribute to increasing the commitment and motivation of employees to become more innovative and productive. Companies that employ CSR related perspectives and tools tend to be businesses that provide the pre-conditions for increased loyalty and commitment from employees. These conditions can serve to help to recruit employees, retain employees, motivate employees to develop skills, and encourage employees to pursue learning to find innovative ways to not only reduce costs but to also spot and take advantage of new opportunities for maximizing benefits, reduce absenteeism, and may also translate into marginally less demands for higher wages.

Socially responsible companies also have less risk of negative rare events. Overlooking negative social and environmental externalities when valuing a company might be equal to ignoring significant tail risk. The risks related to CSR could be grouped into three categories: corporate governance, environmental aspects, and social aspects. Companies that adopt the CSR principles are more transparent and have less risk of bribery and corruption. In addition, they may implement stricter and, thus, more costly quality and environmental controls, but they run less risk of having to recall defective product lines and pay heavy fines for excessive polluting. They also have less risk of negative social events which damage their reputation and cost millions of dollars in information and advertising campaigns. The scandals about child–labor and sweatshops that affect the clothing industry are two fine examples. Thus, socially responsible businesses should have more stable earnings growth and less downside volatility. Since companies that adopt the CSR principles carry less risk, when valuing those companies, a lower discount rate should be used. In the company valuation this lower tail risk should be taken into account.

There are also other cases in which doing what is good and responsible converges with doing the best for the particular business. Some CSR initiatives can dramatically reduce operating costs. For example, reducing packaging material or planning the optimum route for delivery trucks not only reduces the environmental impact of a company's operation, but it also reduces the cost. The process of adopting the CSR principles motivates executives to reconsider their business practices and to seek more efficient ways of operating.

### Empirical Studies of CSR and Financial Performance

Empirical studies of the relationship between CSR and financial performance comprise essentially two types. The first uses the event study methodology to assess the *short-run* financial impact (abnormal returns) when firms engage in either socially responsible or irresponsible acts. The results of these studies have been mixed. Wright and Ferris (1997) discovered a negative relationship; Posnikoff (1997) reported a positive relationship, while Welch and Wazzan (1999) found no relationship between CSR and financial performance. Other studies, discussed in McWilliams and Siegel (1997), are similarly inconsistent concerning the relationship between CSR and short run financial returns. The second type of study examines the relationship between some measure of corporate social performance (CSP) and measures of *long term* financial performance, by using accounting or financial measures of profitability. The studies that explore the relationship between social responsibility and accounting-based performance measures have also produced mixed results. Cochran and Wood (1984) located a positive correlation between social responsibility and accounting performance after controlling for the age of assets. Aupperle, Carroll, and Hatfield (1985) detected no significant relation between CSP and a firm's risk adjusted return on assets. In contrast, Waddock and Graves (1997) found significant positive relationships between an index of CSP and performance measures, such as ROA in the following year.

### Measurement Problems

Determining how social and financial performances are connected is further complicated by the lack of consensus of measurement methodology as it relates to corporate social performance. Significantly, it is unclear exactly what these indicators measure. In other cases, researchers employ official corporate disclosures—annual reports to shareholders, CSR reports, or the like. Despite the popularity of these sources, there is no way to determine empirically whether the social performance data revealed by corporations are under-reported or over-reported. Few companies have their SCR reports externally verified. Thus, information about corporate social performance is open to questions about impression management and subjective bias.

### Measures of Financial Performance

Although measuring financial performance is considered a simpler task, it also has it specific complications. The two measures, which represent different perspectives of how to evaluate a firm's financial performance, have different theoretical implications (Hillman and Keim, 2001) and each is subject to particular biases (McGuire, Schneeweis, & Hill, 1986). The use of different measures, needless to say, complicates the comparison of the results of different studies.

### Conclusions and Implications

There is an extensive debate concerning the legitimacy and value of being a socially responsible business. There are different views of the role of a firm in society and disagreement as to whether wealth maximization should be the sole goal of a corporation. Most people identify certain benefits for a business being socially responsible, but most of these benefits are still hard to quantify and measure. This study did not explore the direction of the causal connections. Nevertheless, the findings indicate that CSR is positively related to better financial performance and this relationship is statistically significant, supporting, therefore, the view that socially responsible corporate performance can be associated with a series of bottom-line benefits.

# Emerging Areas in Corporate Social Responsibility

## *Reforestation*

V. Bergin Prince Bell
A. Antony Britto

### Introduction

This paper gives idea about the Corporate social responsibility that involves in the emerging areas related to the global warming that is Reforestation. Reforestation is the clear solution for the global warming. Many corporations are surviving from the power extracted from our nature but most of the corporations are not interested in giving back, the share of nature. So our planet is in a great danger and it may affect our future generations. Now all the nations of this planet clearly understand the problems due to deforestation.

### Corporate Social Responsibility

Corporate Social Responsibility (CSR) is the decision-making and implementation process that guides all company activities in the protection and promotion of international human rights, labour and environmental standards and compliance with legal requirements within its operations and in its development.

### Carbon Offset

A *carbon offset* is a reduction in emissions of carbon or greenhouse gases made in order to compensate for or to offset an emission made elsewhere.

*The Collins English Dictionary defines a carbon offset as* "a compensatory measure made by an individual or company for carbon emissions, usually through sponsoring activities or projects which increase carbon dioxide absorption, such as tree planting."

## Effect of Industries on Global Warming and Lulucf Project

Industrial pollutants such as hydro fluorocarbons and per fluorocarbons have many thousands of times greater than carbon dioxide by volume. Because these pollutants are easily captured and destroyed at their source, they present a large and low-cost source of carbon offsets.

Land use, land-use change and forestry projects (LULUCF) focus on natural carbon sinks such as forests and soil. It includes the following differences:

- *Avoided deforestation* is the protection of existing forests.
- *Reforestation* is the process of restoring forests on land that was once forested.
- *Afforestation* is the process of creating forests on land that was previously unforested, typically for longer than a generation.
- *Soil management* projects attempt to preserve or increase the amount of carbon sequestered in soil.

## Advantages of Tree-planting Schemes

Some environmentalists have questioned the effectiveness of tree-planting projects for carbon offset purposes Critics point to the following issues with tree planting projects:

- **Surving of living things:** Trees and plants possibilize the great chance for living being existence in this earth, because they intake carbon-di-oxide and out let oxygen for the balance in ecosystem.
- **Timing:** Trees reach maturity over a course of many decades. Project developers and offset retailers typically pay for the project and sell the promised reductions up-front, a practice known as "forward selling".
- **Necessity:** Corporate tree-planting is not a new idea; farming operations have been used by companies making paper from trees for a long time. If farmed trees are replanted, and the products made from them are placed into landfills rather than recycled, a very safe, efficient, economical and time-proven method of geological sequestration of greenhouse carbon is the result of the paper product use cycle. This only holds if the paper in the land fill is not decomposed. In most landfills, this is the case and leads to the fact that more than half of the greenhouse gas emissions from the life cycle of paper products occur from landfill methane emissions.

## Corporate Social Responsibility and Reforestation

CSR and money making sounds like a contradiction. However, not when used to create sustainability for local economic growth in third world countries. Reforestation is the process of restoring forest on land that was once forested.

Corporate social responsibility is a part of contemporary corporate planning to help the community. The social outreach results reported in annual reports receive serious attention. A CSR program making money may be difficult for the community to understand; however, when the process creates sustainable reforestation with profits fueling their replication - with little or no government assistance—the level of controversy may be overshadowed by the immense good to the general public.

### Profit in Reforestation Business

Reforestation is a process that can produce tremendous financial returns. Corporations that have long-term employee benefits programs may find that the time it takes to grow a tree corresponds with the time that it takes an employee to tap the college fund or even longer to draw retirement funds.

A CSR program that works in conjunction with a reforestation foundation may find a long-term relationship that helps local third world development in the long-term and benefits the company's employees. Even climate change mitigation and carbon credit opportunities may develop.

Much of reforestation in the tropical world is getting started and working with the locals. The future value of the trees is in dollars in a western market. The margins are high and permit both worlds to benefit - the first world corporate employee's college or retirement plan is funded and the third world grows the trees sustainably - harvesting only enough to fund the plan(s) and develop the local economy.

### Profits For Individual

The individual may follow the same procedure as the corporate giants once he finds the right value-add agro forestry management services foundation that grows trees sustainably in the third world. Corporate social responsibility is more than just giving. The responsibility portion is the intelligent approach to making the intended purpose of the gift become reality outside of government programs. Both the giving and receiving must have a long-term developmental aim and objective, and it may bring back a goodwill return to the giver, especially if it is to the employee benefits program and helps address climate change mitigation.

### Indian Government and Reforestation

In an effort to meet the costly goal of covering one third of the country with trees by 2012, India's financially-strapped environment ministry is seeking to lease degraded forests to private firms, especially those from the pulp and paper industries, who will be allowed to farm the trees for paper pulp. The paper pulp in turn will be used to feed an increasing demand for paper products from India's burgeoning middle class-from toilet paper to tea bags and cigarette filter papers. Under a scheme named "Multi-Stakeholder Partnership for Forestation", the ministry proposes to entertain private bids for areas with less than ten percent tree cover, in return for paper pulp production.

The government believes that by contracting companies to grow and farm the trees for pulp, the plan will benefit the environment and the growing paper industries, while also providing low-income communities dependent on the forests with a more reliable source of employment. Environmental and social activists aren't buying that though. "The forests do not belong to the state or industry and cannot be owned or traded," says Shankar Gopalakrishnan of the Campaign for Dignity and Survival, an umbrella organization of forest community groups. "An enormous number of people live off minor forest produce and they will lose their homes and their livelihoods if the big corporate move in and get their way."

### Boon for Tribal People in India

It is estimated that 40 million tribal people in India depend upon the resources of forested areas for firewood, simple farming and cattle-grazing. After years of lobbying, paper and pulp corporations will have access to hundreds of thousands of hectares of forest under the scheme. Government authorities say that with the plan these forest dwellers will be the first to get jobs from the pulp industries.

### Role of Private Corporations in Reforestation

SFM-BAM's Campo Verde project in Peru became the first commercial reforestation endeavour using native species to be validated under the Voluntary Carbon Standard (VCS) and following the guidelines for Afforestation and Reforestation. The project, which has planted 919 hectares so far and has a goal of 18,900 hectares, was their main objective.

SFM-BAM is a Peruvian forestry and environmental services company that owns the land they are reforesting and are currently developing several large REDD projects in various regions of the Peruvian Amazon.

Gonzalo Castro de la Mata, Executive Vice-Chairman of Sustainable Forestry Management, explained the profit model of the project. "The revenue comes from 2 sources: carbon (credits) and timber," told Solve Climate. "The timber creates value over the long-term; the carbon is planned to be monetized immediately."

While the project employs 250 men and women (with an equal gender balance), those workers will not share in the ultimate profits of the reforestation in the way that a project like Samboja Lestari is set up to allow. Still, the company argues that there are ongoing social and ecological benefits for the local communities:

> "It is important to recognize the emphasis in training of local workers, as well as the active involvement of local actors as projects partners, in the form of small enterprises which produce the seedlings and provide

services," says Castro de la Mata. "These aspects are fundamental for the long term sustainability of the project."

Earlier this month, The World Bank's Bio Carbon Fund announced that it would purchase 500,000 tons of emission reductions from a reforestation project in the Democratic Republic of Congo (DRC). The Ibi Bateke Carbon Sink Plantation Project will reforest 4,200 hectares of degraded land and trap an estimated 2.4 million tons of carbon dioxide over the next 30 years. French carbon buyer has committed to purchasing a similar amount of credits from the project. It is also the first project in the DRC to benefit from global trade in emission reductions under the Clean Development Mechanism (CDM).

Whether these efforts at reforestation - both private and public - find long term and larger scale success has yet to be determined. Success in forest maintenance seems to rest with creating economic opportunity for the local community. As Willie Smits reiterates throughout his talk, the key is developing local economic value in keeping forests.

## How to Start a Reforestation Company

According to the IRS, the most prominent type of reforestation contract issued by federal and state agencies is for pre-commercial thinning and tree-planting. With 80 percent of the Earth's natural forests already destroyed, and with Brazil and Indonesia's remaining forests being stripped at an alarming rate, reforestation efforts are not only profitable but vital for our human survival. Starting a reforestation company is in some ways similar to starting any other type of company. You need a:

1. Solid financial plan,
2. Qualified personnel,
3. A marketing plan,
4. Business licenses,
5. Business registration with your Secretary of State.

## Conclusion

Businesses today have realized that, in order to continue thriving, they have to adopt a more holistic and focus on transparency and accountability.

Thus, Reforestation is one of the most holistic projects that can prevent the greenhouse gas effect towards living things and earns goodwill to the corporate people and earns lot of profit in the Business. So Reforestation is the best emerging area in the concept of Corporate Social Responsibility.

# Corporate Social Responsibility
## *A Key for Corporate Financial Performance*

R. Mayilammal
M. Rajalakshmi

### Introduction

In the past, a company's merit was solely based on its financial performance. But in the new millennium there is increased pressure from investors, consumers, and employees to consider social and environmental criteria in the way a company carries out its business. This has created momentum for using a "triple bottom line" or "sustainable" approach - social, environmental, and financial data for evaluating the performance of a company. Increasingly, stakeholders are concerned that the company they support has business practices that positively impact society while achieving financial success. Today, financial success is no longer the sole measure by which corporations are judged by their stakeholders, primarily investors, consumers, employees, and communities in which they operate. Companies are now expected to perform well in non-financial arenas such as human rights, business ethics, environmental policies, corporate contributions, community development, corporate governance, and workplace issues. Social and environmental performances are considered side by side with financial performance. In the new global economy, companies that are responsive to the demands of all of their stakeholders are arguably better positioned to achieve long-term financial success.

### Corporate Social Resposibility

Corporate Social Responsibility (CSR) is a concept whereby organizations consider the interests of society by taking responsibility for their activities on customers, employees, shareholders, communities and the environment in all aspects of their operations. It is the continuing commitment by business to behave ethically and contribute to economic development while improving the quality of life of the workforce and their families as well as that of the local community and society at large.

### Four Dimensions of Corporate Responsibility

The following are the four dimensions of corporate responsibility:

1. Economic – Responsibility to earn profit for owners.
2. Legal – Responsibility to comply with law (society's codification of right and wrong).
3. Ethical – Not acting just for profit but doing what is right, just and fair.
4. Voluntary and philanthropic – Promoting human welfare and goodwill and being a good corporate citizen contributing to the community and the quality of life.

### Drivers of Corporate Social Responsibility

The following are the important drivers of corporate social responsibility:

1. Employees and shareholders.
2. Brand equity.
3. Ethical marketing practices and social awareness.
4. The environment consciousness.
5. Energy conservation and global warming.
6. Responsibility towards the government.

### Impact of Corporate Social Responsibility on the Financial Performance

The following are the some of the evidence that demonstrates the positive impact of corporate social responsibility on the financial performance

### Reduced Operating Costs

Some CSR initiatives can reduce operating costs dramatically. For example, many initiatives aimed at improving environmental performance - such as reducing emissions of gases that contribute to global climate change or reducing use of agrochemicals - also lower costs. Many recycling initiatives cut waste-disposal costs and generate income by selling recycled materials. In the human resources arena, flexible scheduling and other work-life programmes that result in reduced absenteeism and increased retention of employees often save companies money through increased productivity and reduction of hiring and training costs.

### Enhanced Brand Image and Reputation

Customers often are drawn to brands and companies with good reputations. Companies operate in a market of opinion. How companies are judged by customers, suppliers and the broader community will have an impact on their profitability and success. A company considered socially responsible can benefit both from its enhanced reputation with the public as well as its reputation within the business community, increasing a company's ability to attract capital and trading partners.

### Increased Sales and Customer Loyalty

A number of studies have suggested a large and growing market for the products and services of companies perceived to be socially responsible. While businesses must first satisfy customers' key buying criteria—such as price, quality, availability, safety and convenience - studies also show a growing desire to buy (or not buy) because of other values-based criteria, such as "sweatshop-free" and "child-labor-free" clothing, lower environmental impact, and absence of genetically-modified materials or ingredients.

### Increased Productivity and Quality

Company efforts to improve working conditions, lessen environmental impacts or increase employee involvement in decision-making often lead to increased productivity and reduced error rate.

### Increased Ability to Attract and Retain Employees

Companies perceived to have strong CSR commitments often find it easier to recruit and retain employees, by offering good working conditions which results in achieving better performance in terms of quality and delivery, and, therefore, experience higher levels of productivity.

### Competitiveness and Market Positioning

CSR will be a source for business opportunities and competitive advantage. It can draw consumers away from the competitors and thereby improve profitability.

### Conclusion

Thus, corporate social responsibility offers manifold benefits both internally and externally to the companies involved in various projects. Externally, it creates a positive image amongst the people for its company and earns a special respect amongst its peers. Internally, it cultivates a sense of loyalty and trust amongst the employees in the organizational ethics. It improves operational efficiency of the company and is often accompanied by increases in quality and productivity and thereby contributes to stronger financial performance and more positive profitability.

# Corporate Social Responsibility as a Business Strategy

R. Janani
T. Gohila

## Introduction

Corporate social responsibility is a form of corporate self-regulation integrated into a business model. All the business has two independent responsibilities. But, the companies lose focus of how social responsibility could have been integrated with the long term business outcomes. Businesses across the world are focused on the immediate results by way of discharging the social responsibility that holds for the long term sustainability of the organizations.

## CSR as Reactive Strategy

CSR has in general been a reactive strategy for reviving drooping fortunes of the company by gaining the confidence of the communities in which they operate. This approach only obscures a business from identifying the real potential CSR holds with respect to their core business. Any complacence by such companies may result in the kind of corporate scandals that we are coming across today.

## CSR as Image Building Exercise

CSR today is seen by companies as an opportunity for building corporate image. Keen on drawing attention of media and general public, companies announce their plans for various kinds of philanthropic activities. Such initiatives are not emphasized in the maze of important and urgent business calls. If a company can develop a systematic and deliberate approach for maintaining the focus on social welfare activities, this will not only enhance its image in the immediate future but consistency on this front will help the company in building a positive reputation of societal concern. Such image will definitely help the company in its future business forays in the region.

### CSR for the Improved Operating Efficiency

The companies take care of environment because it not only helps in operating within the environmental norms set by statutory authorities but also reducing their costs by improving operating efficiency. The operational efficiency in current time frame also results in better environmental conditions that foster better living conditions for future generations. This in fact is a business necessity today for improved profitability for industry and cleverly used by companies for projecting a business case for CSR and showcasing the integration of CSR and business outcomes.

### CSR as A Source of Competitive Advantage

The challenge for industry today is to identify social issues that drive its competitiveness both now and in the future. The managers must believe that social concern or CSR as it is popularly known is a source of business opportunity and competitive advantage. This integration then would pave way for all round sustainability and growth.

### Business Strategies

The business strategies may be in the form of:

- Monetary donations and aid given to local organizations
- Community-based development generally leads to more sustainable development.
- To incorporate the CSR strategy directly into the business strategy of an organization.
- Many companies use the strategy of benchmarking to compete within their respective industries in CSR policy, implementation, and effectiveness.

A business needs a healthy, educated workforce, sustainable resources and adept government to compete effectively. The competitive businesses must be developed and supported to create income, wealth, tax revenues, and opportunities for philanthropy.

### Social Accounting, Auditing and Reporting

Social accounting, a concept describing the communication of social and environmental effects of a company's economic actions to particular interest groups within society and to society at large, is thus an important element of CSR. Social accounting emphasizes the notion of corporate accountability.

Social Accounting refers to "An approach to reporting a firm's activities which stresses the need for the identification of socially relevant behavior, the determination of hose to whom the company is accountable for its social performance and the development of appropriate measures and reporting techniques."

### Potential Business Benefits

The scale and nature of the benefits of CSR for an organization can vary depending on the nature of the enterprise, and are difficult to quantify, though there is a large body of literature exhorting business to adopt measures beyond financial ones However, businesses may not be looking at short-run financial returns when developing their CSR strategy.

### Human Resources

A CSR programme can be an aid to recruitment and retention, particularly within the competitive graduate student market. Potential recruits often ask about a firm's CSR policy during an interview, and having a comprehensive policy can give an advantage. CSR can also help improve the perception of a company among its staff, particularly when staff can become involved through payroll giving, fundraising activities or community volunteering.

### Risk Management

Managing risk is a central part of many corporate strategies. Reputations that take decades to build up can be ruined in hours through incidents such as corruption scandals or environmental accidents. These can also draw unwanted attention from regulators, courts, governments and media. Building a genuine culture of 'doing the right thing' within a corporation can offset these risks.

### Brand Differentiation

In crowded marketplaces, companies strive for a unique selling proposition that can separate them from the competition in the minds of consumers. CSR can play a role in building customer loyalty based on distinctive ethical values.

### Conclusion

Thus, the business concern has many social responsibilities which they want to flourish for the improvement of the society. It also helps the business firm to run its operations smoothly without any government interference. CSR fact is a business necessity today for improved profitability for industry and cleverly used by companies for projecting a business case for CSR and showcasing the integration of CSR and business outcomes.

# Corporate Social Responsibility of Private and Government Institution

## *Airtel Communication Vs. BSNL Communication*

V. Sudha
M. Suhasini

## Introduction

CSR is about how companies manage the business processes to produce an overall positive impact on society. "Corporate Social Responsibility is the continuing commitment by business to behave ethically and contribute to economic development while improving the quality of life of the workforce and their families as well as of the local community and society at large"

## BSNL and Airtel Communication

*Bharti Airtel Limited*, usually referred to simply as *"AIRTEL"*, is a Indian telecommunications company that operates in 19 countries across South Asia, Africa and the Channel Islands. It operates a GSM network in all countries, providing 2G or 3G services depending upon the country of operation. Airtel is the fifth largest telecom operator in the world with over 200 million subscribers It is the largest cellular service provider in India, with over 143 million subscribers Airtel is the 3rd largest in-country mobile operator by subscriber base, behind China Mobile and China Unicom. It has a 29.00% market share of the GSM mobile service in India. Bharat Sanchar Nigam Ltd (BSNL), a public sector telecom operator.

## Corporate Social Responsibilties of BSNL Communication

- When a traveller buys a ticket to travel on board the Rajdhani he/she expects to travel in a clean, friendly and pollution free environment. India's public sector telephone company has taken up a project to maintain and clean some long distance *Rajdhani trains.*
- BSNL will take care for up-gradation, cleaning and maintenance of these trains.

It tries to attract one and half crore eyeballs negotiating 34 locations across eleven states to establish its BSNL3G brand in the mindset of people.

- There are approx 350 Panels, 200 Table Tops and 400 Brochure Holders inside one train, along with audio jingles, announcements, contest and activation by in-train promoters which would create a great impact and engaging communication for the brand BSNL and its services.
- BSNL is using funds in the name of Corporate Social Responsibility. While encouraging companies to become more responsible and undertake enhanced CSR, the Ministry of Corporate Affairs and the Department of Public Enterprises should undertake a study of how money set aside for CSR is being spent. Merely making public announcements upgrading the annual CSR allotments will not ensure increased CSR activity. *BSNL to provide 1000 free mobiles to BPLs under corporate-social* responsibilities.

Minister of State for IT and Communications Sachin Pilot would distribute 1,000 mobile handsets with BSNL connections to below poverty line families near Jaipur on September 8, 2010. "Under the CSR(corporate-social responsibilities), BSNL will provide 1,000 mobiles with connections free to BPL families in Phagi town of the district.

### Airtel

Airtel-Vodafone business has an environmental responsible and reducing carbon footprint highly on the list of corporate social responsibilities in the following aspects :

- conservation of the environment.
- energy conscious company in which that our machines are shut down rather than being left on standby
- office lights are turned off at the end of the working day.
- encouraged the employees to be more environmentally aware by promoting events such as 'Walk to Work' day.

### Eco-Active

It has a registered Eco-Active business in Jersey. It is an environmentally-friendly Channel Island company.

### Partnership

- The production of recycled bags in Jersey.
- In Guernsey, Recycling Scheme to encourage islanders to dispose of their waste in an environmentally friendly manner.

### Education

- Airtel-Vodafone recognises the importance of educating members ofthe community in order to help them to experience life to the full.

- They created and developed courses at both Highlands College in Jersey and the GTA University Centre in Guernsey, which were specifically designed with the local community in mind.
- It supported Guernsey's Elizabeth College in their broadcasting of 'Old School FM'—a short term commercial radio station which provides youngsters with the opportunity to experience first hand how a radio station operates.

### CSR Activities

At Bharti, CSR is a way of life. Each department and employee strives to be sensitive to the stakeholders and environment within their work context. Bharti encourages employees to take decisions and design business-linked processes that are sensitive to communities and environment.

The essence of Bharti's commitment to Corporate Social Responsibility is embedded in the 'Corporate Values', which stem from its deepest held beliefs. These Values are:

1. To be responsive to the needs of the customers
2. To trust and respect the employees
3. To continuously improve the services – innovatively and expeditiously
4. To be transparent and sensitive in the dealings with all stakeholders

It insists its employees that, each employee should understand the importance of environmental, social and economical aspects while taking business decisions. They are :

- Ethics, fairness and being correct
- Meeting and going beyond compliances and legal requirements
- Showing respect and sensitivity towards stakeholders and communities, and
- Nurturing the environment

### CSR Beliefs and Commitments

Through a three-pronged approach it shows the CSR beliefs and commitments:

- Engaging with stakeholders.
- Ensuring stakeholder sensitive policies and practices.
- Undertaking programs for our employees, community and environment.

### Community Initiatives

Each employee is encouraged to take decisions and design business-linked processes that are sensitive to communities and environment. *"We have an obligation to fulfill to society and the communities in which we operate, and help improve the quality of life for everyone, today and in the future."*

Based on the basic guidelines and direction provided in the Code of Conduct, Bharti has undertaken many community programs. Each local office undertakes special programs for the local community. Many projects like:

- material collection drive
- blood donation camps

are organized for the welfare of the underprivileged community.

It searches for new, innovative ways of reducing the consumption of resources, with the aim of leaving a better and greener earth for future generations.

### Response to Disaster - Tsunami

- Built a mobile network in Andaman & Nicobar islands;
- Donated Rs. 1 Crore to the Prime Minister's Relief Fund;
- Created 29 Airtel Crisis Communications centres in Tamil Nadu;
- Raised resources for Tsunami victims by initiatives such as a 'Benefit Cricket Match';
- Employees also contributed through a Donation Collection Drive.

### Response to Assam, Bihar and West Bengal Floods

It also partnered with an NGO to provide relief to the flood victims in the flood hit areas of Assam, Bihar and West Bengal. 'Material Collection Drive' was undertaken across Bharti offices, for collection of material such as clothes, utensils, footwear, blankets, dry ration and monetary donations. 55 cartons of clothes and 65 kilos of ration were dispatched, in addition to monetary contributions.

### Mumbai Floods

Bharti Airtel employees climbed up the towers to restore the networks so that our customers could conveniently reach its employees.

### Earthquake

Bharti airtel's 'rapid response team' responded to the kashmir earthquake by bringing more than 2000 food packets and water bottles to the affected area. money, clothes, woolens and blankets were also collected from employees to distribute among earthquake victims.

### Conclusion

When compared to the social responsibilities of AIRTEL network with the BSNL network, it is evidenced that AIRTEL provides a well planned services to the society than BSNL network. Hence, private communication has provided better society to our society than government institution. They are taking less responsibility on the part of the improvement of the society.

# Corporate Social Responsibility of Private and Government Institution

K. Meena
M. Murugeswari

## Introduction

CSR is an activity which is over and above the compliance of the law. That is any activity that is part of a legal necessity cannot qualify to be called a CSR activity.

Conducting good business is always good for society. To serve best to the customers, we need advanced our commitment to corporate sustainability (CS). Our principles of Corporate Sustainability are based on the premise of creating collective value for enhancing human, natural, social and financial capital. It seeks to demonstrate accountability to all stakeholders, and communicates a fundamental belief in the equilibrium of people, planet and profit. The connections with initiatives that greatly impact people and the environment enriches the lives of others and the lives of the employees.

## Tata Communications and BSNL Communication

Tata Communications believes in the need to enhance the quality of life of people and to serve the communities where it operates. The Company has constantly learning from group initiatives and improving its processes and policies to serve society better. The Company's principles of corporate sustainability are based on the premises of creating sustainable value for enhancing, human, social, natural and economic capital. It lays great importance on being accountable to all its stakeholders. Bharat Sanchar Nigam Ltd (BSNL), a public sector telecom operator.

## Social Responsibilties of Tata Communications

Tata Communications implemented several programmes addresses four major drivers of social equilibrium:

- Education;
- Employability; and
- Entrepreneurship development;
- Encourages a culture of volunteerism to contribute to socio-economic development.

**CSR Partnership**

- The Company continued its partnership with Dr Reddy's Foundation (DRF) in the activities of the Telecom Training Academy for improving skills among the students from the economically weaker sections
- It has the partnership with Victoria Memorial School for the Blind for establishing a recording studio for converting books and other reading materials to digital format in CDs, for use by the visually challenged.
- It established Green IT infrastructures and is constantly improving its data centers and operations to become more and more energy efficient.
- It has an ISO 14001 certified Environmental Management System and a well enunciated Environment Policy in place to guide its activities.
- It was recently awarded a Certificate of Appreciation under Exemplary Innovations in CSR category of the Business World- FICCI-SEDF CSR Award 2009-10.

## CORPORATE SOCIAL RESPONSIBILTIES OF TATA COMMUNICATION NETWORK

• **Protection to the society:** To develop "Green technology" initiatives, it enables the customers worldwide to leverage communications solutions to reduce their company's carbon footprint.

• **Health and Wellness:** The global team participates in initiatives aimed at providing outreach and care to homeless children and children living with HIV and AIDS.

• **Literacy and Education:** Tata Communications and First Book donate thousands of new books to help cultivate the imaginations of low-income children.

• **Sustainable Livelihood:** It aims at building trust, imparting skills, creating capacities and improving the quality of life for communities across the globe.

• **Environmental Clean-up Projects:** Recognizing the importance of protecting nature, employee volunteers participate in environmental clean-up initiatives with children. The project enables our team to connect with and educate young people about the vital need to protect our environment.

• **$CO_2$ Emissions Reduction:** Helping customers to decrease their reliance on business travel reduces CO2 emission rates.

## Corporate Social Responsibilities of BSNL Communication

- When a traveller buys a ticket to travel on board the Rajdhani he/she expects to travel in a clean, friendly and pollution free environment. India's public sector telephone company has taken up a project to maintain and clean some long distance *Rajdhani trains.*
- BSNL will take care for up-gradation, cleaning and maintenance of these trains.

  It trys to attract one and half crore eyeballs negotiating 34 locations across eleven states to establish its BSNL3G brand in the mindset of people.
- There are approx 350 Panels, 200 Table Tops and 400 Brochure Holders inside one train, along with audio jingles, announcements, contest and activation by in-train promoters which would create a great impact and engaging communication for the brand BSNL and its services.
- BSNL is using funds in the name of Corporate Social Responsibility. While encouraging companies to become more responsible and undertake enhanced CSR, the Ministry of Corporate Affairs and the Department of Public Enterprises should undertake a study of how money set aside for CSR is being spent. Merely making public announcements upgrading the annual CSR allotments will not ensure increased CSR activity.

BSNL to provide 1000 free mobiles to BPLs under corporate-social responsibilities.

Minister of State for IT and Communications Sachin Pilot would distribute 1,000 mobile handsets with BSNL connections to below poverty line families near Jaipur on September 8, 2010. "Under the CSR (corporate-social responsibilities), BSNL will provide 1,000 mobiles with connections free to BPL families in Phagi town of the district.

## Conclusion

As far as communication network is concerned when compared to BSNL Communication, TATA Communication provides better services to the society. Rather than government institution, private institutions give their helping hands to the society in a broader way. It shows the responsibility and interest of the private concern towards the society welfare activities.

# Corporate Social Responsibility

## *A Paradigm Shift in the Corporate World*

**M. Rajalakshmi**
**R. Mayilammal**

## Introduction

In India, the term CSR might be new but the concept is not new. It has been there since the earliest times, going back to an age when society itself was in its formative stages. It has been incorporated in the various religious laws where a part of one's earning are donated for the benefit of the poor and community welfare. The Hindus call it 'dharmam', the Muslims call it 'zakatah' the Sikhs call it 'dashaant' whatever name the people used the concept has been imbibed in the society from the very beginning. As individual joined hands to form organizations, the same concept becomes embedded in the organization. In the years since 1991, we have witnessed a dramatic shift in the needs of business and society in general. This was time when many companies in india had started realizing the importance of business involvement in the community. This has been gaining ground since then, and today, CSR has become a part of business process. In the current globalized business world, there exist large multinational as well as small local business organizations. Irrespective of the nature of business organizations, they should be ethically bound to their stakeholders, such as customers, owners/investors, government, suppliers and competitors in order to ensure good will, which in turn assure maximum business growth rates. The social obligations of the corporation were highlighted as a strong reaction to certain practices of business which undermine human rights, health care, labour standards, poverty and minimum education among others etc.

## Corporate Social Responsibility

Corporate social responsibility is understood as the obligation of decision makers to take actions which protect and improve the welfare of the society as a whole along with their own interests. CSR involves a commitment by a company to manage its roles in society – as producer, employers, marketer, customer and citizen - in a responsible and sustainable manner. That commitment can include a set of voluntary principles – over and above applicable legal requirements – that seek to ensure that the company has positive impact on the societies in which it operates. Strategies related to production and marketing of goods and services, business ethics, environmental practices, treatment of employees, approach to human rights and community engagement are all inherent to a comprehensive corporate social responsibility approach.

### Features of Corporate Social Responsibility

The Corporate social responsibility has the following features:

- Conducting business in an ethical way and in the interests of the wider community
- Responding positively to emerging societal priorities and expectations
- A willingness to act ahead of regulatory confrontation
- Balancing shareholder interests against the interests of the wider community
- Being a good citizen in the community

### Role of CSR in Business

Integrating CSR in the company's business model is not just good morals; it also makes good business sense. That can be understood from the following:

- CSR can act as a potential aid to recruiting better talent. When the company stands for something more than just profits or market share, it gains "corporate good karma". And just as the personal good karma attracts benefits, the "corporate good karma" attracts profits in the form of better talent who feel proud to work with the company, and channel partners who want to associate with the company in order to improve their image.
- Any form of CSR that increases the transparency of operation of a company (the internet, for instance) ultimately benefits the company. This is because it creates an environment for the consumers to come together and act as a feedback mechanism which can be tapped by the company to gain valuable consumer insights and criticisms which would otherwise have been lost in the schism between the company and the consumer.
- CSR can help in risk management. In today's world of globalization and information interchange, all the stakeholders of a company are interlinked and are responsible for the actions of each other. So, the image of the company can take a hit if even one stakeholder becomes tainted by allegations of antisocial activity. In such a scenario,

integrating CSR into the business model and encouraging the channel partners and stakeholders to do the same will ensure smooth business in the long run.

- Governments and regulatory bodies are likely to view the firm with more leniency and benevolence if the firm contributes to the society through CSR. This does not mean that the firm has to start doing philanthropy in addition to business. Achievable goals of CSR integrated into the core business model should satisfy.
- Finally, CSR can also help the firm reduce its operational expenses. For instance, the UK based Carillion Company saved £ 4 million pounds by implementing sustainable business practices.

### Corporate Social Responsibility As Business Strategy

CSR is an integral part of long term business strategy. With the help of the CSR the business can get more advantages and the business can run smoothly. The following things gave clarity to us to understand that how for the CSR act as a business strategy.

(*i*) CSR improves public image of the firm
(*ii*) CSR improves stock price of the firm
(*iii*) CSR improves operating efficiency
(*iv*) CSR as reactive strategy
(*v*) CSR as a source of competitive advantage
(*vi*) CSR promote good communities in the business

*(i) CSR improves public image of the firm:* Today many companies view CSR as an opportunity for building their corporate image. Companies announce their plans for various kinds of social philanthropic activities in order to draw the attention of media and general public. In case a company develops a systematic and deliberate approach for maintaining the focus on social welfare activities, this will not only enhance its image in the immediate future but also help the company in building a positive reputation of societal concern. This will definitely help the company in its future business forays in the region. Social initiatives taken by organizations tend to promote goodwill, public favor, and corporate trust, and these may contribute to the long run success of the organization and profit. Therefore, socially responsible would acts enhance an organization's image and business in general.

*(ii) CSR improves stock price of the firm:* The firm having action of social responsibility of an organization would lead to their suppliers, customers, and business associates have more confidence to the organization. The example of social responsibility might include: fair standards of trading, honoring terms and conditions of purchase or sale and settlement dates, for example, payment of accounts, assistance to smaller organization; engagement only inl fair competition; respect for copyright and patents. By doing that, the other

organizations would view the company as less risky. This is in the stock holders' best interest. It will improve the price of stock in the long run because the stock market will view the company as less risky and open to public attack. So, it would reduce the cost of the production of the company. Therefore award it a high price earnings ratio.

*(iii) CSR improves operating efficiency:* There are other set of companies that take care of environment because not only does it help in operating with in the environmental norms set by statutory authorities but also reducing their costs by improving operating efficiency. Operating barely with in the norms set by statutory authorities is being in the compliance mode. As companies deliberately plan and move beyond the compliance mode, find the case for integration of CSR and business goals, where improved productivity or operational efficiency in current time frame also results in better environmental conditions that fosters better living conditions for future generations. This in fact is a business necessity today for improved profitability for industry and cleverly used by companies for projecting a business case for CSR and show the integration of CSR and business outcomes.

*(iv) CSR as reactive strategy:* Generally many companies use CSR as a reactive strategy for recovering from lost fortunes of the company by gaining the confidence of the communities in which they operate. But now companies have started adopting a "proactive approach" in case of CSR by estimating and analyzing the cost of not discharging the social responsibility and as a result they practice the minimum to pull on and thus minimizing their spending on this account. CSR is viewed by these companies as a cost and compulsion. This approach only obscures a business from identifying the real potential CSR holds with respect to their core business.

*(v) CSR as a source of competitive advantage:* The major challenge for any type of industry today is to identify the social issues that drive its competitiveness both now and in the future. Hence the business managers must first believe that social concern or CSR will be a source for business opportunities and competitive advantage. This integration then would pave way for all round sustainability and growth. In the due course of time, the issues relating to climate change and social responsibility in the area of operations will be critical factors for survival of businesses. Thus CSR has the potential to change the way business conducted through out the world.

*(vi) CSR promote good communities in the business:* People and organizations need each other. Social responsibility to employees extends beyond terms and conditions of the formal contract of employment and given recognition to the workers as a human being. People today have wider expectations of the quality of working life, including justice in treatment, opportunities for consultation and participation, training in new skills and technologies, effective personal and industrial relations policies and provision of social

and leisure facilities. A number of leading companies have taken steps to develop more ethical cultures and system by involving individual employees in corporate affaires. To provide or support some benefits to the workers will lead to a good community in the business organizations. Good communication in the internal business will lead to avoid miss understanding of each other. The workers would then enjoy their work and work out more efficiently. The quality of goods and services of the organization therefore increase. This will lead to profitable to the organization's business. Therefore, the CSR is important in internal environment of the business too.

## Conclusion

Corporate social responsibility can generate additional value to the business by supporting business objectives, promoting dialogue with key stakeholders and responding to customer needs.CSR creating and maintaining high reputation to the organization and also it has been securing strong relationships with stakeholders. Now a day many organizations realized that the CSR is a tool for customer retention, increasing share price of the firm and increasing financial performance and profitability of the business. Thus the CSR act as a source for business strategy it simultaneously promotes good communities and co-operation within the organization and develops society.

# Role of Public Sector and Private Sector in CSR

P. Sudha
B. Marilakshmi

## Introduction

"The important thing for business and society at large to understand is the limit to voluntary action, which is the point where government needs to intervene. If we are to live within the earth's capacity and share its resources equitably, economies must be transformed. That cannot be done by business alone"

This paper sets out to describe the role of Corporate Social Responsibility (CSR) in government policy and examine its relevance to a particular sector, the regulated utilities. Current theoretical and political debates and activities conducted at the national and international level, suggest a widespread interest shared by government, industry, civil society and non-governmental organisations (NGOs) regarding the role of government and business for the natural environment, social development and social inclusion.

## The Notion of Corporate Social Responsibility (CSR) and Its Discourse

The notion of corporate social responsibility (CSR) is not new in our society. It was born when corporations were born and societies to accommodate them. The 'soul' of corporate social responsibility is what the French philosopher Rousseau understood to be 'the social contract' between business and society. Rousseau conceptualised the relationship between business and society as being a 'symbiosis'. The Greek word 'symbiosis' means the co-living and co-existence of two parties in a mutually advantageous relationship. Thus, the social contract understands men (social members) as being able to act freely in a civil society that is united by a general will or 'volonte generale': 'The social contract that brings society into being is a pledge, and the society remains in being as a pledged good'.

The social contract signifies the relationship between society and business. Business hosts their operations within society and in return society expects business to show responsibility for aspects of its operations. According to the contract, society recognizes organizations as agents, particularly in the eyes of the law, and authorizes them to use land, natural resources and offer employment. From the business point of view, they improve the quality of life of a society. One can take the argument of the social contract further by adding to it that business is socially, morally and politically 'bounded' to improve the quality of life of society: they are expected to enhance the life of consumers and workers, to promote justice by avoiding deception or fraud, respect their workers and avoid harming any other social groups.

In contrast with public policy arguments, other scholars tried to distinguish between CSR and corporate social responsiveness by arguing that the latter refers to the capacity of an organisation to respond to social pressures. Social responsiveness describes the act of responding to social expectations and consequently, corporate social responsiveness supporters will look for mechanisms, procedures, arrangements and patterns of behaviour that demonstrate the capabilities of an organisation to responding to social pressures (Buchholz, 1993). Both approaches however, public policy and social responsiveness, have been criticised on the basis of ignoring the deeper values involved in CSR that is failure of advancing an understanding of the normative dimension related to corporate social behaviour

## Operational Definition of CSR, Best Practice and Cost-benefit Analysis

From the above it can be argued that the current definition of CSR is developed around two main principles:

- The interests of the firm's stakeholders should be represented at the company board and the decision-making process of the firm;
- Since corporate law protects the interests of the firm's shareholders, a corporate socially responsible or 'corporate citizenship' stance would involve the formulation of decisions that go beyond legal requirements and exceed the law, 'compliance plus'.

Thus, the notion of CSR assumes corporate behaviour that goes beyond legal requirements. CSR is the detailed 'issues' which an organization may be taking into account when developing strategies and on which an organization exceeds its minimum required obligations to stakeholders.20 Traditionally, these issues are both internal and external to the organization ie, employee welfare, working conditions, green issues, products etc. Today, the corporate social responsibility 'handbook' extends to human rights, workplace practices, globalisation practices, corporate power, environmental impact, corruption, community affairs and effective stakeholder dialogue (Cowe, Porritt, 2002). By meeting its legal obligations an organization should not necessarily assume socially responsible behaviour.

## The Role of Government

From the industrial revolution to recent years, social objectives have been almost entirely the responsibility of government. Social movements, NGO activity and pressure groups during the 70s and 80s led to the mobilisation of public opinion demanding from corporations to demonstrate a socially responsible stance. Since the earlier twentieth century, European member states have developed legislation to control the relationship between employee and the firm, health and safety at work, issues of environmental interest, discrimination and equal opportunities at workplace. Across Europe, state owned companies were created to pursue commercial and social objectives, whereas private sector companies were allowed to pursue their commercial objectives almost exclusively.

Legislation, regulation and taxation have been the favourable tools employed by government to promote and protect social objectives. In the area of the environment, 'command and control' techniques have been favoured by the European Union since the 1970s whereas a shift towards 'shared responsibility' between government and industry is another favourable policy approach since the mid 1990s.

In the UK, the government's privatisation programme of the 1980s shifted public expectation of the private sector. Whilst until then, social objectives had been mainly the responsibility of government, the privatisation of gas, water and electricity introduced a new paradigm. It created public companies owned by shareholders pursuing the same kind of financial returns as in any other public company, but the companies had also clear social objectives. In the case of the privatised utilities, these social objectives were managed through the regulatory regime, but the existence of the companies as 'stock market vehicles' demonstrated that financial and non-financial objectives could co-exist (Cowe, Porritt, 2002).

The Labour government has maintained the interest to 'bridge' public and private, social and financial objectives by drawing the private sector into the provision of social goods ie, public-private partnerships. The government has taken steps to reinforce the responsibility of the private sector with regard to its social and environmental impact. A number of legislative measures have been passed to support sustainable development including the climate change levy, the community investment tax credit and the Pensions Act. The company law review (1998-2002) has rejected the concept of 'pluralism' which would have required directors to consider the interests of other stakeholders as well as pursuing the interests of shareholders, but the government's white paper, which incorporated the review's recommendations, has communicated the message that directors would be foolish to omit such matters.

A question of interest therefore in the contemporary debate of CSR is whether government should assist business to exceed its legal obligations and hence commit itself to socially responsible behaviour, as defined in current terms. A second question considers the nature of a potential government role: Should government create the opportunities/enable business to opt for the business case for CSR? Or should government create the environment for business to realise the potentials of seeking legitimacy directly from the firm's stakeholders rather than shareholders alone?

Interestingly, recent published studies suggest that government may play a role to encourage and promote the social responsibility of business. As **Table 58.1** show, the World Bank has identified four principal public sector roles in relation to CSR that are mandating, facilitating, partnering and endorsing roles.

**Table 58.1 : Public Sector Roles**

| **Mandating** | **'Command and control' legislation** | **Regulators and inspectorates** | **Legal and fiscal penalties and rewards** |
|---|---|---|---|
| Facilitating | 'Enabling' legislation | Creating incentives | Capacity building |
| Funding support | Raising awareness | Stimulating markets | |
| Partnering | Combining resources | Stakeholder engagement | Dialogue |
| Endorsing | Political support | Publicity and praise | |

Public sector activities may vary depending on the CSR issue at stake. **Table 58.2** shows potential public sector activities for the CSR issues of corporate governance and community development.

**Table 58.2 : Classification of Public Sector Activities**

| **Public sector role** | | | | |
|---|---|---|---|---|
| **CSR theme** | **Mandating** | **Facilitating** | **Partnering** | **Endorsing** |
| Corporate governance | | Stock exchange regulations and codes; company law | Implementing international principles | Multi-stakeholder code development |
| Community development | Mandating corporate contributions | Tax incentives; 'timebank' schemes; league tables to promote pear pressure | Public-private partnerships | Publishing leading corporate givers |

Cowe and Porritt (2002) call for 'intelligent' government action to ensure that corporate action will contribute towards sustainable development since voluntary corporate action alone will not be enough. This government intervention at the beginning will consist of a set of 'soft' measures such as changing the political environment i.e., mandatory company reporting and hence, building up to 'hard' action - laws and regulations. The authors' belief is that 'the more corporate performance is exposed to the public gaze through effective reporting, the more effective 'civic regulation' can be and the less the need for formal government measures'. Cowe and Porritt's view corresponds to a government role that will increasingly enable companies to seek legitimacy directly from their stakeholders.

## The Development of Corporate Social Responsibility (CSR)

The notion of corporate social responsibility made its appearance almost a hundred and fifty years ago. It emerged in the United States of America as a social and political reaction to the rapid growth of capitalism during the thirty years following the American civil war (1861-65). Big companies, as we know them today, appeared in the United States in the 1870s. But as they grew, an 'anti-trust' movement against the 'robber barons', also grew. McEwan (2001) explains that the rationale for the 'anti-trust' movement was "the new industrial trusts and corporations which had become too powerful, wasted resources, were politically dangerous and socially irresponsible"

The American government assumed responsibility for correcting the social behaviour of big corporations as early as the 1890s and it passed laws on child labour, safety at industrial sites, and on workers' rights to form trusts. Nader et al concede that American corporations became more aware of their public responsibilities after the US Supreme Court announcement in 1906 which condoned that *supervisio*n". The American government extended legislation on labour protection, "the corporation is a creature of the state. It is presumed to be incorporated for the benefit of the public. It receives certain special privileges and franchises, and hold them subject to proper government public utilities and banking services during the nineteenth and in the early twentieth century. Trying to distance themselves from government intervention however, North American entrepreneurs like Francis C Lowell, Ford and Rockefeller laid education in the centre of the relationship between individual entrepreneur and corporate responsibility. For these entrepreneurs education was the means to personal advancement. Their contributions to private universities introduced a culture of private support for public works which still persists in the American thinking today.

## Conclusion

The current practices in the UK regulated companies fall within the 'business case' model of the firm rather than the stakeholder model. The narrow definition of the firm as being an entity that exists to maximise the interests of the firm's shareholders seems to prevail. But the companies examined also begin to realise that the 'licence to operate' is not static and current social trends and attitudes have a direct impact on business conduct and activities. For the UK regulated companies, CSR is a risk management tool that is used to defend company practices in the light of emerging social trends and can be used to explore further the commercial interests of the company, by applying 'best practice'.

For the stakeholder model of the firm to gain more ground, research work and government activity need to concentrate on, and elaborate upon, its legitimacy, accountability and practicability, and provide evidence lending support to the notion that 'CSR is not an activity conducted at the risk of the company owners but, on the contrary, it forms behaviour that contributes to a company's and the society's increased welfare.

# Index

**F**